The poverty of postm

In this book John O'Neill examines the postmodern turn in the social sciences. He rejects the current celebration of knowledge and value relativism on the grounds that it renders critical reason and common sense incapable of resisting the superficial ideologies of minoritarianism that leave the hard core of global capitalism unanalysed. From a phenomenological standpoint (Husserl, Merleau-Ponty, Schutz, Winch), O'Neill challenges Lyotard's post-traditionalist reading of Wittgenstein and Habermas in order to defend common-sense reason and values that are constitutive of the everyday life-world. In addition he argues from the standpoint of Vico and Marx on the civil history of embodied mind that the post-rationalist celebration of the arts of superficiality undermines the recognition of the cultural debt each generation owes to past and post-generations. In a positive way O'Neill develops an account of the historical vocation of reason and of the charitable accountability of science to commonsense that is necessary to sustain the basic institutions of civic democracy. This book will be of interest to anyone concerned to understand the continuing relevance of Marx, Weber, Husserl and Schutz to the debates around Wittgenstein, Lyotard, Foucault and Jameson.

John O'Neill is Distinguished Research Professor of Sociology, York University, Toronto.

SOCIAL FUTURES
Series editor: Barry Smart

The poverty of postmodernism

John O'Neill

London and New York

First published 1995
by Routledge
11 New Fetter Lane, London EC4P 4EE

Simultaneously published in the USA and Canada
by Routledge
29 West 35th Street, New York, NY 10001

© 1995 John O'Neill

Typeset in Times by Mews Photosetting, Beckenham, Kent

Printed and bound in Great Britain by
TJ Press (Padstow) Ltd, Padstow, Cornwall

British Library Cataloguing in Publication Data
A catalogue record for this book is available from the British Library

Library of Congress Cataloging in Publication Data
O'Neill, John
        The poverty of postmodernism / John O'Neill.
            p. cm. – (Social futures)
        Includes bibliographical references (p.   ) and index.
        1. Postmodernism–Social aspects. I. Title. II. Series:
    Routledge social futures series.
    HM73.055 1995
    303.4–dc20 94-7260
                    CIP

ISBN 0-415-11686-4 (hbk)
        0-415-11687-2 (pbk)

For my son
Gregory

Contents

Figures and tables

FIGURES

TABLES

Acknowledgements

My books begin with my graduate students at York University in the Monday night seminar on Contemporary Social and Political Thought. These arguments have travelled to other universities, from Toronto to Cambridge, Edinburgh, Copenhagen, Groningen and Tilburg; then to Arizona, Kansas, South Carolina, Georgia, Indiana, Florida and Hawaii; in Japan they were presented at universities in Tokyo, Niigata, Kyoto and Hiroshima. At every stage I benefited from generous discussion and hospitality. In addition, the arguments have been subject to the usual journal scrutiny and editorial comments. Their final shape owes a great deal to the advice of Barry Smart at the University of Auckland – so, once again, they have another chance to travel.

John O'Neill
Toronto

Introduction
The two politics of knowledge – alterity and mutuality

It is a conceit of postmodernity that it stands on a point of the highest morality achieved through the erosion of all previous moral institutions. Today we are told to jettison the old fashioned belief in unique values that cannot be exhausted by their practice. We consider the practice of any belief constitutes an ultimate value while nevertheless holding that such values are entirely expended in their use. In this, we are wholly ruled by prejudice and politics while believing that never before has the human mind been more open nor the human community more close to the hearts of men or of women. At the same time, we are asked to believe that human beings are now so speciated by gender and race – though we are silent about class – that there can be no universal knowledge, politics or morality. These ideas have not grown up among the masses defeated by the empty hopes of our kind. It is not the masses who have sickened of the injustice and exploitation that grinds their lives, weakens their families, starves their children, murders and terrorizes them each hour of the day and night in every corner of the world. No, it is not these people who have abandoned idealism, universalism, truth and justice. It is those who already enjoy these things who have denounced them on behalf of the others. The two sides, of course, never meet. Each remains on the other side of the great wall of class upon which there flickers the imagery of mass culture, on one side, and the imagery of élite, professional culture, on the other. No one appears to own the wall. This is why those on each side of the wall see only themselves in their own cultures. Worse still, since the masses have no reason to believe they own anything – let alone the wall – those on the élite side have persuaded themselves that the wall is culture rather than property. This idea appeals to the cultural élite since what they own

– as well as what they disown – is largely symbolic capital, especially language and its professional practice.

Nowadays ideas circulate like fast-food and like it are garbaged in favour of the next idea almost without assimilation. To accommodate to such processing, intellectuals are prepared to consider themselves 'bodies without organs', as migratory bundles of pleasure-seeking drives, almost as aimless as those mindless youths whose soft bodies drift through the deafening arcades of pinball machines. The latter devour one another in a parody of the passive self-destructive anger of the consumer who will never knowingly or competently produce anything in which they can mirror self-respect. Dignity is a demand that such lives can only redeem in their struggle with techno-dying. It is a demand that marks their exit once and for all from a society that is incapable of celebrating their birth. In between, living and dying are the slow points of degradation experienced in a sensate culture whose hostility towards itself is the source of all our evils. In such circumstances, to stand for an idea appears to be as foolish as to expect our bread to be bread. What matters, we are told, is what goes with what but not at all what is what. The latter question stalls the merry-go-round. It violates a thoughtless order like the instructions for abandoning an aircraft over water – it being assumed that our trays are not down and laden with food that we must eat because that is the only way to ignore our neighbour eating his way through the heavens. Meanwhile many on earth do not eat at all. But that cannot be the question. There is no justice for them. But that cannot be the question. Nor is there any truth for them. But that cannot be the question. Who, then, owns these questions? Why are they not raised without irritation and scorn, if not impatience and ridicule?

These questions go unasked because those of us who own knowledge, who enjoy literacy, health, self-respect and social status have chosen to rage against our own gifts rather than to fight for their enlargement in the general public. We have chosen to invalidate our science, to psychiatrize our arts, to vulgarize our culture, to make it unusable and undesirable by those who have yet to know it. We honour no legacy. We receive no gifts. We hand on nothing. We poison ourselves rather than live for others. We despise service and are slaves to our own self-degradation.

The current situation requires us to address a number of extremely difficult historical, sociological and philosophical questions. Among these are:

1 *The problem of rationality*: Must reason foreclose in terror and totalitarianism; can its dialectical sources in myth, imagination and embodiment be fostered in the arts and sciences?

2 *The problem of a meta-discourse*: Is there a critical standpoint from which the relationship between the culture of modernity and the institutions of modernization can be evaluated?

3 *The problem of the fragmentation of modernist discourse*: Can the fragment, the ruin, the non-synchronic, the paratactical, the schizophrenic reconstitute sites of local rationality, points at which the decolonization of the life-world can be inaugurated?

4 *The problem of aesthetic-communicative rationality*: Can the humanization of nature remain the norm of social institutions that simultaneously deepen the naturalization of humanity? Is our 'form of life' still thinkable within the modernist paradigm or must it be reconstituted through the paralogical discourses of the life-world (familism, feminism, ecologism, anti-racism, anti-nuclearism) which seek to redefine the grammar of our institutions?

5 *The problem of post-history*: Can 'we' live between the melancholic and joyful options in neo-modernity; what happens among the masses, the intellectuals, in political movements to shape memory, imagination and hope?

I am going to argue against the political current of postmodernism. I shall do so with respect to the core issue raised by the postmodernist claim that *knowledge is no longer power because power is now knowledge*. I believe that if we accept this twist in our conception of the relations between knowledge, power and community, we stand to lose hold of any version of civic democracy.

Lyotard's[1] extraordinary move to jettison the double narrative of knowledge and freedom as, on the one hand, an obsolete theory of science and, on the other hand, a decrepit theory of power is the source of much of the rhetoric of postmodern politics. It suggests that we can live without the twin promise of the Enlightenment and of Marxism because they have somehow overlapped to produce the most deceptive claim of all, namely, that we might reconcile desire and community in a single political economy. Lyotard's minor essay on the strategic nature of science is all the more odd when prefaced by Jameson's efforts[2] to have it refurbish Marxism as the *unconscious* substrate of all political history. While Lyotard reduces politics to a war of minority discourses – ignoring the dark side of the *politics of alterity* by reducing alterity to the model of a language game that never seeks consensus – Jameson clings to the regulative principle that in all class conflict *either* class may desire the collective good! Between them, Lyotard and Jameson have combined random elements of Nietzsche and Freud, to subordinate reason to will and will to desire. The result is a split-subject for whom history and politics are sundered and for whom reconciliation and community are merely specular effects of a dead totality that the modern subject has killed off in 'his' own heart. In Jameson, however, the consequence of this strange alliance is the nearly immediate return of the repressed in celebrations of the despatializing and detemporalizing effects of late capitalism (with a little help from Baudrillard's spin on the seductive signifier).[3]

In my view, Foucault's Nietzscheanism also serves to undermine the subject of politics with the reduction of the subject of knowledge to the docile object of techniques of disciplinary knowledge that intensify political power at the expense of civic democracy. Moreover, the subject of desire becomes the site of a discursive economy that expands control in the name of education, sexuality and health without these staples of a democratic society ever achieving any emancipatory effect. Thus, between them Foucault and Lyotard abandon the subject of politics and history to the history and politics of subjectivity and minoritarianism. Because they abandon the social subject of history – or like Jameson push it into the unconscious – Foucault and Lyotard abandon us to the false alternatives of totalitarianism and minoritarianism, of alterity and difference versus mutuality. Against this view, I shall argue for the reaffirmation of the communicative bias of language, knowledge and power as the template of mutuality in social and political life apart from which we cannot identify our troubles or seek remedies for them. I am quite aware that Habermas[4] is to be credited with the front-line struggle against the political misdirections of poststructuralism and deconstructionism. But whereas I share Habermas' basic claim regarding the regulative principles of the communicative ethic, I am not always convinced by his 'readings' of the principal figures of the play. Certainly, I cannot understand why Habermas[5] ever claimed that Marx had ignored communication in favour of labour as the societal template. This move opened up the way for cultural critics on the Left to abandon Marx for Baudrillard's self-consuming McLuhanism, now sped up by deconstructionism's insistence upon 'difference', or to abandon Marx for neo-Freudian 'desire' which feeds off the spatio-temporality of intrasubjectivity while completely foreclosing upon the narrative claims of inter-subjectivity.

It is a paradox that the current protagonists of authorial death should have achieved such a monopoly upon current social and political theory.[6] It is all the more strange since no one in the social sciences needs to wait upon philosophy and literature to tell us that the sovereign-subject (whether 'supposed to know' or to love) is a myth. This is not because we have no alternative but structuralism. It is because we have no other view upon history and politics than as a series of structures that fault, shift and realign. To rediscover in the video arcade what Darwin, Marx and Freud learned outdoors and indoors is one thing – given contemporary mores – but it is quite another to privilege this electric insight over the Enlightenment. This is because whereas the video privileges surfaces – a risk shared by 'texts' – social structure is unthinkable as appearance. To ignore this difference is to surrender ourselves to cave culture, and to the cultural amnesia that separates us from the long struggle against ideology.

The postmodern fascination with cultural surfaces and its derision of essence, along with its easy deconstructions of super/substructure, centre/margin distinctions – as though these artefacts have ever been employed without a user's sense of the free play in them – makes it difficult to resist the power/knowledge trope that now dominates postmodern political thought. What is at stake are two rival versions of the primal scene of political theory. In the postmodern scene, power is knowledge of our voluntary servitude. In the Enlightenment scene, our knowledge is the power to end servitude. In the first case, we enslave ourselves in the mirror that reflects only our self and not any larger community. In the latter case, the community is a social mirror in which our self is enlarged and enabled through the exchanges of language, labour and communicative exchanges that are ruled by truth, equality and freedom.

I have therefore arranged the following essays around the contrastive device of a first set of essays on the *politics and history of disciplinary knowledge* to which I then oppose a second set of essays concerned with the *politics of mutual knowledge*. In the opening essay, then, I state my position on postmodernism, for better or worse. I then look at the genealogy of the disciplinary society in order not to abandon Marx and Weber for fashionable Foucault. For the same reason, I try to show that the medicalization of the disciplinary society is a political strategy that has its lineage in Parsons/Merton and their concept of the 'professionalization' of the control functions of sociology. The latter largely derives from Parson's recoding of Weber's account of the Protestant ethic and its role in capitalist organization into a set of rational-legal behaviours that are the vehicle for professional/client relations in bureaucratic institutions designed to absorb their own pathologies without resort to political force except in the extreme instance. Consequently, I think it is curious to see how, in response to the postmodern erosion of the control function of the Protestant ethic, two theorists from the current Right and Left (Bell and Jameson), turn up a Durkheimian card in order to stem the secular tide of narcissism with the reaffirmation of the sacred template from which we may still hope to reaffirm community. Here, however, I am not simply playing with a convergence whose incongruity would have amused Parsons. What I try to do in this essay is to show that the narcissization of the body politic has its grounds in corporate techniques of privatizing the public realm.[7] Rather than allow ourselves to be seduced by the postmodern fascination that other cultural critics exhibit, the narcissization of the political body must be opposed with what I call a developmental allegory of the body politic that carries the common-sense values and knowledge of individuals and institutions towards an emancipatory self-knowledge. Here I believe I have fashioned the corporeal complement to Habermas's more cognitivist formulation of the general theory of communicative institutions. By the same token, my insistence upon a developmental model of the integration of corporeal, social and libidinal levels of the body politic redefines the subject of politics in terms of an embodied, gendered, familied and working subject whose values and beliefs are the very stuff of political life.

In order to make clearer the common-sense communicative bias of the essays in Part II, I should point out that they are grounded in the social phenomenology of Merleau-Ponty[8] and Schutz – because I reject the Frankfurt prejudice that phenomenology is inherently subjectivist. In my view, phenomenology after Husserl offers us the possibility of grounding the life-world claims of everyday knowledge and values in our struggle with the disciplinary knowledges whose accountability must be institutionalized in any viable democracy. From this standpoint, the methodological limits of liberal contract theory and its political anthropology may be set out in the following way:

1 liberal contract theory is ahistorical and is unreal in its assumptions about community and individual behaviour;

2 liberal anthropology assumes that its individual agents are disembodied, degendered and defamilied;

3 as a consequence of (2) the constitutive character of the political subject of liberal theory is empty and as such has no grounds for political choice;

4 furthermore, the liberal contractarian distinction between private and public life empties both domains since the private domain is inhabited by disembodied entities (2 and 3 above) that can make no claims upon the political domain whereas our embodiment is the very source of the life of politics;

5 in short, liberal anthropology is incapable of furnishing the ontological grounds of social and political practice.

Inasmuch as liberal atomism claims to break the bonds of patriarchy, whether between man and god or between men and women (children and slaves), it provides the genealogy of postmodernism albeit without its contemporary political unconscious. The difference is that postmodern atomism dislocates individuals from their institutional contexts so that each appears to float freely in an entirely semiotic space. The postmodern political subject is constituted in total isolation while 'society' is correspondingly constituted through the total exchangeability of its atomic subjects. Paradoxically, the grammar of atomism is only complete in a homogenized economy which postmodernism merely translates to the level of politics. To oppose this move, we must spell out an alternative grammar of social justice in which self-interest is not the molecular dynamic of civic life. The grammar of common-sense knowledge and obligation offers an alternative account of the articulation of individual and collective life without the fictions of violent desire or of the permanent absence of the utopian origins and ends of our political commitments.

To my mind, it is an unfortunate result that the phenomenological critique of positivism – which antedates deconstructionism and poststructuralism – later spawned a politics of subjectivity and alterity rather than a politics of inter-subjectivity and mutuality with which it had first blossomed.[9] Perhaps this was an unavoidable effect of the reception-context of the sixties in which many of us believed that the critique of scientism and techno-logocentrism would resolve the basic issues in the drive toward political community. Rather than concede anything to the laments of Lasch[10] and Bloom,[11] I have argued elsewhere[12] and I do so here that the task still remains of reconciling the politics of love's body with the politics of labour, common sense and community. This task has nevertheless become extraordinarily difficult in the present context of the celebration of postmodern fragmentation, on the one side, and of greedy globalism on the other. In Part II I turn to a series of essays on the politics of mutual knowledge. Here I entirely reject Lyotard's and Giddens' acceptance of the strategic or professional disembedding of the natural science and social sciences from the life-world knowledges, crafts and aesthetics. Nor do I accept Jameson's attempt to salvage the life-world by regarding it as the creative basement of an unconscious history of politics. I do not think that the life-world is at its oppositional best when on a merry-go-round of consumerism and addiction from which we may derive a cunning semiotics of postmodern revolt. This is not because I adopt an essentialist view of the everyday life-world. The life-world is a composite of the common-sense worlds of ordinary people, all of whom are reflective actors with a story to tell that is not reducible to the shibboleths of politics, economics or psychoanalysis any more than to the barebones of class, racism and sexism. The life-world cannot be totalized. Nor can it be entirely appropriated in the professional discourses that seek to objectivize, naturalize and computerize it.

The life-world is not a margin; it is not primitive. It is the surrounding sense that anyone has who has any sense of the institutions, customs and know-how into which we are all born. The life-world is not as such resistant to any of the domains – science, art, technology – that are articulated in the course of human history because it is precisely in the life-world that our practical arts and crafts have already been required to develop themselves in ways that are evidently not alien to the later history of humanity. Indeed, it is precisely this link of *tradition* – or *translation*, as I put it – between the two discursive and practical economies of the life-world and the disciplinary worlds of the arts and sciences that must be respected if we are not to be subjected to the abuses of accountability that weaken political democracy. Thus, the life-world is the source of a thick concept of self/other relations that is resistant to the wilfulness of desire whose seat is in the heart or the mind but not in the community. In this concept of things our world is never quite self-centred because we know that others who have and will and do precede us are presupposed in any of our uses of this world. This historical legacy is at the same time a political legacy that enjoins upon us a bias towards communion rather than possessive individualism. Yet, rather than leave the life-world as a court of last appeal – in the way that Husserl,

Schutz and Habermas seem to view it – I am arguing for a radicalization of the life-world thesis on the two grounds of the methodology
of the social sciences and of the communicative praxis essential to
civic democracy. Some such effort is demanded of us if we are not
to leave the public with the poor alternatives of postmodern giddiness
or political tribalism.

NOTES

1   Lyotard, J.-F. (1984) *The Postmodern Condition: A Report on
    Knowledge*, Minneapolis: University of Minnesota Press.
2   Jameson, F. (1984) 'Foreword' to *The Postmodern Condition*.
3   Baudrillard, J. (1981) *For a Critique of the Political Economy of the
    Sign*, St. Louis: Telos Press.
4   Habermas, J. (1987) *The Philosophical Discourse of Modernity*, Ch.
    XI, 'An alternative way out of the philosophy of the subject: com-
    municative versus subject-centered reason', Cambridge: MIT Press.
5   Habermas, J. (1971) *Knowledge and Human Interests*, Boston: Beacon
    Press.
6   O'Neill, J. (1992) *Critical Conventions: Interpretation in the Literary
    Arts and Sciences*, Ch. 1, 'On the practice of literary politics', Norman:
    University of Oklahoma Press.
7   O'Neill, J. (1991) *Plato's Cave: Desire, Power and the Specular Func-
    tions of the Media*, Norwood, NJ: Ablex Publishing Corporation.
8   O'Neill, J. (1989) *The Communicative Body: Studies in Communicative
    Philosophy, Politics, and Sociology*, Evanston: University of
    Northwestern Press.
9   Dallmayr, F.R. (1981) *Twilight of Subjectivity: Contributions to a Post-
    Individualist Theory of Politics*, Amherst: The University of
    Massachussetts Press.
10 Lasch, C. (1979) *The Culture of Narcissism: American Life in an Age
    of Diminishing Expectations*, New York: Warner Books.
11 Bloom, A. (1987) *The Closing of the American Mind: How Higher
    Education Has Failed Democracy and Impoverished the Souls of Today's
    Students*, New York: Simon and Schuster.
12 O'Neill, J. (1985) *Five Bodies: The Human Shape of Modern Society*,
    Ithaca: Cornell University Press.

Part I

The politics of disciplinary knowledge

Chapter 1

Postmodernism and (post) Marxism

A postmodern essay cannot avoid its own exemplarity with respect to the modernity it seeks to situate as an after effect or an abject of its own success. Its exemplarity consists in its wounded subjectivity, its deterritorialization due to its recognition that it lacks any ground outside of its own construction. Nevertheless, the postmodern essay remains a satellite of modernity which in turn remains a star recognized by its distance from the medieval world and the ancient cosmos. In this sense the essayist is a travelling theorist who like Montaigne discovers that all the while he has moved around himself looking for a niche in which to resettle his home.

Nothing much is to be gained from definitions of postmodernism whether as a period concept or as a counter concept. Certainly, nothing can be laid down from the start in such thickets since the pretence of initial clarity would either founder along the way or else catch nothing from its explorations. Postmodernism is a discursive practice with sites in art, architecture, music, literary criticism and the social sciences.

> The word postmodernism is not only awkward and uncouth; *it evokes what it wishes to surpass or suppress* – modernism itself. The term thus contains its enemy within, as the terms romanticism, classicism, baroque and rococo, do not. Moreover, it denotes temporal linearity and connotes belatedness, even decadence, to which no postmodernist would admit. But what better name are we to give this curious age?[1]

We must recognize the will to power at least as much as the will to knowledge in the naming game. Thus any definition will risk the embarrassment of imprecision because of its promise of possession. The poorest map will do provided it can be used to legitimate land sales to eager prospectors. Academics are no less immune to gold-digging than anyone else. So the signs go up: post-historical, post-civilization, postmodernity. Wherever they lead to, such signs lead 'beyond' and naturally recruit followers. One sign alone seems to warn them off the great beyond: anti-modernity. This appears to be the last stop on the autobahn of modern culture: think before you go on, or turn-off!

Well, what sort of cultural highway have we been on and does our culture have alternative paths along which we might just as well proceed? We need to pay some attention to such imagery. We are likening our culture, with all its usages which thicken here and there in our institutions, cities and villages, to a highway along which certain stops stand for places at a remove from the centre of symbolic production. At each stop a phrase in our cultural grammar defines the landscape through which runs the highway of modernism to the left and the road to postmodernism at the right. At best, the two routes function to tell us which road we have been travelling along in our cultural life once a certain number of signs begin to cluster, to become expectable places (*topoi*) in our thought-style.

It may well be that I will not honour my topic. This will depend upon your point of view. In earlier times, I might have presumed upon its direction. Today, however, Marxists are less sure of themselves and post-modernists would be offended by any other certainty than uncertainty. Here is a dilemma we have inherited from modernism, namely, that we cannot start from any certain sense of the public's authority nor of its morality. This is so because a modern public cannot resist the seduction of its own decentring, of its irrelevance and its dispersion. So you would be no more satisfied if I were to presume upon your postmodernism as a perspective upon your Marxism than if I were to treat your Marxism as an antidote for your postmodernism. So I will try to keep the reflections that follow within and against the tradition of modernity, weighing its hopes while marking its melancholy. This, then, is an attempt to honour the question of their relationship by avoiding any dogmatic account of either postmodernism or of Marxism while nevertheless striving within the limits of each perspective to put oneself in question.

I will, however, set forth certain bold assertions at the outset so that they may serve either as a guide to or as a summary review of the places (*topoi*) at which one must engage argument.[2] At the same time, nothing requires that one's development of these issues should be concerned with them in any sequence or priority. They are, then, reminders or remainders of the postmodern condition (Hassan 1971).

THESES ON POSTMODERNISM

1 Novelty is the new conformity; yet
2 the return to history is rather an escape from history.
3 The norms of subjectivity and pleasure are conscriptions of repressive *jouissance*; at the same time as
4 the open history of fashion and style is the end of all histories mirrored in our own.
5 Fashion rewrites the body, assigns its moods, movements, and manageability in order to distract us from the corpse of politics.
6 Style rewrites the mind, appropriates authority and narrativity in order to subject writing to writing – grammatology without end.
7 No attempt to *épater la bourgeoisie* can satisfy the bourgeois capacity for shock, violence, and deception.
8 Alienation and youth are no longer shocking in themselves or even together; this is because alienated youth is the norm – but without any sense of its alternatives.
9 All such observations are met with indifference; this is because –
10 we no longer have the will to difference. Begin again at point one above . . . repeat until the cycle separates into Stations of the Cross but with no Easter.

What is difficult in thinking about postmodernism is that it deprives us of the very resource of parody needed to situate it. This is because postmodernism celebrates the neutralization of all conviction from which even mimicry derives. Our predicament is that neither socialist realism nor bourgeois fictionalism will show our society to itself because its soup cans and its tractors are neither more dead than alive. Moreover, their reproduction actually confirms the production of the ideology of repetition and so convinces us of the foreclosure of history in the narrow future of the self's immediate future. Socialism appears no less to confirm our capacity for boredom than does capitalism. For whether alienation is banned or bastardized, it still eats away at our insides, voicelessly. Thus we are condemned to the present as our future, and no wind truly waves the bright flags of postmodernism or Marxism.

The fact is that our neo-liberalism will not allow institutional substructures to determine cultural superstructures any more than it will allow history to work behind our backs. And the same is true of our liberal politics. We will not prefer class to race or to gender, even if it means moving the political struggle indoors, floating it in the imaginary settings of commissions, television, and the university where insurrection is about as obscene as an erection. This is probably more true of North American practice than of European politics, even though such practice nicely fits with the linguistic excesses and the withering of truth and history celebrated in poststructuralist theory. The awful thing is that our political space has been foreclosed in the name of both theory and practice. Under these circumstances the common sense of British Marxists is little better than the hedonism of their French counterparts or the postmodern puritanism of their American commentators.

However we refer to it, there can be little doubt that we now experiment with postmodernism. Indeed, this may so far be the case that no one can recall – let alone be recalled to – modernism. Yet we know enough to know that despite its mock seriousness, postmodernism could hardly be responsible for itself. Postmodernism displays energy that is frivolous and wasteful. We know that it has solved no historical problem, that it has not come into any utopian end of history and that, above all, it is prematurely aged with its own pretence that youth has neither a past nor a future. Yet there is a complaint, however thin its voice, that postmodernism cannot fail to bring against its parent. It is the charge that it is, after all, nothing but the child of modernism. It therefore cannot be understood unless the compulsion that drove modernism to yield to its own after-effect can be understood. Why do parents weaken themselves with the hope of their offspring who are in turn burdened with a future for which they lack strength and against which they must rage? Viewed in this way, postmodernism wastes itself with the reproduction of the past in an infantile hope of monumentalizing a moment outside of its own memory that might somehow trigger its identity, its past and future now. Postmodernism is therefore extremely verbal, despite its weak capacity for language; it is a master of gesticulation but otherwise inarticulate. Architecture is its empty soul; and film and literature its wandering ghosts.

Yet it appears that modernity (or pre-postmodernism, if you will) has been sick all along with its own dead end. Now it is mocked by its own children for not having delivered their development, their endless progress, their reasonableness, their polymorphous bodies of desire, their love and peace, their seals and whales. The children divide their complaint into consumerism on the right and anti-communism on the left and in between the older children rejuvenate themselves momentarily in Live Aid concerts. Everything testifies to the insanity of postmodernism. Politics, art, and the economy turn into fragments of light spinning off a glass globe at the centre of a dark world where the children dance to their own deafness. Everything glitters in a world without vision. Language fractures in the same way. Our stories do not hold but instead they proliferate without priority. Unable even to order their own elements, our narrative arts begin nowhere, end nowhere, and are a puzzle to their own fictional inhabitants. The farm, the factory, and the family are wastelands of character, order, and progress and no longer serve the engine of postmodernity any better than a disco. Terrorism, racism, and the unofficial wars in Afghanistan, Nicaragua, Lebanon, and Ireland (tomorrow's list will alter the scene but not the horror) divide the political realm, scatter its sites and scramble the language of revolution in the disorders of the disfigured but twin enterprises of capitalism and communism. In such observations we, of course, overwhelm ourselves, entangling ourselves in the ceaseless flux of events without a history or a space – or rather of events that have been deterritorialized and dehistoricized by the failure of modernity to include them in its geopolitical order.

The question that postmodernism turns upon is, how do we justify the repudiation of the past that gives modernism its sense and yet not accept everything around us in the present – including modernism and its generation of anti-modernism, if not postmodernism? Can we really set aside our Cartesianism and Kantianism, or our positivism, as though they haven't withstood our Hegelianism, our structuralism, our mediations and totalities, and although these, too, are worn around the edges, ought we to discard them into the bargain? If the bourgeois humanist tradition is bankrupt, shouldn't we also call in our loans to socialist humanism? Of course, the Left continues to be braver in its philosophy than in its politics. What I mean is that anti-humanism may look well on one's office door while the university enjoys civil liberties and good salaries in exchange for its responsible academic irresponsibility. But where the political consequences of anti-humanism are practised by soulless bureaucracies and state machineries of confinement, censorship, and torture – such a notice would merely mark one's own disappearance. Between the alternatives of philosophical bravado and political impotence, there lies the intermediate realm of the economy, class, race, and illness, as well as the outer horizons of colonialism and nuclearism, where it is harder to pronounce the death of humanism and yet difficult to hold on to the birth of socialism. In a sense, we exclude ourselves through the very practice of such panoramic surveys which are to the intellectual what the supermarket is to the consumer – our ersatz freedom of choice exchanged for abandoning productive choices in the economy and the polity. Of course, the university and the rest of our mass-media culture supplement the shopping centre in the maintenance of a society without history, where everything jostles everything else in an unseasonable present. We suffer our moral poverty as that *embarrass de richesse* we call pluralism and per-spectivism because we no longer assign to the self and its situations any authority beyond its own renunciation, and then we fall into style.

There is in postmodernism a certain will to willessness – a failure of nerve that gives it its nerve. How is that? It reveals itself in the *primacy of language*, in the objectivity of institutions resistant to intention, affect, and hope. Such institutions turn language against itself, making it an autonomous discourse resistant to context and common sense. The dead end of history, the foreclosure of community, and the trivialization of the self and family are the rubble upon which we construct our glass corporations. Here speculation is doubly spectacular. We have gambled against ourselves while constructing glass towers to reflect everything we have lost – a corporate Babel where language holds to no centre. Reflecting our reduced polytheism, the glass corporation miniaturizes us with its welcome, its disposability, its accommodation of our wants generated on its behalf. Such events, so far from being extra-linguistic, are inconceivable without a similar incorporation of language in a self-sufficient structure. Paradoxically, it is then the language paradigm to which appeal is made in order to compre-hend the objectivity of our corporate institutions, whose self-contained discourse is productive of our deepest alienation from meaning, context, and purpose. The naturalization of the language para-digm is the ideological counterpart to the dehistoricization and the depoliticization of the capitalist process. Thus meaning-and-value-production exceed us as much as the ordinary labour of work; and in each case we are dispossessed by what we need. The implicit complaint in this observation, however, cannot be articulated once our language has gone on a poststructuralist holi-day, abandoning its own history to the rituals of meaning without values.

The cry that there is nothing outside of language or that there is not extratextuality (*hors texte*) is insufferable because it is we who are outside of language once the flow of its signifiers exceeds our attempts to identify their referents. It is our history, our community, our hope that is abandoned with the embrace of the quasi-natural language reproduced in the discursive machines of our corporate and governmental institutions. Our commercialism, like our intellectualism, mesmerizes us and, precisely because we make ourselves central to its spectacles, we thereby lose our historical and social bearings. Thus the power of the media over us is the power we have in the media, providing we surrender to its desires as our wants. What else we might truly need will also be supplied by the media in morality plays and subsidized corporate high culture. In the latter, the struggles of the family and the individual with some authority are specularized in compensation for their abandonment in the commercialized and politicized ethics that rule the day. Thus the culture industry produces an ethics of nostalgia which spiritualizes us as passive spectators of the world we have lost, while simultaneously foreclosing any insight into how our past morality might be rendered continuous without future moral needs. The result is that fundamentalism prevails over utopianism. Or else we have to refurbish our religions, and in this regard, Marxism and Christianity are on the same footing in needing to reconnect the events of human suffering with institutional mediations that translate work, reason, and love into meaningful lives for persons, families, and communities fulfilling the present with the continuity of past and future hopes.

The postmodernist rejection of mediations, the search for immediate presence, is haunted by the unfulfilment of this desire. The rejection of Christ's mediation of human history left not only the Jewish people waiting and thirsting in the desert – it has scattered all interpretation. However discreetly we make our assumptions, the dance of polytheism surrounds them and the outer edges of knowledge and value darken. Neither nature nor mind nor the body has replaced the theological text with self-certain readings because in them we have only rediscovered the blind spot in ourselves. For such insight we pay to ourselves a price that disclaims any redemptive value. Having reduced language and history to our own uses, we are as unsure of our place among their shifting signifiers as we are of any other thing no longer signified except as it clings to exchange value. Here nothing stands unless it be style, and then even style must hope it will be recycled, affirming the second time around its celebration of absolute irrelevance. In such contexts, the self loses its depth; everything becomes a surface – our mirrors reflect nothing but a glassy superficiality of looks, arrangement, decor, montage. Between the spaces lie the dead gods of divinity, authoriality and paternity without which grammar itself falls apart. Thus we no longer observe any canon and our master narratives fragment into hysterical case histories whose incompleteness marks our impotent and uncertain point of view. Lacking a storyable literature, we also lack a politics and thereby any sense of history, place, and family except as we append these to madness and exploitation. Or else we retreat to our libraries and blindly explore their labyrinths, entombing desire in dead languages that will never again gather any community beyond the bone heaps of literary criticism.

Postmodern artists reject the aestheticist autonomy of modern art. However, while problematizing both the subjective and objective referents of art, it cannot be said that postmodernism has reduced the élitism of art, escaped from its commercialism, or abandoned itself to the interpretative will of a new political public.[3] Moreover, the gesture of killing off God and ourselves as fellow artists surely no longer astonishes a bourgeoisie that long ago emigrated into the labyrinths of bureaucracy, into the irresponsibility of the market, *realpolitik*, and fashionable histories in which everything is degradable. In short, it is difficult to hang on to postmodernism's claim to be transgressive given the capacity of late capitalism to absorb and to neutralize every shock it imposes upon human truth, justice, equality, and beauty, and even to replay these outrages in anything from a rock video to a commercial or new release. The faster the culture industry runs to outrage its bourgeoisie, the surer it can be of its own embourgeoisement. After all, vulgarity in the appropriation of wealth by those who are successful in the culture industry cannot be considered to have revolutionized our society or its values. When the children of rock video sing out to the starving children of the world, charity itself has been reduced to a postmodern gesture of having fun on behalf of the world's immiseration. We have to ask whether Jesus would have done better as a Palestinian disc jockey. The idiocy of such questions reflects the uncertainty we experience in wanting to believe that any of our institutions work towards our humanity. It may well be that 'we' – intellectuals and artists – are paid to suffer this question without politicizing it in order to square it with our ordinary moral conviction that the world's humanity is still worth working for and that it cannot be trashed by the present disvalues of any major society. Postmodernism is perhaps the penance we pay for abandoning politics. But such a *mea culpa* reverses the order of things. For we have no politics that has not already abandoned us in its pursuit of greed, triviality, and borderline insanity. It isn't just that the king has no clothes – he is naked because he is a corpse, mindless and speechless.

Hal Foster has suggested that we can distinguish two lineages in postmodernism, somewhat as follows:

1 *Neo-conservative* postmodernism;
2 *Poststructuralist* postmodernism.[4]

The nomenclature is, however, a little clumsy. On the one hand, neo-conservatives would probably consider poststructuralism part of the culture of anti-modernism which they deplore. They would also be surprised at being considered postmodernists rather than, say, neo-modernists. This is because they remain enamoured of the modernist will to subjectivity, action, and history. Poststructuralists, on the other hand, appear to be beating the dead horse of modernism whose corpse is perhaps more rotten, even if more recent, when found in the streets of socialism. Poststructuralists seem to believe that the cart of history and politics can lurch along without any horse in front of it – they do not notice the masses pushing from behind. The same is true of the more flamboyant cultural antics of postmodenists. Their pretence to *épater la bourgeoisie* merely starves out the ignorant masses while scarcely feeding the voracious appetite of the bourgeoisie for shock, outrage, and violence. By the same token, the bourgeois consumption of violent culture protects it from its own productions of historyless violence which have colonized the domestic imagination as well as our extraterrestrial dreams. Thus the Super-Id of late capitalism expands in the wasteland created through the collapse of the modernist Super-Ego, giving rise to a neo-conservative lament for lost spiritual authority. Late-capitalist technologies no longer manufacture history and selfhood, any more than the professions and bureaucracy can reproduce society and the family.

Postmodernism is a further expression of what I shall call *creative neotony*. The latter is without training; it relies on instinct which generally serves it badly since the circumstances of action generally change. This affords neotony a continuous lament. But it remains incapable, despite all its resolutions, of creating either society or character. Neotony cannot create institutions because it exhausts itself in starting up, in responding, feeling, adopting its own point of view. Neotony is all entropy, its youth is haggard, wasted because of the intensity with which it locks itself into a single emotion, shibboleth, or discourse. Neotony is therefore a form of death, the repetition of a single desire invoked to cancel the obligations from which it is in flight towards death. The obligations from which neotony is turned away are the exercise of one's limits, the necessity of training, the lesson of patience and the public institution of character and motive committed to a tradition of achievement that cannot be exhausted either in its pleasures or its difficulties.

Late capitalism unleashes an unbounded narcissism for which it simultaneously produces the liquefactions of an ahistorical, asocial mass culture, economy, and politics. Such a culture is marked by its identification of opposites, its ability to collapse contraries, to combine sentimentalism and indifference, exploitation and emancipation, to psychologize the political process while deepening its disciplinary politicizations of the psyche and its therapeutic culture. Thus the psycho-text and the skin surfaces are inscribed within the circuits of symbolic exchange whose own cyclicity of highs and lows provides all there is of orientation, history, and value. Experience surrenders to the autonomy of the instant which in turn cracks all memory. Suffering cannot be recalled except through the rosy glasses of nostalgia. Denunciation sounds manic and, like the bitter critic, excludes itself with an apology. Capital is, after all, self-critical, bitter and self-mocking, cruel and kind, intelligent and zany. How should we exceed this God-term? How are we to refuse it its proper idols?

As Weber saw, our reason has divided once and for all into the subrationalities of science, art, and ethics. But we have not experienced any detotalizing settlement in this process. On the contrary, our science tries to rule our politics and economy, while our economy largely dominates our art and morality, if not our science. At the extreme edge, our art and morality try to impose their rule upon our science and political economy – but they generally lack the stamina, as in the university; or else they scandalize us, as in the case of liberation theology. Surely, we can hardly hope for postmodern literary criticism to rise above these contradictions – to unmask social difference (class, gender, race) and to regenerate 'our' humanism. The more literary criticism achieves social consciousness, the more it dissipates – like everything else in the postmodern experience. To return to Weber, we might say that the crisis of modernity consists in the empty voice of its double vocation for science and politics – men are no longer sure of their ruling knowledge and are unable to mobilize sufficient legitimation for the master-narratives of truth and justice. The fact is that philosophy, history, and religion have lost their authority.[5] This has been known for some time. Yet we seem to need Lyotard and Rorty to tell us this – despite their own bad faith. Lyotard tells us the news, having learned that the physical and biological sciences are tactical, prize-seeking enterprises in which truth is entirely strategic. Rorty chats away in a post-Wittgensteinian room whose mirrors reflect nothing but the lost contexts of his own good sense. The lesson is that we never would have been surrounded by so many corpses – Reason, Desire, Woman, God, Society – had we asked less of the seminar and the bedroom.

Such is the news from Paris and Princeton. We must recognize that words and things have come unstuck. Thus we are all schizophrenics without logos: the flesh writhes, shouts, screams, or sinks into speechlessness. Or perhaps women, hitherto excluded from language, will resuture words and things for us, if there is still time left for such gynesis.[6] For it now looks as though European men have declared themselves as much out of style as Hollywood men. Stallone and Clint Eastwood notwithstanding, the men are no longer as sure as a gun. Rather, the gun itself assures their death – over and over – and the death of the Western (revived, of course, in the new genre of films on pre-post-Vietnam) is on a par with the death of the Western metaphysics that once underwrote it. Whether feminized women can turn themselves into a final metafiction, or at least a fiction that will buy us more time, remains to be seen. In the short run, of course, they are in vogue, talking, writing, and voting themselves into the vacancies advertised for women. Whether these former troglodytes can make the workplace, the university, parliament, and the TV any more true or just remains to be seen. What is currently undecidable about women might then be what is currently undecidable about the exhaustion of modernity and the birth of postmodernism.

Yet, who can say? And when the story begins to take shape, will it be a good one or will we have to put out our eyes for nothing?

NOTES

1 Hassan, I. (1971) *The Dismemberment of Orpheus: Toward a Postmodern Literature*, New York: Oxford University Press, p. 119. Also applies to subsequent references in this chapter.
2 These theses owe something to H. Foster (1985) *Recordings: Art, Spectacle, Cultural Politics*, Post Townsend, Wash.: Bay Press. See also I. Hassan (1986–7) 'Making Sense: The Trials of Postmodern Discourse', *New Literary History*, 18(3): 437–59.

3 Gablik, S. (1984) *Has Modernism Failed?*, New York: Thames and Hudson.
4 Foster, H. '(Post) Modern Polemics', in his *Recordings*, pp. 121–37.
5 Bernstein, R. (ed.) (1985) *Habermas and Modernity*, New York: Basil Blackwell.
6 Jardine, A.A. (1985) *Gynesis: Configurations of Women and Modernity*, Ithaca, NY: Cornell University Press.

Chapter 2

The therapeutic disciplines
From Parsons to Foucault

Sociological discourse was fashioned in the midst of the upheavals and conflicts of an industrializing society in which it was imperative to re-think the grounds of social consensus. Under such conditions, the problem of order was subject to a variety of discursive treatments. Thus religionists, moralists, secularists, reformers, and utopians all vied with one another to invoke past and future orders, to decry conflict and exploitation or to hail the creative and apocalyptic upheaval that could introduce the perfect society. Within this babel of tongues we can now distinguish the particular voices of Marx, Durkheim, and Freud – if not the sombre tones of Weber or the mad cries of Nietzsche. All of these writers were aware of the problem of finding a mode of discourse which would successfully reveal other modes of analysing and prescribing social conduct. Nietzsche aside, we think of Marx, Durkheim, and Freud as founding-fathers because each laid down a science of society. Moreover, they included in their respective sciences an account of ideological and irrational forces of self-interest which prevent the acceptance of the sciences they prescribed for the society they observed. In this Nietzsche has, of course, the final laugh. For he understood the will-to-knowledge as the power of powers which in the modern world can achieve no successful hegemony of virtue.

Like Nietzsche, though with more of a lament, Weber also saw that our times produce no enduring charismatic focus strong enough to resist the thin reasoning of modernization. Thus we all labour within institutions whose subcodes of rationality, utility, and efficiency derive from a master code of rationalization and differentiation. This code is designed to discipline individuals in spheres, or roles and tasks that reproduce society in a series of exchanges between subjective commitments, or expression, and collective necessity, or order. Within this system of exchanges we discourse upon our rationality, our health, our happiness, our sexuality, our families, as well as our sickness, insanity, alienation, and criminality. The result is that, as Foucault (1980) has argued, modern social control has shifted from a largely external threat of execution wielded by cruel but administratively weak state authorities to the self-administered discipline of minds and bodies in the therapeutic state (Rieff 1966). Foucault's often difficult historical studies may be rendered less exotic if attention is drawn to a more familiar sociological corpus – namely, the structural functionalist theories of Talcott Parsons and Robert K. Merton in which we can analyse the discursive production of the concept of social control in terms of cybernetic, monetary, and medical discourse. It is important to do this because the medicalization of the concept of social control is central to the professionalization of sociology itself, and to sociology's claim upon a fiduciary place in the administration of modern therapeutic society.

In the following chapter we will uncover the archaeology of docility that runs from Plato's *Republic* through to Parsons' *Social System* (1951). Such an inquiry does not discover a single strategy for the production of the docile citizen. Rather, what appears is a plurality of discursive strategies in philosophical and medical discourse to achieve hegemony over the body-politic (O'Neill 1985). At the same time, the site of such discourse shifts from the academy to the factory, prison, army, school, asylum, while its protagonists realign – philosophers, physicians, economists, penologists, psychiatrists, and sociologists forming shifting alliances in the production of a docile citizenry. Despite the complexity of these emerging discourses it is possible, as Foucault has shown, to discern since the nineteenth century two major registers in the discursive production of the docile citizen. It is within this double framework that we wish to locate the medicalization of the problem of social control in contemporary sociological discourse:

> The classical age discovered the body as object and target of power. It is easy enough to find signs of the attention then paid to the body – to the body that is manipulated, shaped, trained, which obeys, responds, becomes skillful and increases its forces. The great book of Man-the-Machine was written simultaneously on two registers; the *anatomico-metaphysical register*, of which Descartes wrote the first pages and which the physicians and philosophers continued, and the *techno-political register*, which

which was constituted by a whole set of regulations and by empirical and calculated methods relating to the army, the school and the hospital, for controlling or correcting the operations of the body.

These two registers are quite distinct, since it was a question, on the one hand, of submission and use and, on the other, of functioning and explanation: there was a useful body and an intelligible body. And yet there are points of overlap from one to the other. La Mettrie's *L'Homme-machine* is both a materialist reduction of the soul and a general theory of dressage, at the centre of which reigns the notion of 'docility' which joins the analysable body to the manipulable body.

(Foucault 1979: 136)

The two registers of docility reflect two sides of the problem of social control, namely, how it is that individuals can be induced to commit themselves *morally* to a social order that seeks to bind them to itself *physically*, i.e., in virtue of its discovery of certain laws of association. The conventional critical wisdom holds that Parsons' structural functionalism sublimates the moral question in favour of its analytic resolution, overriding critical consciousness with the normative claims of social consensus. Whether from a Hobbesian or Freudian perspective, sociology has always flirted with the discovery of a social physics. Thus utilitarianism offered it a convenient compromise in the search for a rational theory of compulsion which could also accommodate behaviourist discoveries on the modification of individual conduct. The dream of the social sciences lies in the search for control strategies that would overlap the micro and macro orders of behaviour in a single order of administration. Foucault's studies remind us that the social sciences are historically contrived strategies of social discipline that operate from multiple sites of institutional power/knowledge. In other words, despite the analytic power of the Parsonian vision, the discipline of sociology is not only a cognitive science but a moral science whose object is the social production of a docile citizenry.

It is a truism of social thought that the good citizen is produced by the good society. The difficulty has been to invent a 'moral microscope' which would permit us to view the interaction processes between the two orders of conduct. Here the metaphor of the body-politic has played an important function throughout the history of western social and political thought (O'Neill 1985). Philosophers would long ago have pre-empted social scientists if their window upon the soul had opened upon anything else than the society in which souls are an intractable problem for philosophers. Yet we have no window on society. Rather, what we can learn from Foucault is that we have a history of panoptical strategies for rendering ourselves visible, knowable, talkable. Within this discursive history the metaphor of the body as a source of health and order, as well as of illness and disorder, has generated discourse in philosophy, politics, psychology, medicine, and sociology. Despite the superficial abstractness of Parsonian theory, it is heavily indebted to the basic metaphor of the body as a holistic system of interchanges whose orderliness is constitutive of its health. This basic metaphor is deepened but not altered by later discoveries that the body's internal controls are embedded in a communicative bio-chemistry. Structural-functionalism represents an extraordinary cross-mapping of the functions of the social body and its constituent members, specified to subsystem exchanges on the level of community, politics, economy, and personality. It thereby fulfils the philosopher's dream in casting the sociological theorist as a social physician, doctor of society.

THE MEDICALIZATION OF THE PROBLEM OF ORDER

In the light of recent work by Foucault (1979; 1980), I will show just how the interaction occurs between sociological discourse upon social control and medical discourse upon health and illness. This approach to the problem of social control means that sociologists must find ways of analysing the discursive production of the basic concepts that organize everyday institutional behaviour – not exempting the practices of sociological discourse itself. Here the task is not to produce a genealogy of sociological discourse, as necessary as it might be. It is rather to take a biopsy, as it were, by cutting swiftly and narrowly into the sociological corpus at a point where the greatest diagnostic benefit could be achieved. This strategy has already in part deconstructed itself, of course, in the play of bio-medical metaphors employed to discover the *medicalization of social science discourse*. Nevertheless its value is to draw attention to a key modality of modern power/knowledge.

Speaking of the spread of professional knowledge in the administration of modern society, Parsons himself points to the tendency to treat social control in terms of medical discourse:

This process in turn has been associated with an extension of the focus of ultimate 'responsibility' for the health problems of the society. There was once a sense in which the medical profession shouldered that responsibility virtually unaided except for the basic legitimation of its position in the community. Now it clearly must be shared with administration and trustees, governmental and private, and with universities or organizations. Perhaps above all it is now shared with the various relevant scientific professions, the most recent additions to which are the behavioral.

(Parsons 1965: 355)

Two major discursive strategies in dealing with problems of social control and deviance may be identified in the Parsons/Merton corpus, selected for study because of its dominant place in Anglo-American sociological discourse over the past fifty years: (1) the *clinicalization* of the modalities of socio-political conduct (Merton 1938; 1957: 131–60); (2) the *medicalization* of the mechanisms of social control (Parsons 1965: 257–358). It is in the light of Foucault's attention to discourse production that we can give retrospective force to clinicalization and medicalization as strategies to limit the socio-political space of the American economic order. Thus an unnameable class system functions as a prison without walls, a borderline of reason and unreason, of health and sickness. It simultaneously generates the production of social science discourse in a therapeutic mode. Structural-functionalism is the quasi-natural science of a society whose political discourse is foreclosed through the scientization of its moral life. Weber knew this to his sorrow. Parsons is remarkable for his persistent attempt to underwrite the health of a social order in which the health system forecloses any question of its own reason and justice and is currently a major site for critical reconstruction (O'Neill 1985). Hence there is no argument here for the assimilation of Parsons and Foucault. The task is to analyse how Parsonian discourse produces the concept of social control/power as a health/illness process to be administered as a therapeutic rather than political function.

MERTON'S CLINICALIZATION OF SOCIO-POLITICAL SPACE

The problem of order and conflict, or of commitment and deviance, involves every social and political theorist in some account of the basic propensity to reproduce the social order. Thus there is a long history comprising a variety of discourses, religious, moral, biological, and psychological, in which arguments are made to reconcile either humankind's anti-social nature with civilizing social institutions, or its social nature with anti-social institutions. Parsons and Merton rejected the view that social institutions merely repress an otherwise anti-social human nature. Parsons, certainly, was much too sophisticated in his readings (1965: 17–126) of Freud to adopt any simplistic view of the endemic conflict between the social system and persons or bio-psychological systems. At the same time, the Parsons/Merton theory of social control avoids a crude collective basis. It clinically maps the differential opportunities for the production of conformity and deviance afforded to individuals according to their 'locations' in a social system characterized by a structural bias towards socio-economic success but with inadequately generalized access to legitimate resources and institutions to meet its challenge. The clinical tabulation of individual accommodations to this 'structural strain', as Parsons would express what Marxists call 'class conflict', is contained in Merton's classical typology (Table 2.1):

Table 2.1 A typology of modes of individual adaptation

Modes of adaptation	Culture goals	Institutionalized means
I Conformity	+	+
II Innovation	+	−
III Ritualism	−	+
IV Retreatism	−	−
V Rebellion	±	±

Very briefly, Merton classifies individual responses to institutional strain between goals and means, where (+) means 'acceptance', (-) means 'rejection', and (±) means 'rejection of prevailing values and substitution of new values', and he emphasizes that these are confined to role behaviour in the economy broadly conceived. Although he does not intend to classify personality types as this poses too complex a problem, the scheme has been interpreted in this way pedagogically, if not ideologically. Merton himself claims only that where, as in the United States, there is a cultural bias towards socio-economic success, together with an ideology enjoining universal competition, individuals will construe failure as a self-fault, as a lack of ambition, rather than fault the social system. Only in the exceptional case of 'rebellion' will the social system and its values be rejected in favour of an alternative society:

In sociological paraphrase, these axioms represent, first, the deflection of social criticism of the social structure onto one's self among those so situated in the society that they do not have full and equal access to opportunity; second, the preservation of a structure of social power by having individuals in the lower social strata identify themselves, not with their compeers, but with those at the top (whom they will ultimately join); and third, providing pressures for conformity with the cultural dictates of unslackened ambition by the threat of less than full membership in the society for those who fail to conform.

(Merton 1957: 139)

A Marxist might easily dismiss Merton's topology as nothing but a description of 'false consciousness' in the United States and as such consider it a prime example of the discourse of bourgeois social science. In fact, it is a remarkably prescient (1938) formulation of the sociological mechanisms through which the discourse generated by the 'American ideology' (Wilson 1977) functions so effectively. What Merton shows, from numerous samples of literary and commercial discourse, is how Americans produced a discourse upon individualized success and failure in which everyone ought to participate in order to make any social conspiracy universal. In short, the discursive power of the American ideology does not derive from the so-called 'superstructure', as Marxists claim; it proceeds discursively from everywhere and from nowhere and its moral appeal cannot be reduced to narrow economism. Here Merton really contributes to the specificity of social control theory from which Marxist sociology might well profit in order to increase its explanatory power. Without explicitly saying so, Merton leaves no doubt that it is class position, mediated through the family, which filters individual responses to conformity or deviance with respect to American social goals and values. But since both conservatism and socialism are rival discourses for addressing the basic problems of the social system, the sociologist is obliged to discover a more analytic discourse through which he can subordinate folk accounts of social order and conflict in the encompassing discourse of sociological diagnosis.

What Merton's typology does, in effect, is to *clinicalize the socio-political space of individual responses to the American socio-economic order*. It displays the individual's options in a socio-psychological domain of strenuous conformity, moral defeatism, criminality (alcoholism, drug addiction, gambling, embezzling). While Merton does not intend to classify personality types, he in effect reduces the social control problem to this discursive strategy of psychologizing the stratification process. This is because he does not sufficiently analyse the political space that is foreclosed by the American socio-economic order. To be fair, he recognizes that the rebel, and not just the reformer, might well increase the overall functioning of the social system. On balance, however, the American social system seems to absorb or co-opt its deviants rather than undergo any serious moral transvaluation by them (Bell 1961). What is at issue here is the peculiar nature of the political space within which the American citizen can act. The bias of the American social system is to have its citizens empty their imagination in the economy of success rather than to encourage their political imagination (de Tocqueville 1954).

PARSONS' MEDICALIZATION OF THE CONCEPT OF SOCIAL CONTROL

Parsons and Merton must be regarded as the major architects of contemporary sociological discourse, whatever its variants and despite all critical responses and alternative discourses (conflict theory, symbolic interactionism, Marxism, phenomenology). Structural-functionalism involves a major analytic reduction of classical sociological discourse (see Parsons 1937) to an identifying disciplinary code of fourfold *systemic functions* and an identifying code of *pattern variables* derived from the logic of social interaction. It is necessary to describe these two codes, however briefly, in order to convey their analytic power in bringing to focus an otherwise bewildering variety of social behaviour, contents, and institutions.

What Parsons and Merton have produced in the theory of structural functionalism is a mode of sociological discourse which can shift between vocabularies of ethico-legal systems and bio-cybernetic systems, thereby displaying the interlock between personality and social systems as a normative but quasi-natural mechanism of social control. In *The Social System* (1951) Parsons constructed what can only be considered a sociological holograph, far exceeding the analytic power of Quesnay's *Tableau Economique* (1758), if not Marx's schema of simple and expanded reproduction or Weber's ideal types. The theory of functional prerequisites and of the pattern variables may be considered identifying codes of sociological practice in the double sense that their usage displays holographically a society for analysis at the same time favouring the sociologist as society's diagnostic physician. In the Parsonian social system the professional sociologist's place as a *social physician*, or psychotherapist, is essential to the health of the system just as modern society is unthinkable apart from its valuing of individual health and medical care:

> It is not meant to press the similarity between psychotherapy and other mechanisms of social control too far. Certainly there are just as important differences as there are similarities, but the relationship seems to be sufficiently close, and the common factors sufficiently general, so that then similarities can provide important leads to the recognition and analysis of the operation of control mechanisms which as such are by no means obvious to common sense. . . . An immense amount of research will be necessary in this field.
>
> (Parsons 1951: 319)

The control function

A simple list of the functional prerequisites and the pattern-variables, with a minimum of commentary, serves to give them the appearance of the Mosaic Law, i.e., of a table of sociological commandments laying down the invariants of individual and collective life. We choose to present the 'Parsonian Tables' this way, not only as a pedagogical device but to reproduce the moral effects of Parsons' insistence upon the invariant functions of order. Parsons' understanding of the invariants of social life as bio-systemic properties of the body-politic (Henderson 1917; Cannon 1932) is deliberately moralized in order to show how sociological discourse at this level is inextricably part of a socio-legal and bio-medical imagery designed to give quasi-natural force to its ethico-political imperatives. Parsons starts from the assumption that every social system comprises a series of discursive events as well as several quasi-natural processes. Social systems must reproduce themselves on at least four levels: (1) as a culture (order of meaning); (2) as a society (order of integration); (3) as an economy (order of allocation); and (4) as a polity (order of legitimation). To the extent that social systems meet these functional prerequisites, we can speak of resolving the problem of order in terms of successful interchanges of commitment and motivation from individuals (personality system) and of legitimation and social control (social system). Where these functional prerequisites are disturbed, or are in some way lacking in mutual articulation, the interchange between the social system and personality system are marked by alienation, withdrawal, apathy, rebellion, and possibly revolution.

Consider first the larger social system in which the social control function involves a hierarchy of social controls that operate through sub-system interchanges between persons in roles and roles in institutions. Any social system, then, is identifiably such only in so far as it necessarily maintains intersystemic exchanges between the following four sub-systems:

1 *The Function of Pattern-Maintenance.* 'The function of pattern-maintenance refers to the imperative of maintaining the stability of the patterns of institutionalized culture defining the structure of the system.' This may be called the *fiduciary system*,

2 *The Function of Goal-Attainment.* 'For any complex system . . . it is necessary to speak of a system of goals rather than of a single unitary goal. It concerns, therefore, not commitment of the values of the society, but *motivation* to contribute what is necessary for the functioning of the system . . .' This may be called the *polity* of the system,

3 *The Function of Adaptation.* 'The primary criterion is the provision of flexibility, so far as this is compatible with effectiveness; for the system, this means a maximum of *generalized disposability* in the processes of allocation between alternative uses. Within the complex types of social system, this disposability of facilities crystallizes about the institutionalization of money and markets.' This may be called the *economy* of the system,

4 *The Function of Integration.* 'The functional problem of integration concerns the mutual adjustments of . . . sub-systems from the point of view of their "contributions" to the effective functioning of the system as a whole. . . . The institutionalization of money and power are primarily integrative phenomena, like other mechanisms of social control in the narrower sense.' This may be called the *community* organization of the system.

(Parsons 1961: 30–79)

The social system, Parsons claims, is not concerned with regulating either physical objects or physiological behaviour as such. Rather it is concerned only with allocating rights and duties towards things and persons as symbolic factors, i.e., as the producers of meaningful and legitimate tokens within a broadly shared cultural and value framework. With this reservation in mind, then, we may picture the social system as an input–output system as follows (Parsons 1961: 61):

Table 2.2 Schematic tabulation of societal inputs and outputs

Primary social sub-system	Input and source	Output and destination
Pattern-maintenance	Given structure as institutionalized patterns of normative culture (no external source)	Maintenance of structure and specification of values (no external source)
Integration	Plasticity (from behavioural organism)	Patterns for purposive response (to behavioural organism)
Goal-attainment	Capacity for socialized motiva-tional commitments (from personality)	Goal gratification (to personality)
Adaptation	Codes for organ-ization of information (from cultural system)	Validation of standards of competence (to cultural system)

It is necessary, however, to remain alert to some of the potentially misleading features in this table of an abstract economy of exchanges. The issue is not that it renders the real economy in terms of cybernetic discourse as such, but that the input–output format disarmingly suggests that the social system actually regulates individual conformity without class or psychological conflict. It portrays a cybernetic process without locating its sources of endemic conflict and the necessary control functions designed to meet them. By the same token the metaphors of cybernetic exchange and communication systems theory were attractive to Parsons because he needed to steer himself between the crude economistic discourse of a society conceived as nothing but a field for the pursuit of selfish interest and the political discourse of a society in which collective interests prevailed in every respect at the expense of individual expression. As well as avoiding the extremes of collectivist and individualist discourse, Parsons had also to avoid the two extremes on the theory of human nature and conduct underlying the alternative societies of socialism and liberalism.

Despite Parsons' brilliant sociological critique of the Hobbesian and Freudian interest theories of behaviour, he seems to have remained a liberal utilitarian. In his last years, he undertook a sophisticated analysis of the money market as a generalized medium of exchange. But the result is that the problem of social control is largely re-psychologized through Parsons' analytic focus upon ego/alter exchanges. Thus in his analysis of the role of force in the social process Parsons (1968) argues that force must be seen as one of a number of mechanisms of social control between ego and alter, namely, *inducement, coercion, persuasion,* and *activation of commitments,* understood as a set of positive and negative sanctions operating upon the individual's subjective and objective environments as perceived by alter (see Parsons 1968: 310):

	Sanction type		Channel	
Positive	Intentional Persuasion	3	1	Situational Inducement
Negative	Activation of commitments	4	2	Coercion

Figure 2.1 Four types of strategy

The result of this typology is to undo the common notion that force is the basis of social order and to consider it a factor like non-circulating gold whose function is to keep the other generalized media of social exchange (money, power, and 'conscience') at par. Here, of course, Parsons and Foucault take a comparable stand in dismissing the illusions of possessive power.

The physician function

Parsons' formulation of the *physician role* should now be examined to see how he assigns the social control function to it. Parsons makes it quite clear that he conceived the sick role and the role of the therapeutic agent (doctor, psychoanalyst, social worker) in the framework of social control. In other words, health and illness are reformulated as patterns of motivation towards the social system, i.e., of *commitment* in the 'normal' case and of *withdrawal* in the deviant case. Above all, the social system must make provision so that illness not be allowed to excuse withdrawal or faulting on social tasks:

I should regard deviance and social control as phenomena concerned with the integrative problems of a social system. Illness we may speak of as, at least in one primary aspect, an impairment of the sick person's integration in solidary relationships with others, in family, jobs, and many other contexts. Seen in this perspective, therapy may be interpreted to be predominantly a reintegrative process. To be successful, such a process must take account of adaptive considerations, notably the pathological state of the organism and/or personality and the nature of the patient's adaptive problems in various aspects of his or her life.

(Parsons 1978: 20)

Thus Parsons assigns the social control function to medicine as a necessary consequence of its 'fiduciary' place in society that values health over illness and elevates relevant scientific knowledge and training over ignorance. These features entail an unavoidable asymmetric relation between the professional and the layperson, putting a strain upon trust, the right to consent, participation, and such values that favour individualism in open competition. Any radical questioning of the 'professional complex' would threaten modern society with regressive dedifferentiation, i.e., with individual backsliding or a return to familism over bureaucratic rationality. The physician–patient exchange is therefore a key switching point between the personality and social system, and it must be coded to realize the rational commitments in the respective roles of patient and physician:

Like other professional roles, that of the physician may be categorized in *pattern variable terms*. It has a high incidence of *universalistic* standards, for example, of the generalizability of propositions about diagnosis and probable therapeutic consequences of medical measures. It is *functionally specific* in that the relations of physicians to their patients are focused on problems of the patients' health rather than on other sorts of personal problems. It is *performance oriented* in that the task of the physician is to intervene actively in actual cases of illness and its threat, not to sit passively by and 'let nature take its course.' It is also predominantly *affectively neutral*, though with the kinds of qualifications that Renée Fox (1959) has proposed under her concept of 'detached concern.' Finally, by contrast with the entrepreneur or executive, the professional role generally, including that of the physician, is governed by an *orientation toward collective* values. The most central manifestation of this is the professional ideology that puts the welfare of the patient ahead of the self interest of the therapeutic agents, physicians in particular.

(Parsons 1978: 25; emphasis added)

Every social system exercises its control function through sanctions of reward and punishment which are written into the hearts and minds of its members. As Parsons sees it, the punitive order in modern societies is tied to conditional love at the level of the individual psychic system – mediated by the family – and to a system of differential rewards of power, status, and economic opportunity – mediated by the class system. Such arrangements form the quasi-natural environment in which individuals are motivated to acquire the ordinary competence, skills, values, and aversions that socialize the normal, able-bodied citizen. Because much can go wrong in the interaction between individuals, families, classes, and the social system, society is obliged to find interpretative codes for dealing with sin, rebellion, alienation, illness, retreatism, anomie, narcissism, and the like. For this reason, all societies institutionalize therapeutic practices – magic, religion, ethics, art, and the human sciences – whose function is to reconcile individual and collective life. Broadly speaking, godlessness, illness, crime, and rebellion are most feared by the institutions of legitimate order since their monopoly of knowledge, values, and force is best exercised as rarely as possible if it is to have maximum demonstration effect.

Parsons differentiates these possibilities of individual and collective disturbance along two major 'axes', i.e., in terms of individual orientation to the *situation* acted within and an orientation to the more general *normative patterns* of the collectivity, which raises questions about the moral status of the total person. These orientations may be tabulated into the following clinico-legal space (Parsons 1968: 270) which in turn may be compared with the Mertonian classificatory space (see Table 2.1).

Thus the sociological bias on the problem of social control is to treat threats to the social system as 'deviance' rather than as elements of a distinctly political revolution. That is why it is very difficult to achieve the status of 'political prisoner' for actions that reject the political and economic system. The result is the foreclosure of revolutionary political space in favour of the *clinicalization of rebellious behaviour* as insane terrorist activity outside the boundaries of political culture. This is a favourite strategy in the Soviet Union,

	Disturbance of total person	Disturbance of particular expectations
'Situational' focus	Problem of 'capacities' for task and role performance Illness as deviance Health as 'conformity'	Problem of commitments to collectivities (Barnard's 'efficiency') Disloyalty as deviance Loyalty as conformity
'Normative' focus	Problem of commitments to values, or of 'morality' 'Sin' and 'immorality' as deviance State of grace or 'good character' as conformity	Problem of commitments to norms, or of ' legality' 'Crime' and 'illegality' as deviance Law-observance as conformity

Figure 2.2 Medicalization of deviance/conformity

in Northern Ireland, and elsewhere. In the United States and Europe, a good deal of sociological analysis has treated even the student revolution of the 'sixties' as expressions of alienated youth narcissistically incapable of social commitment. Such discursive strategies, by favouring the medical model of discourse in the treatment of social and political problems, strengthen the place of social science professions in the therapeutic state and increasingly reduce citizens to the role of docile clients or patients. As Foucault has argued at length, there is no need for Orwell's Big Brother or Bentham's Panopticon in such a society. The medical model of social control moves the site of our discontents from the streets into our souls. There we find we need more health, more education, and more welfare. Thus the therapeutic state is the modern soul writ large. Meantime the soul's discourse has been captured from the philosophers by sociologists, psychologists, and their poor cousin economists.

CONCLUSION: PARSONS AND FOUCAULT ON BIO-POWER

The Parsons/Merton strategy that we have identified as the medicalization/clinicalization of the classical problem of social order is remarkable not so much for its abstractive and generalizing power as for its rhetorical effect of a quasi-natural description of society as a bio-system. To the extent that the structural-functionalist discourse of contemporary sociological theory resonates with bio-cybernetic discourse, it assumes the force of the hegemonic language of science in general and of medicine in particular. It thereby tends to by-pass the traditional conflicts and confusions of philosophical, political, and legal discourse concerned with articulating the nature of social order, justice, and the good life. However, what might be welcomed in this cybernetic formulation as progress in the scientific knowledge of society must also be considered from the standpoint of the political and moral life of a society and its citizens. This is so because the communicative competence of citizens with questions of political legitimation and individual motivation may be alienated or expropriated in favour of the diagnostic and prescriptive expertise of social physicians employing bio-cybernetic discourse. Thus Habermas (1984) has commented upon the ability of the social welfare state to absorb class conflict by redefining the political life of the citizen as a client relation. This analysis has intended to show how a key concept of sociological discourse – the social control function – can be seen to make the practice of professional sociology itself indispensable, i.e., a quasi-medical function, in the therapeutic society which it discovers, analyses, and aspires to administer. The *therapeutic state* in turn employs the discourse of the social sciences according to a medico-legal model whose function is to pacify clients, or to produce docile citizens.

Arthur Kroker (1984) has commented upon the curious affinity between Parsons' 'disembodied discourse on power' and Foucault's concrete studies of those discursive strategies for the embodiment of power in the instututions of health, education, work, and penology. What Parsons and Foucault share is the shift from the nineteenth-century *episteme* of physics to the twentieth-century *episteme* of biology which in turn makes the concept of power constitutive of the life struggle and thereby assigns primacy to the life sciences. Power and control are no longer external effects of politics and economics upon the individual who struggles to minimize them. Rather, power, truth, and life are, so to speak, internalized messages encoded in the species to normalize its health, knowledge, and labour (O'Neill 1985). Of course, unlike Foucault, Parsons retains the rhetoric of nineteenth-century bourgeois individualism on the level of action while constraining its commitments toward the dominant control functions on the level of the social system. The personality and social system levels are mediated, as has been argued here, through the discourse of the professional social scientist whose higher individualism is exercised in service of a social system which reproduces the will to reason and value that characterizes its normal members.

The Parsonian social system, despite its apparent abstract structuralism, is in fact a thoroughly *moral* system. Like Durkheim and Freud, however, Parsons conceived the morality of the social system to derive from its *sociological* rather than its ethical nature. Kroker's insight is essential here because he makes it clear that the social sciences could only 'take-off' by abandoning the model of physics for the discourse of biology, medicine, and psychoanalysis. They thereby succeeded in transplanting themselves as previously external organs of power into the internalized organs of *bio-power*. Properly understood, the social system is a moral system and all the social sciences are life-sciences whose control functions, explored in Foucault's studies of the discursive reproduction of health, sexuality, education, and labour, exceed anything previously dreamed of on the physicalist model of power. The biological sciences themselves have, of course, expanded considerably as strategies for the reproduction of the social system conceived in terms of the strategies of bio-power. Parsonian bio-sociology is a step away from Spencer, having absorbed current developments in cybernetics and communications systems thinking. The critical wisdom generally dismisses these developments as evidence of Parsons' hardened conservatism. But this misses the point. The two discursive strategies contained in the clinicalization of the socio-psychic spaces in the American social order and the medicalization of the concept and techniques of social control are not ideological facades concealing bourgeois power relations. Rather, they open up a new field of power relations which we have called the therapeutic state and in which the life-sciences are the hegemonic modes of power/knowledge.

REFERENCES

Bell, D. (1961) 'Crime as an American Way of Life', pp. 127–50 in D. Bell, *The End of Ideology*, New York: Collier.
Cannon, W.B. (1932) *The Wisdom of the Body*, New York: W.W. Norton.
de Tocqueville, A. (1954) *Democracy in America*, New York: Vintage Books.
Foucault, M. (1972) *The Archaeology of Knowledge, and the Discourse on Language*, trans. A.M. Sheridan Smith, New York: Harper and Row.

—— (1979) *Discipline and Punish: The Birth of the Prison*, New York: Vintage Books.

—— (1980) *Power/Knowledge: Selected Interviews and Other Writings 1972–1978*, C. Gordon (ed.) New York: Pantheon Books.

Habermas, J. (1984) *The Theory of Communicative Action: Reason and the Rationalization of Society*, 1, Boston: Beacon Books.

Henderson, L.J. (1917) *The Order of Nature: An Essay*, Cambridge: Harvard University Press.

Kroker, A. (1984) 'Modern Power in Reverse Image: The Paradigm Shift of Michel Foucault and Talcott Parsons', pp. 74–103 in J. Fekete (ed.) *The Structural Allegory: Reconstructive Encounters with the New French Thought*, Minneapolis: University of Minnesota Press.

Merton, R.K. (1938) 'Social Structure and Anomie', *American Sociological Review* 3 (5): 672–82.

—— (1957) *Social Theory and Social Structure*, New York: The Free Press of Glencoe.

Morrison, K.L. (1981) 'Some Properties of "Telling Order" Designs in Didactic Inquiry', *Philosophy of Social Sciences* 11 (2): 245–62.

—— (1987)'Some Researchable Recurrences in Disciplinary Specific Inquiry' in J. Mehan and A. Rawls (eds) *New Directions in the Study of Social Order*, New York: Irvington.

O'Neill, J. (1981) 'The Literary Production of Natural and Social Science Inquiry', *The Canadian Journal of Scoiology* 6 (2): 105–20.

—— (1982) 'Defamilization and the Feminization of Law in Early and Late Capitalism', *International Journal of Law and Psychiatry* 5 (3/4): 255–69.

—— (1985) *Five Bodies: The Human Shape of Modern Society*, Ithaca: Cornell University.

—— (1986) 'A Realist Model of Knowledge: With a Phenomenological Deconstruction of its Model of Man', *Philosophy of Social Sciences* 16 (1): 1–19.

Parsons, T. (1937) *The Structure of Social Action*, New York: McGraw-Hill.

—— (1951) *The Social System*, New York: The Free Press of Glencoe.

—— (1965) *Social Structure and Personality*, New York: The Free Press.

—— (1968) *Sociological Theory and Modern Society*, New York: The Free Press.

—— (1978) *Action Theory and the Human Condition*, New York: The Free Press.

Parsons, T., Shils, E., Naegele, D. and Pitts, J.R. (eds) (1961) *Theories of Society*, New York: The Free Press of Glencoe.

Rieff, P. (1966) *The Triumph of the Therapeutic: Uses of Faith After Freud*, London: Chatto and Windus.

Wilson, H.T. (1977) *The American Ideology: Science, Technology and Organization as Modes of Rationality in Advanced Industrial Societies*, London: Routledge and Kegan Paul.

Chapter 3

The disciplinary society
From Weber to Foucault

Here I want to show through an historical rather than analytic sketch how the formidable works of Weber and Foucault may be considered in terms of their convergence upon a single question, namely, *what are the techniques by which humankind has subjected itself to the rational discipline of the applied human sciences* (law, medicine, economics, education, and administration)? Clearly, it is not possible to pursue this question in the same historical and comparative detail to be found in either the Weberian corpus or in Foucault's recent archaeological studies. Rather, it will be argued that certain developments in Foucault's studies of the disciplinary society (1979a; 1979b) may complement Weber's formal analysis of the modern bureaucratic state and economy – despite Foucault's different conception of social rationality. Thus, the formal analytic and historical features of Weber's account of the bureaucratic state and economy may be related to Foucault's analysis of the discursive production of the human sciences of government, economics and social policy and to the concomitant regimentation of *docile bodies* under the disciplines of the prison, the workhouse and the factory. Despite Foucault's critical stance on the Marxist theory of state power, we cannot overlook Marx's attention (as well as that of more recent social historians) to the rise of factory discipline since this is an essential presupposition in the theory of discipline and power espoused both by Foucault and Weber. An historical sketch of the struggle over the work process, labour discipline, Taylorism and the bureaucratization of controls backed ultimately by the State which also guarantees rights to work, health and education, is necessary to understand how labour is rendered docile in the disciplinary culture of the therapeutic state (Miller and Neussus 1979; Hirsch 1979).

STATE POWER, BUREAUCRACY AND BIO-POLITICS

It is not far-fetched to consider Weber an archaeologist of the power man exerts over himself, and thus to see him as a precursor of Foucault's conception of the disciplinary society. In each case, history is not ransacked for its rational essence, even though it is only understood as a process of increasing rationalization. Nor is history seen as the story of individual freedom, even though western political history is only intelligible as its invention. What intervenes is the logic of the institutions that bring together rationality, individualism and freedom in the large-scale disciplinary enterprises of capitalism, bureaucracy and the modern therapeutic state. Modern society makes itself rich, knowledgeable and powerful but at the expense of substantive reason and freedom. Yet neither Weber nor Foucault are much beguiled by the socialist diagnosis of these trends. Of course neither thinker is entirely intelligible apart from Marx's analytic concerns. But both are closer to Nietzsche than to Marx in their grasp of the radical finitude of human rationality (Foucault 1970). In this, Weber and Foucault part company with Marx's ultimately romantic rationalism and its sad echoes in the halls of socialist state bureaucracy. Both of them are resolutely separated from any transcendental rationality, although Weber seems at times to have yearned for the desert winds of charisma to blow through the disciplinary society. But Foucault, distinguishing himself from Weber, shows no such equivocation.

> One isn't assessing things in terms of an absolute against which they could be evaluated as constituting more or less perfect forms of rationality, but rather examining how forms of rationality inscribe themselves in practices or systems of practices, and what role they play within them. Because it's true that 'practices' don't exist without a certain regime of rationality. But rather than measuring this regime against a value-of-reason, I would prefer to analyse it according to two axes: on the one hand, that of codification/prescription (how it forms an ensemble of rules, procedures, means to an end, etc.) and on the other, that of true or false formulation (how it determines a domain of objects about which it is possible to articulate true or false positions).
>
> (Foucault 1981: 8)

The only possibility of any reversal in the discursive production of the disciplinary sciences and their technologies of administrative

control, as Foucault sees it, is that archaeological studies of the
knowledge/power complex will simultaneously unearth the *subjugated
knowledge* of those groups (not simply identifiable with the proletariat)
who have been condemned to historical and political silence (under
socialism no less than capitalism). If Weber, on the other hand, saw
no relief from his vision of the *bureaucratic production of the state,
economy and society,* it is because he regarded science in general,
and the social sciences in particular, as 'factions' in the production
of the rationalization process they simultaneously discover as a topic
and deploy as a resource for their own disciplinary organization
(Wilson 1976; 1977). Thus Weber carried out his own vocation as
a 'specialist', limited by his reflections upon a politics and history
unable to transcend positive finitude. Weber's commitment to his
discipline did not represent a mode of self-alienation or of political
bad conscience, so much as the responsible ethic of an individual
who had seen the limits of our faith in science as an objective belief.
The alternative is a leap into the barbarism of reflection and a utopian
invocation of the cycle of history to deliver new men on the back
of the old man.

   Weber's distillate of the formal features of bureaucratic organization
and discipline (1947; 1967) is intended to assist in the study of
hospitals, armies, schools, churches, business and political organizations, as well as of the institutions for the production of scientific
knowledge of nature and society. Legal order, bureaucracy,
compulsory jurisdiction over a territory and monopolization of the
legitimate use of force are the essential characteristics of the modern
state. This complex of factors emerged only gradually in Europe and
is only fully present where legitimacy is located in the body of
bureaucratic rules that determine the exercise of political authority.
It should be noted that Weber's concept of the legitimacy of the modern
legal state is purely formal: laws are legitimate if procedurally correct
and any correct procedure is legal. Of course, Weber did not ignore
the actual value-contexts of political legitimacy (Schluchter 1981).
He saw the historical drift moving from natural law to legal positivism
but could not see that the events of the twentieth century would lead
to attempts to reinstate natural law in an effort to bridle state barbarism.
Foucault's studies of the rise of the modern state apparatus do not
alter Weber's conception of the legitimation process but they are much
more graphic. This is meant quite literally. Although Weber sees the
documentary growth of the legal and bureaucratic administrative
process, he does not judge its effects upon the *body politic.* By

contrast, like Marx, Foucault never loses sight of the body as the ultimate text upon which the power of the state and the economy is inscribed. By the same token, Foucault is able to go beyond Weber's legal-rational concept of legitimacy to capture the medicalization of power and the therapeutic mode of the legitimation function in the modern state:

> In concrete terms, starting in the seventeenth century, this power over life evolved in two basic forms; these forms were not antithetical however; they constituted rather two poles of development, linked together by a whole intermediary cluster of relations. One of these poles – the first to be formed, it seems – centered on the body as a machine; its disciplining, the optimization of its capabilities, the extortion of its forces, the parallel increase of its usefulness and its docility, its integration into systems of efficient and economic controls, all this was ensured by the procedures of power that characterized the *disciplines*: an *anatomo-politics of the body*. The second, formed somewhat later, focused on the species body, the body as the basis of the biological processes: propagation and longevity, with all the conditions that can cause these to vary. Their supervision was effected through an entire series of interventions and *regulatory controls: a bio-politics of the population*.
>
> (Foucault 1980: 139)

Weber's discussion of bureaucracy is largely framed in terms of the legal and rational accounting requirements of political and economic organization which in turn give to legal domination its administrative rationality and adequacy. The formal-analytic features of the Weberian concept of bureaucracy are to be found as constitutive practices in the operation of the army, church, university, hospital and political party – not to mention the very organization of the relevant discovering social sciences. Although Foucault (1975; 1979a) does not study the bureaucratic process in the Weberian mode, his studies of the prison, hospital and school go beyond Weber in grounding the legal-rational accounting process in techniques for the administration of corporeal, attitudinal and behavioural discipline. Foucault thereby complements Weber's formal-rational concept of bureaucracy and legal domination with a *physiology of bureaucracy and power* which is the definitive feature of the disciplinary society. It is for this reason that, despite the difficulties in his style, Foucault deserves the attention of social scientists. There is a tendency in

Weber's account of bureaucracy to identify it with a ruling class, dominating the economy and the bourgeois democratic state. There are a number of overlapping issues here regarding the demarcation of the economy and the polity, of classes and élites, but especially of the distinction between the *state apparatus* and state *power*. Bureaucracy is the dominant mode of operation of the state apparatus, as it tends to be in the economy. But it is neither a class in itself nor is it the state power. Rather, bureaucracy might be treated as a *strategy* for the reproduction of the state's relation to the economy, and for the reproduction of socio-economic relations between individuals in the state. Thus we have to review, however briefly, the history of the separation of labour from the ownership of the means of production. In other words, we have to see how the bourgeois state assigns to the juridical individual his/her legal rights whereby he or she freely contracts into systems of exploitation and discipline (patriarchal, paternalist and bureaucratic) which the state defends even when it corrects its abuses. The ideological function of the state and legal process is to constitute individual agency at the juridical level precisely in order to reproduce the social division of labour and its bureaucratic rationalization independent of 'individuals' and their particularistic attributes (Poulantzas 1973). The sociological codification of this effect is to be found in the Weberian and Parsonian (1951) analysis of the rational-legal accounting process and its pattern variable schematization of required conduct from adequately motivated, i.e., disciplined individuals concerned solely with role-specific functions which we examined in the previous chapter.

What the ideological isolation of the independent juridical subject achieves is the *inversion* of the economic dependency of the subject who freely contracts into a system of labour dominated by the market. Or rather, precisely because the issue of independence is removed from the level of economy to the level of the polity, the economy can subject itself to the 'independent' discipline of external laws of the market before which capitalists are as unfree as labourers. These features are preserved when we replace the 'market' with 'bureaucracy' as a gloss upon the isolation of the state and socio-economic processes of capitalist production. By the same token, the bourgeois state limits itself to the integration of the isolated effects of the underlying class system of production and labour discipline but without seeking to radically alter it beyond the defence of individualized rights and duties. But this argument needs to be considered in an historical perspective in order to recapture (however briefly) the movement from which Weber, Marx and Foucault drew their theoretical insights into the stratagems of power that shape the disciplinary society.

THE RISE OF INDUSTRIAL DISCIPLINE

It may be worthwhile to consider the middle ground between Weber and Foucault by taking even a brief look at the history of *industrial discipline*. This will enable us to weigh the difference between Weber's formal-analytic approach to the rationalization of social and political control and Foucault's approach via the discursive strategies and physiology of *disciplinary power* which were devised in the context of the shift to the factory and its gradual bureaucratization of the work process. By the same token, this will put in perspective Foucault's (1980) critique of the Marxist theory of power by reminding us that industrial and bureaucratic discipline arise from the historical struggle between capital and labour over control of the technical means and social organization of production (Braverman 1974; Burawoy 1984; Pollard 1963; Reid 1976; Thompson 1967). This is necessary since, while Foucault scores nicely against certain Marxist conceptions of state power, his own views are in danger of leaving us the victims of power that is everywhere and nowhere.

Although, as we know from Laslett (1965) and Wall (1983), it is no longer possible to indulge the myth of the family as a natural economy, it is generally agreed that in the mid-eighteenth century the family-based putting-out and domestic system of manufacture came under pressure as the industrial revolution got under way. In the specific case of the cotton industry, the family system had to adjust to a new pace, increasingly independent of the agricultural seasons (Smelser 1959; Edwards and Lloyd-Jones 1973; Anderson 1976). The pull in this direction showed itself in productive bottlenecks, imbalances between spinning and weaving, and the master's increasing dissatisfaction with the independence, self-pacing and casual character of the workers engaged in the putting-out system (Reid 1976). The putting-out system compared unfavourably (Landes 1969) with the factory system of control and discipline and with the Methodist values which serviced the interests of continuous production (Burrell 1984). Thus workers were plagued with charges of idleness, dishonesty, drunkenness and immorality in the courts and the press. The factory masters responded in opposing ways to this perception of wayward labour, namely, with the imposition of harsh and cruel conditions, as a general rule, and with proposals for 'model communities', to transform the old rule. In either case, worker *discipline* was the main ingredient aimed at improving the moral habits of the labouring poor, to make them orderly, punctual, responsible and temperate:

> In all these ways – by the division of labour; the supervision of labour; fines; bells and clocks; money incentives; preachings and schoolings; the suppression of fairs and sports – new labour habits were formed, and a new time discipline was imposed.
>
> (Thompson 1967: 90)

Further stress fell upon the domestic system and the family economy with the differential impact of technological changes in spinning and weaving. The spinning jenny and the water-frame moved spinning into the factory and, by simplifying the labour, at first displaced men with women and children. This, of course, seriously challenged the moral economy of the family, although a modified apprenticeship and family hiring survived in the factory for quite a while. Thus, as Smelser observes:

> the water-frame factory of the late eighteenth century moved only 'part way' toward the ideal conditions of economic rationality. Workers were segregated from their means of production, but the remnants of job appropriation by workers remained in the form of a modified apprenticeship system and family hiring. Discipline proved a major problem to the early capitalists, but its enforcement had not differentiated entirely from the more diffuse family ties of the pre-factory social structure.
>
> (Smelser 1959: 107)

With the introduction of mule-spinning and steam power, the factory system and its discipline became more pronounced. The separation of the workers from the ownership of the means of production increased capital's control over labour. By the same token, workers lost control over their own pace (Thompson 1967) and became increasingly subject to entrepreneurial discipline. The changes we have observed on the spinning side of the cotton industry could not continue without building pressure for similar changes, differentiation and realignments in the weaving trades. As spinning began to outstrip the weavers, pressure grew to separate weaving from its basis in the domestic putting-out system, moving it into hand-loom factories and eventually power-loom factories. The big difference here is that power-loom weaving, as opposed to mule-spinning, displaced males with women and children. Workers in the cotton industry responded to the changes in their family economy with machine breaking, strikes and riots. They struggled to come to terms with piece rates, child labour and the ten-hour day, always trying to preserve their skilled status (Penn 1982). The hand-loom weavers turned to pleas for relief, violence, political agitation and were attracted to the utopian movements of Cobbett, Owen and the Chartists. The Acts of 1833 and 1844 combined to reduce child labour and thereby to separate the adult and child working day, putting pressure once again on the family and state agencies to be concerned with child education and family welfare. Thus the workers turned to the organization of unions, friendly societies and savings banks as means of adjusting to circumstances that could no longer be handled by the old poor law relief system.

We cannot pursue these histories. Moreover, the complexity of the issues surrounding the evolution of the working class (Form 1981; 1983) and its paths towards reformism or revolution (Burawoy 1984) remains unresolved even by a host of empirical studies. Here it is enough to remark that in most instances worker discipline, even where it involves self-discipline, is always a ruling concern – food riots and strikes being taken as evidence of the naturally undisciplined nature of workers outside of administrative controls, while the workers struggle to maintain their skills and concomitant social status. The fact remains that industrial discipline has never wholly conquered the working classes. Workers have hung on to many pre-industrial values, they have learned to sabotage, slow down, quit and take off (Palmer 1975; Stark 1980; Littler 1982). Thus labour discipline continues to challenge management and government to this day. It is therefore necessary to avoid a naïve economism when thinking of the capitalist control of the means of production. Such control may be more or less efficient when viewed from a strictly technical standpoint and there may even be some competitive push in this direction. But capitalism is a social system concerned to reproduce itself. In other words, any form of social control over the means of production must reproduce the class system of capitalism – and this rule must apply to bureaucracy no less than to technocracy: 'all means for the development of production transform themselves into means of domination and exploitation of the producers' (Marx 1906: 709). Thus capitalists had also to bring themselves into line with the requirements of industrial rationalization (Pollard 1963). It is one thing to be Protestant in outlook and quite another to be so in narrow practice. For this reason, capitalists as entrepreneurs resisted feeding themselves into Taylorism as much as their workers, preferring, as Littler (1978; 1982) points out, to subcontract worker discipline and management. It fell to the engineers to devise for them the book-keeping and cost-accountancy functions that increased control over expenses, stocks, overheads, productivity and profitability (Hill 1981). The engineers and middle managers, then, made themselves the servants of capital in this respect. Its prospective control of the work process, craft knowledge and labour solidarity further extended the appeal of scientific management and professional engineers (Rodgers 1979). Here it is vital to see that what was at stake was capitalist hegemony over the primary work process and not some abstract attachment to scientific efficiency. Taylorism was morally alien to the values and dignity of independent labour. Taylor's conception of the labouring man as lazy, bestial and intemperate, working only under the threat of discipline and strict supervision was hostile to self-paced labour. However, Taylorism was gradually adjusted to accommodate unionism, collective bargaining and various paternalistic and welfare concessions to labour, and owners came to terms with working-class struggles against premium systems, piecework, and loss of control of pace and decision in the smallest of tasks. Indeed, the union movement itself incorporated features of scientific management, particularly during World War II. Whenever management fails to negotiate between labour and capital, labour returns to its historical struggle and capital will call upon the police and, if necessary, the army to maintain law and order. It is, however, in the interest of both the state and capital to reserve legal force for exceptional use. This can be achieved so long as the disciplinary society, to which we now turn, can be relied upon to operate with quasi-natural effect, i.e., removed from historical and political consciousness. How this can be uncritically assumed will be seen in some closing remarks upon the liberal conception of bureaucracy (Crozier 1964) and power.

THE PRISON AND THE FACTORY

The labour history we have briefly sketched needs to be relocated in the original framework of classical political economy and its concerns with 'policing' an impoverished, unhealthy, rebellious and criminal population created by the new industrial economy. The autonomy of modern economics was achieved at the expense of abstracting its concerns from the original disciplinary science of government and morals that occupied classical political economy. Thus it is necessary, in the light of Foucault's studies, to review how industrial discipline arose in relation to prison discipline in the production of a docile labour force suited to the needs of early industrial capitalism. It is then possible to see how the bureaucratic discipline of late capitalism presupposes this early history of bodily discipline which, so to speak, funds society's more superficial attitudinal controls. The formal (contractual) freedom of labour expresses its separation from the ownership of the means of production.

The decline of feudalism, the enclosure movements and the confiscation of monastic property at first released large numbers of former peasants into vagabondage and criminality. Fifteenth- and sixteenth-century legislation was faced with the task of separating 'the impotent poor' from the anomalous 'able bodied poor'. The former were authorized to beg; the latter were lucky to find their way into the workhouse and forced labour, a slight-step away from prison. In part, the segregation of forced labourers functioned to regulate the supply of free labour; but, in a broader way, it set the model for the discipline and surveillance of former peasants and artisans while they resisted their new freedom. Early capitalists needed not only to depress wages as far as possible; they also needed wage-labour disciplined to accept long hours and harsh conditions of work. They had also to destroy the popular culture and habits of pre-industrial labour, yet to avoid entirely destabilizing the social order (Ignatieff 1979: 183–4). Thus Calvinism was nicely instrumental as a substitute for Catholic attitudes to charity, holidays and the like. It might be said that if Protestantism removed religious authority from the community, it restored it inside the factory. In fact, Protestantism reinvigorated patriarchy both in the family (Stone 1979: 103–5) and in the workhouse which it ran on family lines, as it would later the hospital and prison:

> If prison is a model of society – and here one is still concerned with metaphor – it will not take many years for the Protestant and above all the Calvinist view of society to create a model of the prison of the future in the shape of the workhouse.
> (Melossi and Pavarini 1981: 28–9)

In England, despite the challenge to law and order and the ineffec-tiveness of its terrible punishments, the propertied classes were not in a hurry to embrace rationalist and utilitarian penal reforms. Such reluctance may well have been inspired by a better sense of the workings of law and authority that enabled the eighteenth-century bourgeoisie to exercise its hegemony without either a large army or a police force. Between them patronage and pardon seem to have increased respect for the law in its mercy and through the very arbitrariness that might strike equally at rich and poor gave rise to a general sense of justice. A curious balance was attempted between the law as an instrument of class privilege and the panoply of its impartiality (Hay 1975).

However, it was inevitable that the increasing demand for labour at lower wages would destroy the Elizabethan Poor Laws, replacing charity with forced labour in the workhouse. But the confusion between the workhouse and the house of correction continued – they were often parts of the same building. When labour became increasingly plentiful, unemployed and driven to crime and rebellion, the houses of correction became even more punitive, while labour in the houses of correction was limited to grinding and useless tasks so that no one would enter them voluntarily. The overall effect was to teach free labour the discipline of the factory both outside and inside the factory, in prisons and workhouses. Thus the employed and the unemployed learned their respective disciplines. Thereafter, we might say that in the bourgeois social order the prison, the factory and the school, like the army, are places where the system can project its conception of the disciplinary society in the reformed criminal, the good worker, student, loyal soldier, and committed citizen. In every case, it is a question of reproducing among the propertyless a sense of commitment to the property system in which they have nothing to sell but their labour and loyalty. The articulation of the disciplinary society in the factory, prison, army, schools and hospitals represented a response to social and moral problems arising from industrial change and conflict:

> the new science called political economy arises out of the registering of the new network of constant and multiple relations between population, territory and wealth; and this corresponds to the formation of a type of intervention characteristic of government, namely intervention in the field of economy and population. In other words, the transition from an art of government to a political science, from a regime dominated by structure of sovereignty to

one ruled by techniques of government occurs in the 18th century
around the theme of population and consequently centres on the
birth of political economy . . .

We must consequently see things not in terms of the substitution for a society of sovereignty by a disciplinary society
and the subsequent replacement of a disciplinary society by
a governmental one; in reality we have a triangle; sovereignty-
discipline-government, which has as its primary target the
population and its essential mechanism apparatuses of security.

(Foucault 1979b: 18–19)

However repressive these disciplinary strategies may look to
us, in their own day they were part of the reformist, humane and
enlightened discourse that responded to the needs of the times
and were often inspired by a pedagogic intention to transform
individuals into able-bodied citizens. The broad issue here is
a complex, shifting relationship between industrialization, law,
criminality and the labourers in the town and countryside (Tobias
1967). Thus it is not always easy to decide whether such responses
as food riots, poaching, machine breaking, reform movements and
trade unionism were popular politics or mob crimes. From the
standpoint of the propertied classes, such activities were more
likely to be criminalized than politicized, so to speak, since the
propertied class had trouble in imagining the kind of political
order that might be built upon a propertyless mass. From the
standpoint of the peasants and urban labourers faced with immiseration, certain criminal activities were often desperate strategies
of maintenance, however colourful they may have made London
life. Although the law was used to enact severe and terrible
punishments for crimes against rural and urban property, it
nevertheless seems to have been employed also to teach lessons
of mercy and a universal sense of order. In other words, the bourgeois
state tempered the force of law with the ideology of respect for
the Law. To the extent that this was achieved, the labouring
class also won from the bourgeoisie extensions in the rule of
law, freedom of speech and assembly, as well as the right to
strike and to organize in the work place. The law, therefore, is
not simply the oppressive agency for the bourgeois state. Inasmuch
as capitalism must be concerned with its own social reproduction,
it will be driven to motivate moral consent as well as sheer physical
compliance. Thus the class struggle will propel the law to universalize

its prescriptions in the search for solutions on a higher level of control.

In the eighteenth century, the role of the state was at first minimal in the sense that it served to sweep away the feudal order and to institute the necessary discipline of the new industrial labour force. Later, it began to adjust the conditions of labour, passing the factory legislation that to some extent restricted capital while accommodating labour. At this stage, the state's task in softening domination with education is shared by humanitarian, paternal and religious welfare in helping the poor, sick, criminal and ignorant. Foucault (1979a) argues that the disciplinary institutions were conceived to open up a field for the practices of evaluating, recording and observing large populations in order to administer them through the therapeutic institutions of health, education and penality. This is the original matrix of the human and social sciences, rather than any abstractive generalization such as Comte's Law of the Three Stages. Instead, we might speak of the social sciences as *strategies of power* designed to minimize the cost of power, to maximize its coverage and to link 'economic' power with the educational, military, industrial, penal and medical institutions within which the docility and utility of populations can be maximized. In a disciplinary society power works by a sort of capillary action, drawing itself up from individual conduits. Thus, in a certain sense, the operation of power is individualized in order to achieve its maximum concentration:

> In a disciplinary regime . . . individualization is 'descending': as power becomes more anonymous and more functional, those on whom it is exercised tend to be more strongly individualized; it is exercised by surveillance rather than ceremonies, by observation rather than commemorative accounts, by comparative measures that have the 'norm' as reference rather than genealogies giving ancestors as points of reference, by 'gaps' rather than deeds. . . .
> All the sciences, analyses, or practices employing the root 'psycho-' have their origin in this historical reversal of the procedures of individualization. The moment that saw the transition from historico–ritual mechanisms for the formation of individuality to the scientific–disciplinary mechanism, when the normal took over from the ancestral, and measurement from status, thus substituting for the individuality of the memorable man that of the calculable man, that moment when the sciences of man became possible

is the moment when a new technology of power and a new political anatomy of the body were implemented.

(Foucault 1979a: 193)

BEHIND THE STATE: BUREAUCRACY AND THE DISCIPLINARY SOCIETY

When Weber considers the historical roots of bureaucratic discipline, as well as of the factory, he traces them directly to the model of military discipline. 'The discipline of the army gives birth to all discipline' (Weber 1967: 261). This emphasizes the uniformity of obedience and command in an impersonal office. Emotions, status, devotion and charisma are subordinated to a rational calculus of success or profitability from the objective standpoint of the organization. At the same time, Weber concedes that there is no direct link between military discipline and various economic institutions such as the Pharaonic workshops, slave plantations and the factory. He remarks upon the intensification of rational discipline achieved through the American systems of 'scientific management'. But his observations on these topics are not developed and his interest is absorbed by the most general features of formal bureaucratic administration. Thus it may be argued that, while Weber (1950) saw the direct line from monastic discipline through Luther and Calvin to bureaucracy and scientific management, he did not pay sufficient attention to the circuits of the factory, workhouse and prison in the creation of industrial discipline and social control. Discipline in the factory, prison and school involves much more specific strategies of corporeal discipline than is captured by the generalized attitude of Protestant asceticism. In this respect, Weberianism implies a too cognitivist version of capitalist, state and bureaucratic controls. Moreover, it leaves the impression that in late capitalism the state only employs brute force, of a police or military nature, in the last instance. Thus the history we have reviewed makes it possible to see how the Weberian approach can result in Crozier's (1964) portrayal of enlightened bureaucracy produced by taking for granted the *disciplinary society* (family, schools, hospitals and prisons) that underwrites discipline in the workplace and allows the State to reserve its violence on behalf of the property system:

Modern organizations, in contrast to their predecessors, use a much more liberal set of pressures. They deal with people who, through

their education, have already internalized a number of basic con-
formities and a general ability to conform easily to an organization's way. . . . Most important of all, human behaviour is now
better understood and therefore more predictable. Because of this,
a modern organization does not need the same amount of conformity to get as good results as did earlier organizations. The modern
organization can tolerate more deviance, restrict its requirements
to a more specialized field, and demand only temporary commitments. For all these reasons, it can and does rely more on
indirect and intellectual means to obtain conformity: communication structure and work flow, the technical setting of jobs, economic
incentives, and also, perhaps, rational calculus of a higher sort.
The punitive aspect of the conformity achievement process has
declined. Direct coercion is still in reserve as a last resort, but
it is very rarely used, and people apparently no longer have to
see it operate often to retain it in their calculations.

(Crozier 1964: 184–5)

Crozier's view of workers' compliance will seem plausible only to
the extent that it can presume upon the *natural discipline*, so to speak,
of the work place and of the wage system. But this, as we have seen,
is always the arena of a struggle with formally free labour to accept
its substantive lack of freedom due to the persistent efforts of capitalism
to separate labour from control of the work process. Thus the rights
of labour to freely contract for wages guaranteed before the law is
reproduced in the system of punishment calculated in retribution for
crimes against property, against property in persons and ultimately
against the crime of propertylessness (Melossi and Pavarini 1981).
The legal contract is therefore the sacred fiction of the bourgeois social
and political order since it simultaneously reproduces formal freedom
and equality with substantive inequality and oppression. The discipline
of the factory and the wage system, however much it is bureaucratized,
remains the ultimate source of labour's docility. Indeed, it is the work
place discipline that funds the apparent organizational effectiveness
of state and bureaucratic controls. In fact, these controls also require
for their effectiveness that the greater part of the bureaucratic structure be itself subject to the very discipline its middle management
employees imagine they are supervising with respect to labour. What
is called bureaucratic control must be seen to involve a continuous
struggle over:

(a)   the *technical control* over the work process, and
(b)   *disciplinary and punitive control* over the social relations of production

Whereas in early capitalism paternalist power derived from the personal relationships between the owner and his labourers, technical and bureaucratic control grow out of the formal structure of the firm. The difference is that technical control is embedded in the production process and, as such, may be employed to *naturalize* bureaucratic controls which are embedded in the social organization or power structure of the firm. In practice, paternalistic, technical and bureaucratic discipline will be found to coexist and, while they may be regarded as stages of industrial discipline (Perrot 1979), they have arisen in a pragmatic way as responses to owner/worker struggles for control. Although it is preferable from the standpoint of management to address control issues in terms of a Weberian vocabulary of rational accounting, efficiency and universalistic-achievement requirements – in fact to naturalize the social relations of production to technical relations of production – the reality is that it is relations of power and ideology that are at stake. Where labour freely contracts to meet the wage discipline, it thereby subordinates itself to the conditions of mental and bodily control (Sohn-Rethel 1978) arising from its separation from the ownership of the means, pacing and purpose of production in a substantively rational social enterprise. In detail, this means that workers submit to the direction of their tasks, their nature, method, pace and quality of work (Edwards 1979; Thompson 1961). They thereby simultaneously submit themselves to a system of worker evaluation, punishment and reward. It is, of course, in the interests of bureaucratic management to make worker discipline, punishments and rewards, appear to flow from naturally established organizational rules and procedures. Analytically, there occurs a kind of progression in industrial discipline moving from paternalistic controls to assembly line, machine paced routines and, finally, to bureaucratically imposed discipline. What is involved is a shift from heteronomous paternalist controls to autonomous, internalized discipline, and identification with corporate goals and values. To achieve this, worker evaluation is concerned less with physical productivity than with workers' attitudes to the corporation. In a certain sense, the modern corporation seeks to refamilize the workers while cutting them off from their own class culture. Since such a disciplinary achievement takes time, corporations seek to minimize labour turn-over and to maximize loyalty, ever solicitous of worker attitudes:

> What distinguishes bureaucratic control from other control systems is that it contains incentives aimed at evoking the behaviour necessary to make bureaucratic control succeed. It is this *indirect* path to the intensification of work, through the mechanism of rewarding behaviour relevant to the control system, rather than simply to the work itself, that imposes the new behaviour requirements on workers.
>
> (Edwards 1979: 148–9)

These considerations suggest further political studies of the internalization of discipline in the enucleated family, in schools, sports and much of modern entertainment. The family has long ceased to be the natural scene of work discipline, while still charged with the production of able-bodied citizens. It has fallen to the schools, social and medical agencies, and the media – inasmuch as the message is still the ordinary society – to provide the secondary socialization which Crozier takes for granted in shifting the disciplinary burden from modern bureaucracy onto an 'educated' citizenry. In short, we need to re-examine the division between public and private conduct in terms of historically variable strategies of discipline – even in so-called leisure – which subserve the social and political imperative of a disciplined labour force and its current levels of manual, mental and emotional 'education'. Such a tactic would treat social discipline as a socio-political strategy whose organizational features are historically and institutionally variable. Moreover, it would avoid any retrospective myth of an undisciplined state of nature generated from a Freudian or a Hobbesian perspective. At the same time, it would not reduce political discipline to a work place activity, nor indulge prospective fantasies of an undisciplined society ruled by play and the absence of the state. By the same token, the approach recommended here might give social scientists direction in the empirical study of the embodiment of power as it is achieved in the lives of individuals, families and educational institutions.

CONCLUSION

Weber's formal theory of bureaucracy needs to be complemented by the history of factory discipline, the latter overlapping with prison discipline and eventually overlaid with bureaucratic discipline.

Thus we return to Weber via Foucault and Marx. The benefit of this approach is that it makes it clear how Weber's concept of state and bureaucratic discipline alternates between (i) obedience based upon the observation of rules of technical efficiency, and (ii) obedience required as a governmental end in itself, or what Gouldner (1954: 216–17) calls 'punishment centered' bureaucracy. In reality, the sphere of the technical expert is subordinate to that of the true bureaucrat whose administration derives from a presumption of power. For this reason, the disciplinary tasks of punitive bureaucracy are directed to the industrial control of minds and bodies, of attitudes and behaviour. Here the studies of Foucault and the social historians we have cited broaden the Weberian concept of administrative power into the embodied strategies of industrial power. Bureaucrats cannot make the Prussian assumption that their goals are beyond criticism and resistance (Gouldner 1976). Industrial bureaucracies are less privileged than government bureaucracies in this respect. For this reason, the two bureaucracies of state and economy share an interest in depoliticizing the perception of their power and ideology by subordinating them to the neutral image of disciplined technology and expertise. With this strategy, the two bureaucracies seek to manufacture public docility and in this way have citizens support the state which in turn supports them with a modicum of legal force exercised against their occasional disobedience.

REFERENCES

Anderson, M. (1976) 'Sociological History and the Working Class Family: Smelser Revisited', *Social History* 3: 317–34.
Braverman, H. (1974) *Labour and Monopoly Capital, The Degradation of Work in the Twentieth Century*, New York: Monthly Review Press.
Burawoy, M. (1984) 'Karl Marx and the Satanic Mills: Factory Politics Under Early Capitalism in England, the United States and Russia', *The American Journal of Sociology* 90(2): 247–82.
Burrell, G. (1984) 'Sexual Organizational Analysis', *Organizational Studies* 5(2): 97–118.
Crozier, M. (1964) *The Bureaucratic Phenomenon*, Chicago: The University of Chicago Press.
Edwards, M. and Lloyd-Jones, R. (1973) 'N.J. Smelser and the Cotton Factory Family: A Re-assessment', in N.B. Harte and K.G. Ponting (eds) *Textile History and Economic History*, Manchester: Manchester University Press, 304–19.
Edwards, R. (1979) *Contested Terrain: The Transformation of the Workplace in the Twentieth Century*, New York: Basic Books.

Form, W. (1981) 'Resolving Ideological Issues on the Division of Labour', in H.M. Blalock, Jr. (ed.) *Theory and Research in Sociology*, New York: The Free Press, 140–61.

—— (1983) 'Sociological Research and the American Working Class', *The Sociological Quarterly* 24, Spring: 163–84.

Foucault, M. (1970) *The Order of Things: An Archaeology of the Human Sciences*, New York: Vintage Books.

—— (1975) *The Birth of the Clinic: An Archaeology of Medical Perception*, trans. A.M. Sheridan Smith, New York: Vintage Books.

—— (1979a) *Discipline and Punish: The Birth of the Prison*, trans. A. Sheridan, New York: Vintage Books.

—— (1979b) 'Governmentality', *Ideology and Consciousness (I and C), Governing the Present*, 6: 5–21.

—— (1980) *The History of Sexuality Volume I: An Introduction*, trans. R. Hurley, New York: Vintage Books.

—— (1981) 'Questions of Method', *Ideology and Consciousness (I and C), Power and Desire: Diagrams of the Social*, 8: 3–14.

Gouldner, A.W. (1954) *Patterns of Industrial Democracy*, Glencoe, Ill.: The Free Press.

—— (1976) *The Dialectic of Ideology and Technology: The Origins, Grammar and Future of Ideology*, New York: The Seabury Press.

Hay, D. (1975) 'Property, Authority and the Criminal Law', in D. Hay, P. Linebaugh, J.G. Rule, E.P. Thompson, C. Winslow (eds) *Albion's Fatal Tree, Crime and Society in Eighteenth Century England*, London: Allen Lane.

Hill, S. (1981) *Competition and Control at Work: The New Industrial Sociology*, Cambridge: The MIT Press.

Hirsch, J. (1979) 'The State Apparatus and Social Reproduction: Elements of a Theory of the Bourgeois State', in J. Holloway and S. Picciotto (eds) *State and Capital: A Marxist Debate*, Austin: University of Texas Press, 57–107.

Ignatieff, M. (1978) *A Just Measure of Pain: The Penitentiary in the Industrial Revolution 1750–1850*, New York: Pantheon Books.

Landes, D.S. (1969) *The Unbound Prometheus: Technological Change and Industrial Development in Western Europe from 1750 to the Present*, Cambridge, Cambridge University Press.

Laslett, P. (1965) *The World We Have Lost – Further Explored*, London: Methuen and Co. Ltd.

Littler, C.R. (1978) 'Understanding Taylorism', *British Journal of Sociology* 29(2): 185–202.

—— (1982) 'Deskilling and Changing Structures of Control', in S. Wood (ed.) *The Degradation of Work? Skill, Deskilling and the Labour Process*, London: Hutchinson, 122–45.

Marx, K. (1906) *Capital, A Critique of Political Economy*, Chicago: Charles H. Kerr and Company.

Melossi, D. and Pavarini, M. (1981) *The Prison and the Factory*, New York: Macmillan.

Miller, W. and Neussus, C. (1979) '"The Welfare State Illusion" and the Contradiction Between Wage Labour and Capital', in J. Holloway and

S. Picciotto (eds) *State and Capital. A Marxist Debate*, Austin: University of Texas Press: 32–9.

Palmer, B. (1975) 'Class, Conception and Conflict: The Thrust for Efficiency, Managerial Views of Labor and the Working Class Rebellion, 1903–22', *The Review of Radical Political Economics* 7(2): 31–49.

Parsons, T. (1951) *The Social System*, New York: The Free Press of Glencoe.

Penn, R. (1982) 'Skilled Manual Workers in the Labour Process, 1856–1964', in S. Wood (ed.) *The Degradation of Work? Skills, Deskilling and the Labour Process*, London: Hutchinson, 90–108.

Perrot, M. (1979) 'The Three Ages of Industrial Discipline in Nineteenth Century France', in J. Merriman (ed.) *Consciousness and Class Experience in Nineteenth Century Europe*, New York: Holmes and Meier, pp. 149–68.

Pollard, S. (1963) 'Factory Discipline in the Industrial Revolution', *The Economic History Review* XVI, 2: 254–71.

Poulantzas, N. (1973) *Political Power and Social Classes*, London: NLB.

Reid, D.A. (1976) 'The Decline of Saint Monday 1766–1876', *Past and Present* 71: 76–101.

Rimlinger, G.V. (1971) *Welfare Policy and Industrialization in Europe, America and Russia*, New York: John Wiley.

Rodgers, D.T. (1979) *The Work Ethic in Industrial America 1850–1920*, Chicago and London: The University of Chicago Press.

Schluchter, W. (1981) *The Rise of Western Rationalism: Max Weber's Developmental History*, trans. G. Roth, Berkeley: University of California Press.

Smelser, N.J. (1959) *Social Change in the Industrial Revolution: An Application of Theory to the British Cotton Industry*, Chicago: The University of Chicago Press.

Sohn-Rethel, A. (1978) *Intellectual and Manual Labour: A Critique of Epistemology*, London: Macmillan.

Stark, D. (1980) 'Class Struggle and the Transformation of the Labour Process: A Relational Approach', *Theory and Society* 9: 89–130.

Stone, L. (1979) *The Family, Sex and Marriage in England 1500–1800*, New York: Harper & Row.

Thompson, E.P. (1967) 'Time, Work, Discipline, and Industrial Capitalism', *Past and Present* 38: 56–97.

Thompson, V.A. (1961) *Modern Organization*, New York: Alfred A. Knopf.

Tobias, J.J. (1967) *Crime and Industrial Society in the 19th Century*, New York: Schocken Books.

Wall, R., Robin, J. and Laslett, P. (eds) (1983) *Family Forms in Historic Europe*, Cambridge: Cambridge University Press.

Weber, M. (1947) *The Theory of Social and Economic Organization*, trans. A.M. Henderson and T. Parsons, New York: Oxford University Press.

—— (1950) *General Economic History*, trans. F.H. Knight, Glencoe, Ill: The Free Press.

—— (1967) *From Max Weber: Essays in Sociology*, trans., ed. and with an Introduction by H.H. Gerth and G. Wright Mills, New York: Oxford University Press.

Wilson, H.T. (1976) 'Reading Max Weber: The Limits of Sociology', *Sociology* 10: 297–315.
—— (1977) *The American Ideology, Science, Technology and Organization as Modes of Rationality in Advanced Industrial Societies*, London: Routledge & Kegan Paul.

Chapter 4

The phenomenological concept of modern knowledge and the utopian method of Marxist economics

I now propose to examine the split between power and freedom in Western knowledge by returning to Husserl's[1] formulation of it and by situating its phenomenology in the context of Marxist–Weberian political economy. In attempting to show these connections, I hope to point the way to a synthesis of phenomenology and critical theory which I think Habermas attempted too late in his battle against post-rationalism. Rather than take on the philosophical and literary postmodernists and have them teach us our business, I think we must stand firmly upon our own ground of sociological knowledge and not import it second-hand from literary critics whose sense of social institutions is often very thin as I show elsewhere (O'Neill 1992 – See Ch. 1, note 6). It is for this very reason that here I deliberately develop my argument from the nature of economic knowledge, critically related to its own institutional and value assumptions. The argument will move from the works of Husserl and Heidegger onto Marcuse, Weber, Hegel and Marx. My study of this constellation represents an effort to integrate the grounds of rational knowledge and freedom in an 'originary' matrix of the human praxis which sustains Western knowledge and its regional sciences of nature and society. In particular, it responds to Husserl's call for a new kind of philosophical method, which I have called 'documentary work';[2] this method has already borne fruit in the historical and social sciences, where it is suited to the hermeneutic problem which arises from the essentially reflexive nature of human knowledge and praxis. Finally, I shall develop the notion of documentary work in connection with Merleau-Ponty's concept of 'institution',[3] in order to relate the reflexive features of knowledge to the dialectic of institutional order and individual freedom, which is the ground of critical theory as I understand it.

Husserl's description of the crisis of Western knowledge is clearly not a prophecy of its impending failure. Western knowledge is methodically successful. Indeed, we can so take for granted the expansion of the physical and social sciences that what is at stake is not their phenomenal success, but our residual capacity to raise any questions about their nature. This is the transcendental question which Husserl sees can no longer be raised outside history and still be efficacious, or, as he would say, 'responsible'. The successes of the physical and social sciences accumulate by means of a method of objectifying, specializing, and technifying, which makes it possible for the practitioners, working in teams, bureaucracies, and planning agencies, to proceed without raising any radical questions about the foundations of their knowledge. It is important to understand that to raise such fundamental questions by no means implies any need to take the house of science apart brick by brick. Nor does it mean the desire to leave it to rot and decay. Such interpretations merit the impatience and anger of scientists of all kinds, who are concerned to get on with the job and able to appeal to a generalized philosophy of the improvement of mankind through science. Perpetual philosophical beginnings are no better than the dark night of Hegel's cattle.

In speaking of a crisis of Western knowledge Husserl is quite aware that he is engaged in a paradoxical exercise. The increasing rigour of the sciences appears indeed to leave philosophy itself in a backwater. But Husserl's logic is to raise a question, not about the success of the physical and human sciences, but about their meaning for human existence. In other words, Husserl is questioning the fact-value separation which has been integral to the pursuit of science. This is the same question with which Max Weber struggled in his essays on the respective vocations of science and politics, and, of course, in his historical studies of capitalist and non-capitalist social orders. Moreover, Husserl states explicitly that his question of the meaning of the sciences is a historical question, since scientists themselves have not always made a rule of the irrelevance of social and political values to science, as witness the Renaissance and Enlightenment conceptions of science. 'Thus the positivistic concept of science in our time is, historically speaking, a *residual* concept.'[4] The dominance of the positivist concept of science is, therefore, the problem of a cultural order whose self-aspiration is something less than the traditional aspiration toward a rational civilization. Rationality is reduced to the microprocesses of scientific and technical rationality, and is unconcerned to raise any questions about its consequences for civilized reason and humanity.

> We have also become aware in the most general way ... that human philosophizing and its results in the whole of man's existence mean anything but merely private or otherwise limited cultural goals. In *our* philosophizing, then – how can we avoid it? – we are *functionaries of mankind*. The quite personal responsibility of our own true being as philosophers, our inner personal vocation, bears within itself at the same time the responsibility for the true being of mankind; the latter is, necessarily, being toward a *telos* and can only come to realization, *if at all*, through philosophy – through *us, if* we are philosophers in all seriousness. Is there, in this existential 'if', a way out? If not, what should we, who *believe*, do in order to *be able* to believe? We cannot seriously continue our previous philosophizing; it lets us hope only for philosophies, never for philosophy.[5]

It is easy to misunderstand Husserl's reflections here as another attempt to raise philosophy, if not phenomenology, by its bootstraps. Such an exercise leads to understandable irritation but will in any case leave all but the philosophical virtuosi behind. However, I do not think this is the underlying method of Husserl's reflections. Rather, I think that Husserl here understands philosophy, in its seriousness *pro nobis*, as a collective enterprise in which social scientists must do their part to reflect on the *telos* of civilized humanity. Given this, I think *we* can find a tradition of reflection on social science knowledge which is complementary to Husserl's intentional history of the scientific method, if we take as our topic rationality in its socioeconomic and political contexts. Like Hegel, we shall then be able to avoid a metaphysical alienation of reason by preserving 'the labour of the notion' of rationality within the dialectic of historically specific social structures.[6]

THE CONCEPT OF MODERN KNOWLEDGE AND THE UTOPIAN METHOD OF MARXIST ECONOMICS

An essential feature of modern knowledge is its *infinitude*. It has been the central theme of Goethe's *Faust*, Hegel's *Phenomenology of Mind*, Marx's *Capital*, as well as the motive of the reflections of Husserl and Weber. However, Husserl remarks:

But with the appearance of Greek philosophy and its first formulation, through consistent idealization, of the new sense of infinity, there is accomplished in this respect a thoroughgoing transformation which finally draws all finite ideas and with them all spiritual culture and its [concept of] mankind into its sphere. Hence there are, for us Europeans, many infinite ideas (if we may use this expression) which lie outside the philosophical-scientific sphere (infinite tasks, goals, confirmations, truths, 'true values', 'genuine goods', 'absolutely' valid norms), but they owe their analogous character of infinity to the transformation of mankind through philosophy and its idealities. Scientific culture under the guidance of ideas of infinity means, then, a revolutionization [*Revolutionierung*] of the whole culture, a revolutionization of the whole manner in which mankind creates culture. It also means a revolutionization of [its] historicity, which is now the history of the cutting-off of finite mankind's development [*Geschichte des Entwerdens des endlichen Menschentums*] as it becomes mankind with infinite tasks.[7]

The infinitude of modern knowledge constitutes a problem for social science knowledge, which I shall focus as the Hobbesian problem of order. First, however, I shall follow Husserl in presenting a schematic outline of the shift between the ancient and modern conceptions of knowledge and the essence of being, with attention to the consequences for human praxis.

The post-Renaissance scientific approach to nature and its laws of motion no longer ascribes permanence through change to the work of the Platonic demiurge. The rationality of form in motion no longer requires that nature be pervaded by intelligence or a hierarchy of being. In part, this is the legacy of the Judaeo-Christian conception of a mindless nature, subject only to the rationality of God and the human being made in his image, the latter for that reason being in but not of the world. Transcendental monotheism abolished the 'souls' or spirits of nature, paving the way for the strictly quantitative dynamics of nature unleashed in the seventeenth century. The Cartesian dualism of *res cogitans* and *res extensa* reduces a cosmological principle to a methodological subjectivity which is the source of the alternatives of materialism and idealism that have struggled for philosophical and scientific dominance to this day. However, the price which the Cartesian ego pays for certainty is to remain an enigma to itself, without intelligible principle, since all lifeforms fall outside the study of inertial motion, unless reduced to the behaviourist study of the animal and human 'machine'.

The notions of 'mathematics', 'creation', and 'universe' belong together, but, as Hans Jonas has observed, they do not refer to the same constellation of meaning and purpose in Greek philosophy and in modern physics.[8] 'Thus it is wonderfully made known to us how in the very origination of things a certain Divine mathematics or metaphysical mechanics is employed and the determination of the greatest quantity takes place.'[9] What appears to be a return in the seventeenth century to the Pythagorean-Platonic tradition of mathematics is in fact a radical change in the conceptions of mathematics and ontology, as a result of the idealization of knowledge as an algebraic calculus of functions or processes. The ancient hierarchy of forms is replaced by an inverted order of complex and simple functions. The idealization of knowledge proceeds, therefore, in terms of an ontological reduction of nature to its simplest and least rational (in terms of classical ontology) parts.

> It was the paramount interest in *motion*, as against the satisfaction with pattern, which prompted the ascendance of algebraic method in physics: motion instead of fixed spatial proportions became the main object of measurement. This marks a radically novel attitude. In the early stages of modern science, analysis of becoming supplants contemplation of being. The role of 't' in physical formulae indicates the new attitude. The 'forms' here envisaged are no longer those of the terminal products, but those of the continuous processes of nature. Process, as such, is defined solely by its own form, the law of the series, and in no way by its end (of which there is none) or any temporary formulations en route. Greek geometry had considered the relations of unchanging figures and bodies – intuitive ultimates: the abstract algebra of analytical geometry and of the infinitesimal calculus made it possible to represent the geometrical form itself as a function of variables, that is, as a phase in their continuous growth, and so to formulate the laws of its 'generation'. These generative, determining laws became the true objects of mathematical cognition, instead of the descriptive, determinate forms, which had lost their independent status for that of transitional limits.[10]

Marcuse has commented on the contrast between the results of the ancient and medieval approaches to the 'essence' of being and the consequences of the modern reduction of being to the object of authentic and certain knowledge.[11] The medieval and Platonic conceptions of essence, of the unity and universality of being, were not purely epistemological, but included critical and ethical elements. The pre-modern conceptions of being were concerned with the tension between essence and existence, in which *eidos* was a dynamic constituent of things moving toward their 'true being' and 'good', and subject to the moral critique of their unrealized potential, or bad facticity. In modern philosophy, the problem of essence is reduced to a problem of logic and epistemology. The authentic potentiality of being is now the exercise of subjective thought seeking absolutely certain knowledge in a nature subject to mathematical calculation and the domination of applied science. Henceforth, the method of philosophy is the transcendental organization of experience and nature in the 'concept of the unconditioned'. The transcendental reduction in its various stages from Descartes and Kant to Husserl represents, in Marcuse's judgement, a progressive abandonment of the critical task of philosophy.[12] In this respect phenomenology and positivism, however differently they view themselves and one another, are surpassed by materialist theory, which restores the real dynamics of essence and appearance, thus continuing the legacy of Hegel.

In the materialist dialectic the tension between essence and appearance becomes a historical theory of the development of humankind through specific forms of social and economic organiza-tion. The Hegelian-Marxist conception of essence does not refer to an immutable ontological difference, but to a historical relationship between individuals, which is the motive for knowledge and for the transformation of praxis. The mode of materialist knowledge is to relate particulars to wholes, which are masked in inessential relations that determine immediate practice, but which can be seen historic-ally to be disproportions (*Missverhältnis*) of the true development of our kind.

In truth, an *a priori* element is at work here, but one confirming the historicity of the concept of essence. It leads back into history rather than out of it. The immemorially acquired image of essence was formed in mankind's historical experience, which is preserved in the present form of reality, so that it can be 'remembered' and 'refined' to the status of essence. All historical struggles for a better organization of the impoverished conditions of existence, as well as all of suffering mankind's religious and ethical ideal concep-tions of a more just order of things, are preserved in the dialectical concept of the essence of man, where they have become elements of the historical practice linked to dialectical theory.[13]

It is important to understand the materialist theory of essence if we are to have any adequate grasp of Marx's economic analysis. For Marx did more than flirt with the Hegelian method in *Capital*. The determination of human essence has traditionally governed idealist philosophy through historical contingencies external to its own formal interests. However, once reality is conceived as the totality of the relations of production – material, social, political, and ideological – then the interests of domination and recognition provide a structural organization in which form and content, essence and appearance, are separate only within particular historical patterns of community and class interests. The result of this materialist conception is that its theory functions at two levels: at one level concepts deal with the relations between reified phenomena, and, at another, they deal with the real or essential relations between reified phenomena whose subjective constitution has been revealed as a historically specific praxis. Marxian economics therefore employs a first set of concepts, such as profits, wages, entrepreneur, and labour, in order to present the real but 'phenomenal' forms of the processes of production and reproduction. At the next level, the processes of production and reproduction are regarded as an antagonistic unity aimed at the realization of capital, which then requires concepts such as surplus value to bring out the essential relations of class exploitation and to reveal the true content of the formal analytic categories employed at the first level.

The two levels of analysis, however, are dialectically related through the intentional structure of the first level, which is to 'produce' humankind. The historical alienation of this first-level intentional structure can only be grasped through a second-level analysis in which the materialist dialectic furnishes a critical theory of economic reification.

> The dialectical concepts transcend the given social reality in the direction of another historical structure which is present as a tendency in the given reality. The positive concept of essence, culminating in the concept of the essence of man, which sustains all critical and polemical distinctions between essence and appearance as their guiding principle and model, is rooted in this potential structure. In terms of the positive concept of essence, all categories that describe the given form of existence

as historically mutable become 'ironic': they contain their own negation. In economic theory this irony finds its expression in the relationship of the two sets of concepts. If, for instance, it is said that concepts such as wages, the value of labor, and entrepreneurial profit are only categories of manifestations behind which are hidden the 'essential relations' of the second set of concepts, it is also true that these essential relations represent the truth of the manifestations only insofar as the concepts which comprehend them already contain – their own negation and transcendence – the image of a social organization without surplus value. All materialist concepts contain an accusation and an imperative.[14]

What Marcuse adds to our understanding of the concept of essence and the subjectivity of modern knowledge is the Hegelian unity of reason and freedom which is demanded by the concept of the essence of humankind. This concept is therefore as much an ethical as a rational one; it is critical as well as descriptive, and in this respect its historical and political dimensions are effectively utopian. This utopian conception of the essence of humankind is opposed to the idealization of freedom and reason outside the real world in which the palace of ideas sits next to the hovels of the poor and hungry. Nor is it a simple materialism, although it rests on economic foundations in so far as these are transcendentally oriented to the 'production' of a human world. It rests on science and technology; but its utopian nature asks questions about science that are beyond the pale of idealist and positivist reason. Its concern with the future *as human future* lies beyond the predictive controls of science in general, and, needless to say, of economics in particular.

I have appealed to Marcuse's critical analysis of the concept of essence because what I have called its *utopian* feature emphasizes an element in the teleology of reason which otherwise appears to be purely cognitive. By stressing the utopian nature of knowledge and rationality, we may be reminded that the crisis of reason is not just a matter of philosophical ennui or failure of nerve. It is a crisis in the utopia of social-scientific knowledge, which is the form philosophical reason assumes in order to mediate human praxis. Moreover, it is through its utopian dimensions that the concept of the essence of humankind can be adequate to its intentional universality and to the present need to hold in theory what in the future will be an everyday reality.[15]

RATIONALITY, ORDER, AND THE
CRITIQUE OF POLITICAL ECONOMY[16]

The change in the ends of knowledge between the ancient and modern world, that is, the shift from speculative to practical knowledge, pushes theory toward practice and away from contemplative wisdom. Modern knowledge is knowledge of 'works', through the knowledge of the laws of nature's motion. Such knowledge is intrinsically tied to technology. Its values are utilitarian, aimed at the reduction of human misery, if not the production of happiness. Aristotelian knowledge produced happiness in the soul of its possessor by reason of the nobility of the objects of its contemplation; it lifted the individual soul into the cosmic order. The uses of Aristotelian knowledge are intrinsic to its possession and its effects upon the soul. But the pursuit of wisdom leaves unsolved the problem of freedom as freedom from necessity; indeed, it presupposes the slavery of the household economy and the idiocy of its inhabitants, who are excluded from the *polis* and thus from philosophical and political life.[17] Baconian knowledge puts nature to the sovereign use of humankind, but without any other wisdom than the necessity of humanity's mastery of nature, which is otherwise the source of its miseries. The calling of modern science entails unremitting toil on the part of the scientist to relieve the misery of his or her fellow beings. In short, far from presupposing leisure, modern knowledge becomes essentially a work which is, moreover, never finished and which never produces harmony in the soul of the scientist, except as a wager on progress and posterity.

We need to understand how the metaphysics of modern knowledge shapes and is in turn shaped by the modern world, its economy, its political and moral structures of the self, and its institutional orders. There are various ways of presenting the constellation of knowledge, technique, and social order which constitutes the dynamics of the modern world. Our effort must be to tie together the transcendental understanding of knowledge with the life-worlds of economics and politics – to grasp the meaning of the accumulation of knowledge, values, and power.

The problem of knowledge and values involved in the methodological success of modern rationality is sometimes expressed as the problem of value-free knowledge. The Platonic philosopher's return to the cave is a necessity because of the cosmological ties between the orders of knowledge, the soul, and the world. The philosopher's knowledge is intrinsically responsible: it requires no felicific calculus to justify its action on society. Moreover, as wisdom, it works on souls and not on an empty nature. The dualism of humankind and nature is, however, essential to the practice of modern knowledge. The result of this dualism is the conquest of nature, which as a praxis treats its own transcendental presuppositions as an enigma. Utilitarianism is both a metaphysics and a method for the resolution of the implications for the moral and political orders of the dominance of technical rationality. What is usually referred to as the Hobbesian problem of order derives from the reduction of substantive rationality to a deterministic theory of the conditions of rational conduct based on the model of mechanical physics. It is assumed that the ends of action are random, and that under these conditions rationality consists in the most efficient pursuit of whatever ends individuals propose to themselves. Hobbes's so-called 'state of nature' is indeed a historical fiction, in the sense that it reveals the sociological preconceptions of modern civil society.[18] In Hobbes's view, the basic problem of rational egoism is to command the services and recognition of other people, so equal in nature and 'equality of hope' that there is nothing to restrain them from fraud and violence in the pursuit of their own ends.

The fiction of a social contract fails to solve the question raised by Hobbes, since, as Marx later pointed out, the costs of keeping promises can be shifted onto a class which lacks the freedom to contract, and thus Hobbes's 'state of war' becomes 'class war'. The problem of order is, therefore, ultimately a problem of power, which could not be solved within the liberal utilitarian tradition. But theoretical difficulties are often patched in practice, and in this case Locke's postulate of the natural identity of interests matched the early experience of liberal individualism better perhaps than Hobbes's more consistent fears. Thus the problem of order came to rest in the doctrine of the natural identity of interests, until Marx demonstrated that the capitalist system of social exchange and division of labour produces a class which recognizes itself only in the conditions of its own dehumanization.

The Hobbesian problem must be considered in the context of the challenge to modern knowledge raised by the collapse of the feudal community. The loss of a natural basis for community raised the question of whether it was possible to construct a community out of the principles of individualism and rational egoism. It had always appeared, from the medieval standpoint, that only chaos could result from slipping the divine anchor and allowing the passions free play.

This was the fearful prospect of Renaissance and Reformation freedom, especially once it had found in the market an infinite field for the expansion of desire and the accumulation of power. At the same time, this sudden and terrible expansion of moral and political freedom was being transformed into an orderly system of economic exchanges which in turn rested on the growth of mathematical and physical knowledge and its applications to technology and commerce. But there is a subtle yet profound change between the ancient and medieval conceptions of order and the Hobbesian conception. It is a change which stems from the shifts in the definitions of truth and knowledge which occur between ancient, medieval, and modern philosophy.[19]

Modern rationality and its institutional organization rests on the axiom of human domination of nature, which radicalizes the subject–object split and propels knowledge toward quantification and the creation of a moral and political arithmetic. Socrates, it will be remembered, turned away from the study of physical nature in favour of the study of human nature. In this manner Socrates raised the question of the unity of human knowledge as a praxis whose values are revealed in the effects on the soul of the kinds of knowledge pursued in a given social order. With the Renaissance discovery of the experimental method, the dramatic affinity of Western knowledge for power was revealed, unfettered by the moral universals of the ancient and medieval world. Yet to Erasmus the Baconian equation of knowledge and power appeared to be a pagan reversal rather than the intensification of the inherent logic and axiology of Western knowledge. 'Never forget', he remarked, 'that "dominion", "imperial authority", "kingdom", "majesty", "power", are all pagan terms, not Christian. The ruling power of a Christian state consists only of administration, kindness and protection.'[20] Erasmus' comment is a reflection of the crisis of community fought out in the political and religious controversies of the late sixteenth and early seventeenth centuries. In the face of the collapse of church unity and the rise of individual conscience, the normative grounds of community could no longer be presumed upon; and yet it became clear that any particular covenant or contract was nothing more than, in Milton's words, 'the forced and outward union of cold, and neutral, and inwardly divided minds'. Hobbes's concept of philosophy as the pursuit of clear and precise discourse on the model of geometry dictates his aim of bringing peace and order into civil life by a set of political definitions founded on sovereign authority which would put an end to the anarchy of values and opinions.

For I doubt not, but if it had been a thing contrary to any man's right of dominion, or to the interest of men that have dominion, *that the three angles of a triangle, should be equal to two angles of a square*; that doctrine should have been, if not disputed, yet by the burning of all books of geometry, suppressed, as far as he whom it concerned was able.[21]

Henceforth, rationality is never a substantive concept based on the 'nature of things'; the task of reason is confined to providing conclusions 'about the names of things'. The standard of rationality furnished by Hobbes's science of politics is totally divorced from the traditional sentiments and usages of reason.

This dilemma faced by Hobbes was partly owing to a failure to realize what other apostles of 'scientific' politics have not yet seen, that one of the basic reasons for the unsurpassed progress of science was that scientific discourse, unlike political discourse, had rejected not only the common vocabulary of everyday life, but also the modes of thought familiar to the common understanding.[22]

In the end Hobbes failed to solve the problem of order in any but an external fashion. Hobbes's citizens live in a common, mutual fear which corrodes their private lives and leaves society dependent on the sovereign whose power can never be anything but the exercise of fiat because the civil order lacks any sense of community or constituency.

The Hobbesian problem prefigures the crisis of reason of which Husserl spoke and illuminates his rejection of Enlightenment rationalism. However, in order to appreciate the weight of Husserl's arguments for social science rationality, we need to be aware of the Hegelian and Marxist critique of the utilitarian and Enlightenment conceptions of reason and social order. Hegel and Marx made it explicit that the metaphysics of reason determine the methodology of the social sciences, and thus the preconceptions of utilitarian economics and politics.

Hegel regarded history as a process which unfolds through living ideologies, such as the Enlightenment, utilitarianism, and the Absolute Liberty of the French Revolution. Each of these ideologies is related to a definite cultural and social reality, through which the nature of human rationality and freedom is progressively revealed. Once the Enlightenment had won its struggle with religious superstition, the question arose as to the nature of the philosophical truth which the Enlightenment was to set in its place. The truth of the

Enlightenment is utilitarianism, which judges everything by its usefulness to humankind; but utilitarianism is unable to solve the dilemma of one individual's utility to other people, which raises the problem of exploitation, insoluble within the utilitarian tradition.

> As everything is useful for man, man is likewise useful too, and his characteristic function consists in making himself a member of the human herd, of use for the common good, and serviceable to all. The extent to which he looks after his own interests is the measure with which he must also serve the purposes of others, and so far as he serves their turn, he is taking care of himself: the one hand washes the other. But wherever he finds himself there he is in his right place; he makes use of others and is himself made use of.[23]

Marx seizes upon this dilemma in utilitarianism in a passage characteristic of his own development of Hegelian insights:

> Hegel has already proved in his *Phänomenologie* how this theory of mutual exploitation, which Bentham expounded *ad nauseam*, could already at the beginning of the present century have been considered a phase of the previous one. Look at his chapter on 'The Struggle of Enlightenment with Superstition', where the theory of usefulness is depicted as the final result of enlightenment. The apparent stupidity of merging all the manifold relationships of people in the *one* relation of usefulness, this apparently metaphysical abstraction arises from the fact that, in modern bourgeois society, all relations are subordinated in practice to the one abstract monetary-commercial relation. This theory came to the fore with Hobbes and Locke, at the same time as the first and second revolutions, those first battles by which the bourgeoisie won political power.[24]

Once the physiocrats had demonstrated the nature of the economic process as a circular flow, all that remained to complete classical political economy was to give an account of individual attitudes and motivations within that economic framework. This was Bentham's contribution, although, as Marx observes, the theory of utility could not have the generality it claimed because it ignored its own institutional assumptions. For a time, the utilitarian theory of the natural identity of interests had some empirical basis in the facts of the social division of labour and exchange. It was not until Marx adapted Locke's labour theory of value to demonstrate that it contained the working principles for the exploitation of formally free labour that the sociological framework of classical economics was shattered. For utility is subject to appropriation in the form of capital, which is then able to command the services of others to their disadvantage, whatever the circumstances of a formally free contract. Hence the attempt to base the social and political order on the postulate of the natural identity of interests fails once and for all.

Between them, Hegel and Marx developed a thorough critique of the social and political foundations of utilitarian economics. Classical liberalism depended on the protection of a sphere in which the values of personal integrity, property, and contract could be realized as the expression of market society. But, as Hegel showed in the *Philosophy of Right*, in a society conceived solely as a field for market behaviour, economics cannot provide the only framework for law, if personality, property, and contract are to be preserved as anything more than instruments of civil society. The political principles of liberal utilitarianism can only be preserved by a system of state laws based on Reason, which differentiates them from the laws of the market.[25] In other words, Hegel argues that the utilitarian conception of economic society based on economic laws grounds civil society (*bürgerliche Gesellschaft*) in positive but not substantively rational law. The laws of economic society and civil society are in turn distinct from the state, which is the highest stage of the realization of Reason and the ethical will.

Marx's critique of the liberal bourgeois concept of the state, society, and individual rights is substantially the same as Hegel's. The difference is that Marx's argument also contains a destructive critique of Hegel's own concept of the state and its bureaucratic rationality. Marx's critique in many ways anticipates Max Weber.[26]

If power is taken as the basis of right, as Hobbes, etc. do, then right, law, etc. are merely the symptom, the expression of *other* relations upon which State power rests. The material life of individuals which by no means depends merely on their 'will', their mode of production and form of intercourse, which mutually determine each other – this is the real basis of the State and remains so at all stages at which division of labor and private property are still necessary, quite independently of the *will* of individuals. These actual relations are in no way created by the State power; on the contrary they are the power creating it. The individuals who rule in these conditions, besides having to constitute their power in the form of the *State*, have to give their will, which is determined by these definite conditions, a universal expression as the will of the State, as law – an expression whose content is always determined by the relations of this class, as the civil and criminal law demonstrates in the clearest way.[27]

The utilitarian conception of society, i.e., of civil society, is characterized by the separation of state and society which reduces the enforcement of law to the preservation of property and those personal rights necessary for its acquisition and alienation.[28] Thus the utilitarian conception of society enforces a radical dualism between private and public personae which is the basis for all other forms of individual and social alienation.

THE SUBJECTIVE MEANING OF THE ECONOMIC WORLD

The objective and methodological nature of modern knowledge is an essentially subjective praxis, with specific historical and institutional bases. This is especially true of knowledge in the social sciences; I shall return to this point as part of the discussion of the views of Marx and Weber on the process of rationalization. I shall first, however, deal with the question of the subjective grounds of the modern economic world as developed in Hannah Arendt's argument concerning the hybridization of the realms of politics and economics, and then turn to the discussion of these phenomena in Marx and Weber.[29]

In the Graeco-Roman world the boundary between the public and private realms was clear, and everyone was conscious of the threshold that separated the two. Although the ancient city-state grew at the expense of the family household and kinship group, the boundary between these realms was never erased. Indeed, the definition of the public realm as an area of freedom and equality presupposed the recognition of 'necessity' in the household economy. The needs of maintenance and reproduction defined the social nature of man and the family and the sexual and social division of labour between man and woman, master and slave. In the modern period this ancient boundary between public and private realms was dissolved with the emergence of 'society' and the liberal concept of mini-government. A whole new world – the social universe – emerged, confounding public and private life.

The public aspect of the social universe has its roots in the subjectivization of private property and the limitation of government to the minimal agenda of social equilibration of individual and public interests. Seventeenth-century politics originated the narrow limits of 'government' in order to exploit the boundless domain of possessive individualism, which C.B. Macpherson has described as the central impediment of modern liberal-democratic ideology.

Its possessive quality is found in its conception of the individual as essentially the proprietor of his own person or capacities, owing nothing to society for them. The individual was seen neither as a moral whole, nor as a part of a larger social whole, but as an owner of himself. The relation of ownership, having become for more and more men the critically important relation determining their actual freedom and actual prospect of realizing full potentialities, was read back into the nature of the individual. . . . Society becomes a lot of free individuals related to each other as proprietors of their own capacities and of what they have acquired by their exercise. Society consists of relations of exchange between proprietors. Political society becomes a calculated device for the protection of this property and for the maintenance of an orderly relation of exchange.[30]

Liberal practicality shied away from any utopian conception of the public domain and was content with an order that seemed to emerge through non-intervention in the natural processes, or rather the metabolism, of society. As Hannah Arendt argues, the extraordinary identification of the notions of society and economy may be traced in part to the liberal devaluation of politics.

What concerns us in this context is the extraordinary difficulty with which we, because of this development, understand the decisive division between the public and private realms, between the sphere of the polis and the sphere of household and family, and finally, between activities related to a common world and those related to the maintenance of life, a division upon which all ancient political thought rested as self-evident and axiomatic.[31]

The separation of public and private experience which characterizes modern society derives from the essential nature of its processes of work and intellectual activity. Ancient knowledge possessed intrinsic ties to action and purpose, that is, to human initiative and the realm of politics and history. By contrast, modern knowledge is without such limits; it consists only of the self-infinitizing labour of the person of culture, as well as of the person of property. But we cannot speak of knowledge outside the context of human action and purpose, or apart from human initiative and the bonds of promise and forgiveness. The accumulation of modern knowledge, the self-infinitizing labour of the person of culture and the person of property, is the labour of modern self and its alienation from the world. As Kafka put it, modern man 'found the Archimedean point, but he used it against himself; it seems that he was permitted to find it only under this condition'. The modern age is built upon the paradox that its expansion of technological, economic, and social activity has produced a massive alienation and domination of the world, coupled with universal migration, which are motivated by what Weber called 'inner-worldly asceticism'. The release of these forces was preceded, as we have shown, by the collapse of the ancient and feudal conceptions of the world as a political realm of public deeds and public speech resting on the citizen's or the lord's control of his own household and its private economy. So long as the household economy was embedded in the political order, labour served to produce objects whose value was subordinate to the social values created by the thoughts, deeds, and speech of political man. The modern world, however, is built on an inordinate expansion of individual utilities, which subordinates labour and production to a cycle of consumption and destruction divorced from the political order. This is the source of the modern conception of 'society' as solely a field of individual interests, which inspired Hobbes's nasty vision, and whose essentially contradictory features were later analysed, as we have seen, by Hegel and Marx.

The question which underlies the 'crisis' of the social sciences is the question of the meaningfulness of the subjectivization of the bases of need and utility, once these are broken off from their political matrix. It is this issue which focuses the socio-logical tradition through Marx, Durkheim, and Weber. The relevance of these classical theorists for our problem is that they were concerned with the historical process whereby legal and economic rationality undermines the traditional, sentimental bonds of association in favour of market freedoms or property rights. Both Marx and Durkheim elaborated critiques of the utilitarian theory of conduct in order to raise the transcendental question of the meaningfulness of individual behaviour in different orders of society. In other words, they raised the question of the substantive basis of the legitimacy of social and political orders *as a problem of economic knowledge.*

Classical utilitarian thought from the time of Hobbes through Locke, Marx, and Durkheim, must be understood in the light of the constitutional, class, and industrial crises in which the doctrine of the natural identity of interests, however logically objectionable, provided a metaphysical prop for the drama of modern individualism and market rationality. As the framework of market society, class, and property gradually evolved, the shift from the sentimentalities of kinship to the rational social division of labour can be seen as the articulation of modern self-consciousness. The problem of order is historical as well as sociological. It is the problem of the origins and teleology of civilization, and was seen in this light by Marx, Durkheim, Weber, and, of course, Freud. Another aspect of the same question comes into modern consciousness through Nietzsche, Dilthey, Burckhardt, and Husserl;[32] for them, the problem of order is the riddle of history, that is, the problem of humankind's estrangement through civilization, the need to set restraints on the infinitude of wants. Durkheim attempted to draw a distinction between individuality and personality in order to cope with the ways in which society at once provokes and ennobles individual aspirations. Moreover, Durkheim was aware that these problems were wider than the limits of law and the bonds of solidarity. He sensed their origins in the ambivalence of modern knowledge, including sociology, despite his hopes for the latter as a social remedy.[33] Marx argued that the forces which divide humankind against itself derive from the division of property on the basis of class, which is prior to the problems of specialization and division of labour. But the deeper question is, what is the meaning of the 'surplus repression',[34] or the value set on value accumulation, which provides the driving force, the glory, and the misery of modern civilization?

The understanding of Western rationality demands a structural analysis as well as a phenomenological description of the dialectic of humankind's fundamental historical and social nature and its alternations between freedom and determinism. It is necessary to start from the institutional matrix in which specific norms of action shaped, and were in turn shaped by, a particular conception of human nature. With the rise of capitalism, human rational nature was increasingly understood in terms of an instrumental orientation toward the domination of physical nature. At the same time, this orientation toward nature involved an expressive as well as cognitive reorientation of perception of self, society, and the elements of nature. The essence of this shift was grasped by Hegel and Marx in their conception of human freedom as 'man making himself'. Between Hegel's *Phenomenology of Mind* and Marx's *Communist Manifesto* the 'world' has become the immanent term of human thought and activity which sustains the alternation of freedom and determinism. The significance of Marx's critique of the relationship between ideologies and philosophical thought is that it brings human ideas into a permanently efficacious present, shaped by and giving shape to the processes through which a society endures and changes. Thus the weight of the past, articulated in the social division of labour and the ideological superstructure of past religions and philosophies, is not just the residue of historicism or relativism. It is the phenomenological reality of truth as the product of social life and the creation of *homo faber*.[35]

Benefiting from Hegel, Marx grasped the internal logic of knowledge and action in modern society. Furthermore, with the advantage of a more detailed knowledge of the nature of capitalist institutions, Marx was able to show that the logical connection between human technological domination of nature and the complete integration of humankind's individual and social experiences lay outside the utilitarian conception of rationality. Marx's analysis of capitalist society is directed primarily to the connections between social norms and economic systems. Marx, no less than Weber, makes very clear the ascetic basis of capitalist rationality and its motivation toward the accumulation of value.

In a remarkable passage from the *Economic and Philosophical Manuscripts*, Marx explains how political economy develops against the background of the breaking away of labour and property from their anchorages in use values. The emancipation of labour makes possible the substitution of exchange values for use values, which leads to the subordination of all forms of life and property to the accumulation and expansion of wealth. In their endlessly reproducible forms, as the prices of capital and the power of labour, private property and labour alienate human needs in favour of market wants. Marx concludes that the impulse to modern individualism is the subjectivization of the bases of feudal community, which simultaneously supplies the orientation toward market behaviour. The physiocrats identified all wealth with land and cultivation, which, while leaving feudal property intact, shifted the definition of land to its economic function and thereby exposed feudal property to the later attacks on ground rent. The objective nature of wealth was also in part shifted to its subjective basis in labour, inasmuch as agriculture was regarded as the source of the productivity of land. Finally, industrial labour emerged as the most general principle of productivity; the factors of production, land, labour, and capital, became nothing but moments in the dialectic of labour's self-alienation.

Thus, from the viewpoint of this enlightened political economy which has discovered the *subjective* essence of wealth within the framework of private property, the partisans of the monetary system and the mercantilist system, who consider private property as a *purely objective* being for man, are *fetishists* and *Catholics*. Engels is right, therefore, in calling Adam Smith the *Luther of political economy*. Just as Luther recognized *religion* and *faith* as the essence of the real *world*, and for that reason took up a position against Catholic paganism; just as he annulled *external* religiosity while making religiosity the *inner* essence of man; just as he negated the distinction between priest and layman because he transferred the priest into the heart of the layman; so wealth external to man and independent of him (and thus only to be acquired and conserved from outside) is annulled. That is to say, its *external* and *mindless* objectivity is annulled by the fact that private property is incorporated in man himself, and man himself is recognized as its essence. But as a result, man himself is brought into the sphere of private property, just as, with Luther, he is brought into the sphere of religion. Under the guise of recognizing man, political economy, whose principle is labor, carries to its logical conclusion the denial of man. Man himself is no longer in a condition of external tension with the external substance of private property; he has himself become the tension-ridden being of private property. What was previously a phenomenon of *being external to oneself*, a real external manifestation of man, has now become the act of objectification, of alienation. This political economy seems at first, therefore, to recognize man with his independence, his personal activity, etc. It incorporates private property in the very essence of man, and it is no longer, therefore, conditioned by the local or national *characteristics of private property* regarded as existing outside itself. It manifests a cosmopolitan, universal activity which is destructive of every limit and every bond, and substitutes itself as the *only* policy, the *only* universality, the *only* limit and the *only* bond.[36]

Marx and Weber raised a common question: what is the human value of the mode of social organization called capitalism; what is its *raison d'être*; what is the sense in its universality? Admittedly, Weber may have gone further in the comparative study of the conditions under which the normative and institutional bases of capitalism emerged. But each took the same view with regard to the major task of understanding the historically unique role played by the rational domination of nature and the accumulation of values in determining human action in capitalist society.

We need to understand the 'vocation' of Western science and rationality. Modern science is chained to progress through invention and discovery. Every scientific finding asks to be surpassed in the light of accumulated knowledge. Each scientist resigns himself to making only a partial and fleeting contribution to a task that is conceived as limitless.

> And with this we come to inquire into the meaning of science. For, after all, it is not self-evident that something subordinate to such a law is sensible and meaningful in itself. Why does one engage in doing something that in reality never comes, and never can come to an end?[37]

Weber compares his own question of the meaning of science to Tolstoy's question about the meaning of death in modern civilization.[38] Civilized humankind has broken with nature. Cultural values have replaced use values, and the cycle of life familiar to the peasant and the feudal lord has exploded into a self-infinitizing progression of the accumulation of cultural values. The peasantry could encounter the totality of meaning ordained for them in the feudal order and die at peace with their station in life because their daily life was congruent with the whole of their life. But the modern individual pitted against an ever expanding universe of ideas, problems, and values, though they can be weary of life, always encounters death as meaningless, for death robs them of infinity. 'And because death is meaningless, civilized life as such is meaningless; by its very "progressiveness" it gives death the imprint of meaninglessness.'[39]

For want of a science of ends which might illuminate the ideal of Western rationality and its affinity for power and accumulation,

Weber turned to the notions of 'calling' and the 'ethic of responsibility'. It is implicit in Weber's 'ideal type' method that the growth
of rationality in science, politics, and economics is a meaningful way
of representing Western experience only so long as we choose to
understand it *in its own terms (verstehen)*. But as soon as we consider
Western rationality from the standpoint of comparative history it loses
its self-evidence. In other words, the increasing rationality of modern
science and technology becomes an enigma.

HISTORICAL RESPONSIBILITY AND THE
VOCATION OF REASON

Modern consciousness is greatly affected by the standpoints of
anthropology and historicism, which reveal that all knowledge about
humankind and nature presupposes some metaphysical stand on the
relation between human facticity, knowledge, and values. Thus we
need, as Husserl observes, 'a new method of philosophical work',
which will explore the reflexive ties between rational subjectivity
and the regional ontologies of science, economics, politics, and
everyday life.[40] Instead of pursuing the ideal of an objective
mathésis universalis, a complete mathematical formalization of
biological, linguistic, and economic values, which still lures modern
structuralists, we need a philosophical method which we may
call, borrowing from Husserl, 'documentary work'. This work
would be profoundly anthropological and archaeological, provided we recover the historico-intentional origin of these modes
of work. At the same time it will be necessary to translate the
transcendental question of the possibility of rational knowledge
and freedom into a question about the *institution* of science and
the social sciences as a human praxis, a collective endeavour,
which develops a tradition while still remaining open to rebellion
and change. We must turn the transcendental question of the possibility
of knowledge and freedom into a question of the 'origins' (*Ursprünge*)
of critical thought. In this way we shall be true to the ultimately
ethical responsibilities of phenomenological and social-scientific
knowledge. To Weber's reflections on the vocations of science
and politics, in so far as these vocations are stoically responsible
and not plunged into nihilistic despair, may be joined the notion
of 'tradition' in Husserl and Heidegger, which integrates the question of the origins of reason with the nature of human authenticity.
Such a conception is worthy of attention as a propaedeutic to

the discussion of institutional alienation, which I shall not otherwise treat, though it provides an obvious gloss on the problem we are about to consider.

I have argued that the alienation of the world inherent in capitalism, as well as its innerworldly asceticism, is due to the classical utilitarian reduction of the world to a calculus of utilities, from which our kind itself could not be saved as an ultimate standard of value. Kant's categorical imperative raised a standard of action and personal conduct which had no foundations in the context of class inequality and exploitation that reduced most people to the status of means and not ends. Marx drew from Hegel the essence of modern subjectivity, the notion that people produce themselves. But, as Hegel pointed out in his *Phenomenology of Mind*, modern subjectivity consumes itself in an unstable utilitarianism, which destroys the substantive rationality of things and the orders of nature and society, at the same time that it represents the greatest release of subjective rights and freedoms. More recently, Hannah Arendt has described the processes of destruction of the world, the cycle of meaningless labour, and the activity of 'science' which designs the landscape and invents the scenarios of modern violence.[41] The disenchantment of the world and the devaluation of nature are the results of a consistent utilitarianism, driven by the rational asceticism of modern subjectivity guessing at a hidden God. Once humankind no longer has an end beyond itself, nothing stops it in the relentless exploitation of the world and itself. In this project the vocabularies of liberal individualism and progress provide motivational supports for the private appropriation of world resources and the unthinking pollution of alternative human environments. It is no longer possible within this ideological framework to separate the processes of production and destruction. For modern labour is the inspiration of a divine madness, working upon a promised land, where abundance feeds rapacity and denies conservation.

We need to generate a counter-myth to the ideology of world domination. To this end it is necessary to separate the notion of work from the self-infinitizing logic of utilitarianism. The human world is an artifice built upon everyday passions, but also against time and eternity. Much of human life is spent in incessant labour aimed at the simple reproduction of life and the satisfaction of bodily needs; these labours consume a good part of the mental energies of the individual, so that it is necessary to distinguish, Arendt argues, that 'science' which serves wants from 'thought', whose aim is nonutilitarian. *Thought* serves no obvious purpose; it is the riddle of human activity, the source of religion, magic, myth, and art. Thought produces objects for their own sake; pre-eminently in art it draws from time and destruction a world of essence, an immortal home for mortals. Of itself thought produces nothing without human hands, eyes, ears, and tongues; these materialize thought and embody its creations, which would otherwise lose humankind in reflection, dream, and imagination. Thought transcends science, logic, and intelligence; it can never be expropriated by computerized homunculi, who merely aid mental labour in the service of wants. The prevalence of thought demands the reversal of modern utilitarianism and the subordination of economics to politics. Upon this reversal hangs the question of the humanization and conservation of the world, not as an emporium, but as a public space in which an individual's words might be memorable and their deeds glorious. Without such a space history and politics are polluted, and the human story reduced to an insane series of commercials.

If the *animal laborans* needs the help of *homo faber* to ease his labor and remove his pain, and if mortals need his help to erect a home on earth, acting and speaking men [*political men*] need the help of *homo faber* in his highest capacity, that is, the help of the artist, of poets and historiographers, of monument-builders or writers, because without them the only product of their activity, the story they enact and tell, would not survive at all. In order to be what the world is always meant to be, a home for men during their life on earth, the human artifice must be a place fit for action and speech, for activities not only entirely useless for the necessities of life, but of an entirely different nature from the manifold activities of fabrication, by which the world itself and all things in it are produced. We need not choose here between Plato and Protagoras, or decide whether man or a god should be the measure of all things; what is certain, is that the measure can be neither the driving necessity of biological life and labor, nor the utilitarian instrumentalism of fabrication and usage.[42]

The radical and monumental feature of thought, as Hannah Arendt speaks of it, requires as its world-historical medium a viable conception of tradition and criticism distinctly different from the liberal anti-tradition of change and criticism.

The ill repute of speculative philosophies of history has generally caused the social sciences to neglect the temporal and historical features of individual conduct and institutional life. Husserl's concern with the structures of the life-world brought his attention to the temporal dimensions of interpersonal conduct and the continuity of tradition. The horizon-structure of experience requires that its temporal organization, as a field of retrospective and prospective concerns, is its own intrinsic historicity. The problem presented by Husserl's transcendental ego is to relate its own inner time-consciousness to the communal structures of human history, within which there is no such transcendental standpoint. But even to put the problem this way is to misrepresent it with respect to Husserl's task in the *Crisis*.[43] For the *Crisis* requires that the consciousness of the historicity of human knowledge and specific scientific praxes be grasped as an existential structure, always open to forgetfulness and recovery. However, Husserl and especially Heidegger offer the bridging notion of an intersubjectively open horizon of 'things', interests, and activities, which through their capacity for repetition (*Wiederholung*) become a living tradition of recollection and projection of future work, values, and meaning.[44] Our communal life, its beliefs and practices, is 'world-historical' through and through, that is, it involves the integration of the realms of predecessors, contemporaries, and successors as temporalized regions of our collective life. The integration of these domains of our communal being is achieved by means of an explicit repetition or recovery of the Dasein that 'has been', in the sense of 'having been there' (*dagewesen*). The past of a living communal tradition is thus not a determinate weight so much as a legacy, a 'handing down' (*Überlieferung*) of the authentic possibilities of Dasein that has been. Moreover, the authentic repetition of the past is critical to the present inasmuch as it is grounded in an anticipatory resoluteness, which is the recovery of Dasein from its circumscriptive, falling concern with everydayness.

Understood in this way, Husserl and Heidegger present a concept of tradition as a structure of 'monumental, antiquarian and critical' concerns.

As historical, Dasein is possible only by reason of its temporality, and temporality temporalizes itself in the ecstatico-horizontal unity of its raptures. Dasein exists authentically as futural in resolutely disclosing a possibility which it has chosen. Coming back resolutely to itself, it is, by repetition, open for the 'monumental' possibilities of human existence. The historiology which arises from such historicality is 'monumental'. As in the process of having been, Dasein has been delivered over to its thrownness. When the possible is made one's own by repetition, there is adumbrated at the same time the possibility of reverently preserving the existence that has-been-there, in which the possibility seized upon has become manifest. Thus authentic historiology, as monumental, is 'antiquarian' too. Dasein temporalizes itself in the way the future and having been are united in the Present. The Present discloses the 'today' authentically, and of course as the moment of vision. But in so far as this 'today' has been interpreted in terms of understanding a possibility of existence which has been seized upon – an understanding which is repetitive in a futural manner – authentic historiology becomes a way in which the 'today' gets deprived of its character as present; in other words, it becomes a way of painfully detaching oneself from the falling publicness of the 'today'. *As authentic, the historiology which is both monumental and antiquarian is necessarily a critique of the 'Present'*. Authentic historicality is the foundation for the possibility of uniting these three ways of historiology. But the *ground* on which authentic historiology is founded is *temporality* as the existential meaning of the Being of care.[45]

Reflecting upon the sources of the crisis of Western rationality, Husserl called for a method of philosophical and scientific thought which would be monumental, world-building, and at the same time 'poetic' in the exchanges between itself and the world. The consequence of history is that the universality and truth pursued by thought are not an intrinsic property of the idea, but an acquisition which must be constantly established with a community of knowledge, which calls for and depends on the free response of its members. Merleau-Ponty has remarked how well Husserl's notion of *Stiftung*, foundation or institution, captures the fecundity of cultural works, through which they endure into the present where they open new relevances and options on the future.

It is thus that the world as soon as he has seen it, his first attempts at painting, and the whole past of painting all deliver up a *tradition* to the painter – *that is*, Husserl remarks, *the power to forget origins* and to give to the past not a survival, which is the hypocritical form of forgetfulness, but a new life, which is the noble form of memory.[46]

It is important for us to retrieve the notion of the fecundity of tradition, craft, and thought, if we are to avoid the Weberian alternation between cultural pessimism and charismatic fatality, the alternatives of ineffectual alienation and unfulfilled utopianism. These are considerations which bear on economic and sociological knowledge, inasmuch as these must be grounded in an adequate conception of human institutions. Human experience, its labours and visions, accumulates only in the circle of institutions which enlarge and deepen the meaning of our sentiments, our deeds, and our work. This is the circle of alienation, but also of freedom, provided we do not lose our sense of the collectivity, whose history knows of tradition and of a future. In this sense, human institutions are never wholly reified; they are made and unmade in each of us according to his grain. As I understand it, then, the consequence of this conception of institution is that it grounds criticism itself in tradition and membership. The critic labours in the same fashion as anyone else in the community of work, language, and politics. This is not to say that the critic is not rebellious; it is merely to draw the consequences of solidarity and of the responsibility of reason under which Hegel and Marx, as well as Husserl and Weber, lived, worked, and which they left for us as a legacy.

NOTES

1 Husserl speaks of the crisis of European knowledge, but the intentionally broader notion of a crisis in Western knowledge and civilization is endorsed by A. Gurwitsch (1966) in 'The Last Work of Edmund Husserl', in his collected *Studies in Phenomenology and Psychology*, Evanston, Ill.: Northwestern University Press, and it is also supported by Husserl's remarks on 'spiritual Europe', in *The Crisis of European Sciences and Transcendental Phenomenology: An Introduction to Phenomenological Philosophy* (1970), trans. D. Carr, Evanston, Ill.: Northwestern University Press, pp. 273–6 (hereafter cited as *Crisis*).
2 Husserl, *Crisis*, pp. 389–95. This notion is kin to Harold Garfinkel's 'documentary method of interpretation', developed in his *Studies in Ethnomethodology* (1967) Englewood Cliffs, NJ: Prentice-Hall.
3 O'Neill, J. (1970) *Perception, Expression and History: The Social Phenomenology of Maurice Merleau-Ponty*, Evanston, Ill.: Northwestern University Press, pp. 46–64.
4 Husserl, *Crisis*, p. 9.
5 Ibid., p. 17.

6 Here I would like to draw attention to a series of studies by Benjamin Nelson on the fusion of the 'rationales of conscience' underlying the Protestant Reformation and the scientific and philosophical revolutions of the sixteenth and seventeenth centuries. Professor Nelson's patient studies, together with the literature cited in them, are absolutely essential to the full understanding of the complex history that forms the background to the question of the meaning (*Selbstbesinnung*) of social science rationality. See B. Nelson (1968) 'Scholastic Rationales of "Conscience", Early Modern Crises of Credibility, and the Scientific-Technocultural Revolutions of the 17th and 20th Centuries', *Journal for the Scientific Study of Religion*, VII: 157–77, Fall.
7 Husserl, *Crisis*, p. 279.
8 Jonas, H. (1968) 'Is God a Mathematician? The Meaning of Metabolism', in his *The Phenomenon of Life: Toward a Philosophical Biology*, New York: Dell.
9 von Leibniz, G.W. (1697) 'On the Ultimate Origin of Things', in *The Monadology and Other Philosophical Writings*, trans. R. Latta (1898) Oxford: Clarendon Press, p. 342.
10 Jonas, H. *Phenomenon of Life*, pp. 67–8.
11 Marcuse, H. (1968) 'The Concept of Essence', in his *Negations: Essays in Critical Theory*, Boston: Beacon Press, pp. 43–87.
12 Marcuse's judgement here would seem to overlook the *Crisis*, where, as I shall show, Husserl is concerned precisely with the historical responsibility of phenomenological philosophy as a communal aspiration.
13 Marcuse, *Negations*, p. 75.
14 Ibid., p. 86.
15 'In the history of revolution, deep faith in man and deep faith in the world have long gone hand in hand, unmoved by mechanistics and opposition to purpose. But militant optimism, as the subjective side of real progress, also implies searching for the where-to and what-for on the objective side – of forwardmoving being without which there is no progressive consciousness. And the *humanum* is so *inclusive* in the *real possibility* of the *content of its goal, that it allows all movements and forms of human culture location in the togetherness of different epochs. The humanum is so strong that it does not collapse in face of a wholly mechanistically conceived cyclic time*', E. Bloch (1970), *A Philosophy of the Future*, trans. J. Cumming, New York: Herder and Herder, p. 140 (italics Bloch's).
16 In this section I have drawn on my argument (1972) in 'The Hobbesian Problem in Marx and Parsons', in *Explorations in General Theory in the Social Sciences*, J. Loubser, R.C. Baum, A. Effrat and V.M. Lidz (eds), New York: Free Press, forthcoming.
17 Aristotle, *Politics* 1252 a. 2.
18 Macpherson, C.B. (1962) *The Political Theory of Possessive Individualism: Hobbes to Locke*, Oxford: Clarendon Press.
19 Oakeshott, M. (1946) Introduction to *Leviathan*, by T. Hobbes, Oxford: Blackwell.

20 Quoted by Erich Hula in his Comment on Hans Jonas (1963) 'The Practical Uses of Theory', in *Philosophy of the Social Sciences: A Reader*, M. Natanson (ed.) New York: Random House, p. 151.
21 Hobbes, *Leviathan*, p. 68 (italics Hobbes's).
22 Wolin, S.S. (1960) *Politics and Vision: Continuity and Innovation in Western Political Thought*, Boston: Little, Brown, p. 261.
23 Hegel, G.W.F. (1910) *The Phenomenology of Mind*, trans. with an Introduction and notes by Sir James Baillie, London: Allen and Unwin, pp. 579–80.
24 Marx, K. and Engels, F. (1964) *The German Ideology*, trans. Ryazanskaya, Moscow: Progress Publishers, pp. 448–9.
25 Hegel, G.W.F. (1942) *Philosophy of Right*, trans. with notes by T.M. Knox, Oxford: Clarendon Press, Pt. 3, (2) 'Civil Society', pp. 122–55.
26 Lefebvre, H. (1968) *The Sociology of Marx*, trans. N. Guterman, New York: Random House, Pantheon Books, Ch. 5, 'Political Sociology: Theory of the State', pp. 123–85.
27 Marx, *German Ideology*, p. 357.
28 Franklin, M. (1960) 'On Hegel's Theory of Alienation and Its Historic Force', *Tulane Studies in Philosophy*, IX 50–100.
29 I shall not give any detailed refutation of Arendt's interpretation of Marx's conceptions of labour and the human world, since she mistakes Marx's analysis of these concepts under capitalist conditions for his own views. See W.A. Suchting (October 1962) 'Marx and Hannah Arendt's *The Human Condition*', *Ethics*, LXIII, pp. 47–55.
30 Macpherson, C.B. *Political Theory of Possessive Individualism*, p. 3. The liberal concept of 'society' provoked the counterconcept of 'organic society' in conservative and Marxian thought, which have more in common with each other than either has with liberalism. See K. Mannheim (1953), *Essays on Sociology and Social Psychology*, New York: Oxford University Press, Ch. 2, 'Conservative Thought'.
31 Arendt, H. (1958) *The Human Condition*, Chicago: University of Chicago Press, p. 28.
32 Bendix, R. (April 1965) 'Max Weber and Jacob Burckhardt', *American Sociological Review*, XXX, pp. 176–84.
33 Bendix, R. (1966) 'The Age of Ideology: Persistent and Changing', *Ideology and Discontent*, D.E. Apter (ed.) New York: Free Press, Ch. 8, pp. 294–327.
34 Marcuse, H. (1955) *Eros and Civilization: A Philosophical Inquiry into Freud*, New York: Umlage Books, p. 32.
35 Wolff, K.H. (1951) 'On the Significance of Hannah Arendt's *The Human Condition for Sociology*', *Inquiry*, IV, Summer, 67–106.
36 Marx, K. (1963) 'Economic and Philosophical Manuscripts', *Early Writings*, trans. and ed. T.B. Bottomore, London: Watts, pp. 147–8.
37 Weber, M. (1958) 'Science as a Vocation', in *From Max Weber: Essays in Sociology*, trans., ed., and with an Introduction by H. Gerth and C. Wright Mills, New York: Oxford University Press, p. 138.
38 Tolstoy, L. (1964) *The Death of Ivan Ilych*, trans. Aylmer Maude, New York: New American Library.
39 Weber, M. 'Science as a Vocation', p. 140.

40 Husserl, *Crisis*, p. 351.
41 Arendt, H. *Human Condition*, Ch. 6, 'The *Vita Activa* and the Modern Age', pp. 225–97.
42 Ibid., p. 153
43 Ricoeur, P. (July–October 1949) 'Husserl et le sens de l'histoire', *Revue de métaphysique et de morale*, LIV, 280–316.
44 Husserl, *Crisis*, pp. 358–60.
45 Heidegger, M. (1962) *Being and Time*, trans. J. Macquarrie and E. Robinson, New York: Harper & Row, pp. 448–9 (italics Heidegger's).
46 Merleau-Ponty, M. (1964) *Signs*, trans. R.C. McCleary, Evanston, Ill.: Northwestern University Press, p. 59; and Ricoeur 'Husserl et le sens de l'histoire', pp. 293–5.

Chapter 5

Orphic Marxism

I now want to give the preceding introduction to the historical rationality of human institutions – which I think must be opposed to contemporary post-rationalist and minoritarian doctrines – a positive reformulation in Marxist humanism. This exercise benefits from the critique of alienation in both socialist and capitalist societies since Marxism has itself practised scientism and a crude Prometheanism. My reformulation of Marxist humanism gives emphasis to its civility over its industrialism.

Since I have at several points rejected the postmodern fragmentation of cultural myth and narrative, I propose to put the opposite case in terms of the mytho-poetics of an Orphic mythology of the self-civilizing functions of the human body. Whereas in postmodernism the body is reduced to the sensory register of fleeting simulacra of desire without end, I believe it can be argued that the human body is also the figure of a great civilizing narrative that cannot be separated from the equally humanizing figure of work. In short, I shall develop from Vico and Marx an Orphic Marxism which I believe to be the necessary complement to the largely Promethean mythology that has underwritten Marxism, for better or worse. In this way, we may oppose the easy postmodern rejection of 'historism', i.e., the notion that history can be subject to a technical practice (although it sometimes celebrates this very error) on the ground that it loses sight of the more difficult concept of 'historicism', namely, that we never achieve an absolute distance between our history and our modes of historical understanding. This must be recognized not because history shapes us through forces larger than ourselves, whether institutional or unconscious, but because even our ability to formulate these modifications in our understanding never places us out of ourselves. Certainly, men and women make their own history, but they do so in the same way that they make music or art, i.e., with a religious sense that they exceed us and are therefore inexhaustible gifts to the whole of humankind:

> The human mind is naturally inclined by the senses to see itself externally in the body, and only with great difficulty does it come to understand itself by means of reflection. This axiom gives us the universal principle of etymology in all languages: words are carried over from bodies and from the properties of bodies to signify the contributions of the mind and spirit.[1]

Vico and Marx are two great naturalists. They are, by the same token, two great humanists. Today, such a claim would seem paradoxical inasmuch as nothing threatens humanism so much as the naturalist method of the human and social sciences in their embrace of a universal scientism. Yet Vico and Marx rejected both materialism and idealism because of their inadequate conception of humankind's embodied mind and sensuous history.

Alienation, as Marx understood it, is neither a spiritual condition nor the lament of the soul imprisoned in the body. The human mind would not be more efficacious if its operation were unmediated by language, sensory perception and corporate, i.e., incarnate and collective life. Wherever the mind constructs its own heavenly palace, the body lives in a neighbourly hovel. But neither is alienation the lament of the natural body, uninhibited by thought and the confinements of collective life, labour and language. Rather, Marx, like Vico before him, argued that human beings are thinking bodies whose nature is entirely second nature. Human nature is the historical and civil achievement of ways of thought, perception, language and labour through which we mediate our own humanity. Understood in this way, alienation is a necessary moment in the history of our lived-being. To refuse alienation is to suspend our living, to imagine ourselves as wholly spiritual beings, as divinities, or full-time philosophers. Yet to embrace alienation is not to embrace animality, nor to content ourselves with the world as a pasture in which we graze as innocently as sheep or with as little foresight as the birds. Alienation does not adorn us; the civil beauty of our kind is at once far less and greater than the beauty of the lilies of the field.

As early as the 'Economic and Philosophical Manuscripts' of 1844, Marx had developed an unswervingly Viconian conception of the historical nature of human nature:

But man is not only a natural being, he is a human natural being. This means that he is a being that exists for himself, thus a species-being that must confirm and exercise himself as such in his being and knowledge. Thus human objects are not natural objects as they immediately present thenmselves nor is human sense, in its purely objective existence, human sensitivity and human objectivity. Neither nature in its objective aspect nor in its subjective aspect is immediately adequate to the human being. And as everything natural must have an origin, so man too has his process of origin, history, which can, however, be known by him and thus is a conscious process of origin that transcends itself. History is the true natural history of man.[2]

It follows from such passages that Marx rejected equally the idealist and materialist conceptions of subjectivity and objectivity. The human world is neither an idea nor an organism, neither a given nor a projection. The human world is at every level of sensation, perception, thought and action a *social praxis* in which our inner and outer worlds are mutually articulated. The human eye is civilized by what it sees in the field of art as is the human ear by the music to which it listens. In each case, human physiology is inserted into a hermeneutical field whose own historical articulation includes the relatively autonomous praxes of optics, acoustics, art and music. In this way, vision and art are entirely relativized by one another, and the same can be said of the rest of the human senses and their correlative institutions and histories. Thus the body has a history because human history has a body:

> Only through the objectively unfolded richness of man's essential being is the richness of subjective human sensibility (a musical ear, an eye for beauty of form – in short, senses capable of human gratification, senses affirming themselves as essential powers of man) either cultivated or brought into being. For not only the five senses but also the so-called mental senses – the practical senses (will, love, etc.) – in a word, human sense – the human nature of the senses – comes to be by virtue of its object, by virtue of humanized nature. *The forming of the five senses is a labour of the entire history of the world down to the present.*[3]

If Marx separates himself from the Hegelian vision of spiritual alienation – and we shall argue against that view – it is on the ground that epistemological alienation, or the irreducible excess of the spirit beyond its fall into matter, is merely an idealist lament incapable of redeeming the history it has constructed out of its own self-alienation. In keeping with this argument, Hegel deprives history of its body and thereby reduces the spirit to an unhappy history of unmediated self-reflection. In turn, Hegel's disembodied history can only imitate life by absorbing its history into the abstract laws of logic, while continuing to grasp at reality through the mirror of dialectics. Consequently, Hegel's sublimation of the historical movement of alienation arises from his substitution of a mistaken separation of mind from matter – which can only occur on the level of philosophy – with the immoral separation of human beings from their humanity – which can only occur on the level of political economy:

> What is supposed to be the essence of alienation that needs to be transcended is not that man's being objectifies itself in an inhuman manner in opposition to itself, but that it objectifies itself in distinction from and in opposition to, abstract thought.[4]

But against this critique of Hegel, which Marx himself fostered, there is another reading of Hegel which Marxism has more recently espoused in order to revise its own potential for positivism and bureaucratized alienation. Here the convergence beween Marxism and phenomenology is necessary, despite Althusser's strenuous attempts to separate them on behalf of scientific Marxism. It is often remarked that Hegel spiritualized action where Marx materialized it. Marx himself believed this to be the substance of his critique of Hegel. But I think there is some evidence for the argument that Hegel and Marx are engaged in a similar critique of alienation as estrangement from action as expression; and thus there is a continuity between Hegel's *Phenomenology of Mind* and Marx's *Economic and Philosophic Manuscripts*.

In his remarks on physiognomy Hegel argues that the externalization of consciousness is not contingently related to its purpose but is essential to consciousness as embodied being. Thus the human hand and human speech are essential organs of conscious expression and it is by means of them that we establish a common world of artefacts and meanings. It is through the body that we give to our immediate surroundings 'a general human shape and form, or at least the general character of a climate, of a portion of the world', just as we find regions of the world characterized by different customs and culture. It is through the expressive organs of the hand and speech that we realize a unity of purpose and object which conveys our presence in the world and to others. The human body is thus the expressive instrument of spirit and not its simple objective alienation; it is the instrument whereby there can be culture and history which in turn shape human sensibility, thought, and perception.

> For if the organs in general proved to be incapable of being taken as expression of the inner for the reason that in them the action is present as a process, while the action as a deed or (finished) act is merely external, and inner and outer in this way fall apart and are or can be alien to one another, the organ must, in view of the peculiarity now considered, be again taken as also a middle term for both.[5]

Thus self-consciousness is not estranged by its natural being, for the human body is an expressive organ through which meaning is embodied in speech and the work of human hands which together articulate the nature of humankind:

> That the hand, however, must exhibit and reveal the inherent nature of individuality as regards its fate, is easily seen from the fact that after the organ of speech it is the hand most of all by which a man actualizes and manifests himself. It is the animated artificer of his fortune; we may say of the hand it is what a man does, for in it as the effective organ of his fulfilment he is there present as the animating soul; and since he is ultimately and originally his own fate, the hand will thus express this innate inherent nature.[6]

The ultimate goal of self-consciousness is to recover the unity of the self and the world which it discovers abstractly in the unity of the mind and its objects. The recovery of the world is mediated by desire which reveals the world as my praxis. But this is still only abstractly a world until my interests are recognized by the other. The dialectic of recognition appears as a life and death struggle because of desire which binds consciousness to the world of things and simultaneously reveals its transcendence as the negation of things and the Other. But the categories of subject and object, negation, self, other and recognition are not a priori categories of experience. They arise in the course of the self-interpretation by consciousness of its modes of lived experience which involve consciousness in a dialectic between intentionality and an irreducible ontological difference which generates the world and the recognition of the Other. For if consciousness did not encounter the resistance of things and others,

it could only know things perceptually and others by analogy and
it would have no organic or social life. But this means that consciousness can never be satisfied in a desire for objects and the Other.
For in this it would only consume itself whereas it needs a common
world in which things and others reflect consciousness back upon
itself: 'Self-consciousness, which is absolutely *for itself*, and
characterizes its object directly as negative, or as primarily desire,
will really, therefore, find through experience this object's independence.'[7] Desire, then, is not the actuality of self-consciousness but
only its potentiality for actualizing itself in a common world and inter-
subjectivity. Hence the struggle to the death which originates in desire
is exteriorized in the relation to objects established between the Master
and the Slave which preserves their independence in the form of a
living dependency: 'In this experience self-consciousness becomes
aware that life is as essential to it as pure self-consciousness.'[8]

With respect (fear) for life that is born from the struggle to the
death there is initiated a further dialectic in which the Slave's
apprenticeship to things makes possible the practical observation of
the laws of their operation. Though he works for another, the Slave
learns to work with objects whose independence now submits to his
production though not to his consumption. By the same token the
Master's independence of things mediated by the Slave becomes his
dependence upon the Slave's cultivation:

> Labour, on the other hand, is desire restrained and checked,
> evanescence delayed and postponed; in other words, labour shapes
> and fashions the thing. The negative relation to the object passes
> into the form of the object, into something that is permanent and
> remains; because it is just for the labourer that the object has
> independence.[9]

Thus from the recognition of the value of life and the fear of death,
expressed in submission to things for the sake of life, the experience
of domination and servitude opens up the cycle of culture as the
objective mediation of self-expression and the world. It is through
work that the world is revealed as conscious *praxis*, as a field of
individual interests which are in turn opened to the interests of others
and hence to a common measure of good and evil. As a field of practical intentions the world is the element of consciousness, its 'original
nature' which the activity of consciousness moulds to its purposes.
Hegel is quite explicit that there is no room for the experience of
estrangement in the act whereby the self externalizes itself in the

world of objects. It is the very nature of consciousness to act to externalize itself in the deed, or work.

Marx's own theory of alienation is, of course, idealist in its critique of any theory of cultural objects, such as rent, or of social relations, such as poverty, where these phenomena are treated as quasi-natural objects in a world external to their social and historically produced effect. His theory is equally materialist in the sense that it involves the history and social production of ideas and values in its critique of idealist ideologies of the determination of the human world. In short, Marx insisted that the human mind is historical and social because it is an embodied mind and that the human body is similarly social and historical because it is intelligent. People are thinking bodies whose humanity is their own historical achievement. Human nature is neither given nor a singular possession, although this may appear to be the case within certain theophilosophical ideologies and in fact be the case within a socio-economic system dominated by private property:

> Private property is only the sensuous expression of the fact that man is both objective to himself and even more becomes a hostile and inhuman object to himself, that the expression of his life entails its externalization, its realization becomes the loss of its reality, an alien reality. Similarly the positive supersession of private property, that is, the sensuous appropriation by and for man of human essence and human life, of objective man and his works, should not be conceived of only as direct and exclusive enjoyment, as possession and having. Man appropriates his universal being in a universal manner, as a whole man. Each of his human relationships to the world – seeing, hearing, smelling, tasting, thinking, contemplating, feeling, willing, acting, loving – in short all the organs of his individuality, just as the organs whose form is a directly communal one, are in their objective action, or their relation to the object, the appropriation of this object. The appropriation of human reality, their relationship to the object, is the confirmation of human reality. It is therefore as manifold as the determinations and activities of human nature. It is human effectiveness and suffering, for suffering, understood in the human sense, is an enjoyment of the self for man.[10]

We may now summarize the basic propositions in Marx's humanist theory of alienation. Before we do so, however, a terminological distinction is required with respect to the usage of the term 'alienation' since, unless we are aware of its double reference, we unwittingly reduce the theory of alienation to an idealist dimension. Thus the humanist theory of alienation which we are developing has nothing to do with a lament over mind's embodiment or that the exercise of every human faculty involves world shaping activity that is reciprocally anthropomorphizing. Thinking bodies necessarily express themselves in a 'world'. We call this the movement of externalization (*Entäusserung*) to the necessary worldly expression of incarnate minds. Only entirely angelic beings could lament alienation as externalization since even God seems to have emptied himself into the created world. Having said as much, both God and man find themselves in a world they have made but which nevertheless is not entirely responsive to their designs for it. We must set aside God's patience with this state of affairs. In man's case we speak of alienation or estrangement (*Entfremdung*) in respect of man's freely creative self-image failing to be reflected and amplified in the social institutions through which our kind preserves its own humanity. Therefore, while it is essential to humankind that its incorporation is realized in a historically and socially produced world of institutions, it is a contingent but corrigible fact that the anthropomorphizing design of those constitutions is distorted by the socio-economic system of private property. This corrigible history of estrangement is in turn the matter for an analytic social science to which Marx gave his own name.

We conclude, then, that Marx's humanist theory of alienation is, first of all, a philosophy of anthropomorphosis that, like Vico's *New Science*, is discovered as both nature and norm, or as *quasi-nature* and absolute *norm* of all human history. But this means that Marxism is simultaneously the discovery of a history within history that humanizes our condition. However, we cannot overlook the need to restate the categorical claim in Marx's humanist theory of alienation as one that applies equally to the history of socialist and communist societies. In this regard, we consider the weakness of Marxist social science to derive from its fundamental tenet that, whereas the system of private property is the source of human estrangement, the common ownership of the means of productions would constitute the end of human alienation. Rather, socialist societies seem to have engendered their own specific modes of alienation deriving from the hegemony of state capital, single Party politics, the suppression of civil liberties including the practice of physical and mental torture, as well as socialist colonialism and nuclearism. Much of this history of alienation exceeds Marx's vision. It now falls to contemporary socialist discussion to rethink the nature of political power and its modes of alienation as universal effects of collective life whose corrigibility is the test of any humane society, an issue we pursue in the following chapter.

Ultimately what is at issue in Marx's theory of alienation is not so much its claims as a social science but its conception of humanism. Everyone can recall the exhilaration of Marx's claim that all previous history is the pre-history of our kind hitherto unable to develop its humanity until it has delivered 'species-man', the universal essence of humanity, a model of sensuous and intelligent integrity whose capacities are playfully exemplified in socialist society:

> The ancient conception, in which man always appears (in however narrowly national, religious or political a definition) as the aim of production, seems very much more exalted than the modern world, in which production is the aim of man and wealth the aim of production. In fact, however, when the narrow bourgeois form has been peeled away, what is wealth, if not the universality of needs, capacities, enjoyments, productive powers, etc. of individuals, produced in universal exchange? What, if not the full development of human control over the forces of nature – those of his own nature as well as those of so-called 'nature'? What, if not the absolute elaboration of his creative dispositions, without any preconditions other than antecedent historical evolution which makes the totality of this evolution – i.e., the evolution of all human powers as such, unmeasured by any previous established yardstick – an end in itself? What is this, if not a situation where man does not produce himself in any determined form, but produces his totality? Where he does not seek to remain something formed by the past, but is in the absolute movement of becoming? In bourgeois political economy – and in the epoch of production to which it corresponds – this complete elaboration of what lies within man, appears as the total alienation, and the destruction of all fixed, onesided purposes as the sacrifice of the end in itself to a wholly external compulsion.[11]

In short, the *radical anthropomorphization* of the fundamental concepts of theology, philosophy, and political economy must stand as the central dogma of Marxist humanism. However, this anthropomorphic dogma is more than a renaissance trope of creative hierarchy in view of what we may call its *deconstructive power*. By the latter, we refer to the analytic power of Marx's tireless critique of every binary usage which separates our kind from its humanity by compounding the separations of mind and body, male and female, owner and non-owner, individual and society. In short, every discursive production of our self-estrangement is seized upon in Marx's emancipatory prose – in passage after passage from which anyone of us can recall the exhilaration of our first vision of socialist man and of human reason cleared of thought fetishes. The 'thing-ification' (*Verdinglichung*) of social practices and relationships to which men and women subordinate themselves is deconstructed in Marx's complete rejection of the *metaphysics of absence*. Man's absence from man is circulated throughout the commodity system and its property relations, in the state, and in all the ideological discourses of philosophy, the arts and social sciences that expand upon the absence of integral discourse for human conduct and community:

> We have seen that the whole problem of the transition from thought to reality, hence from language to life, exists only in philosophical illusion, i.e., it is justified only for philosophical consciousness, which cannot possibly be clear about the nature and origin of its apparent separation from life. This great problem, insofar as it at all entered the minds of our ideologists, was bound, of course, to result finally in one of these knights errant setting out in search of a word which, as a *word*, formed the transition in question, which, as a word, ceases to be simply a word, and which, as a word, in a mysterious superlinguistic manner, points from within the language to the actual object it denotes; which, in short, plays among words the same role as the Redeeming God-Man plays among people in Christian fantasy . . . thus the triumphant entry into 'corporeal' life.[12]

Marx's critique of classical political economy is a tireless deconstruction of its capital-logical discourse. It unmasks the hegemony of capital over labour through which the life-force of labouring individuals is expropriated and assigned to the driving force of capital shaping its materials of nature in and around humankind.[13] By the same token, the expropriative logic of capital fearfully engenders its own deconstruction in the proletariat whose social conditions and historical intelligence opens up the possibility of revolution, i.e., the expropriation of the expropriators. Thus capitalism can never achieve the closure that marked feudalism since it cannot foreclose the discourse of humanism once it is appropriated by the proletariat and amplified in the deconstructive analytic of Marxism. In *The German Ideology* Marx and Engels decisively undermine any notion of ideas and social objects or process which assigns to them a singular, external, and quasi-natural constitution. All conceptual languages are articulated within the longer 'material intercourse of men, the language of real life'[14] which is the practical ground of collective life and history whose effects of externality are abstracted into the ideologies of a quasi-natural or ideal society. The movement of human history is grounded in the double reproduction of human needs as culturally and biologically open circuits that continuously redefine one another. Hence, 'the "history of humanity" must always be studied and treated in relation to the history of industry and exchange'.[15] However, it is the social production of *humane* life which Marx treats as the basic framework of all modes of intellectual and manual production. It is this anthropomorphic principle which provides the basic humanist norm of every other economy of effort through which it is articulated. In fact, it constitutes the highest form of the pragmatics of language and the historical development of *'universal* intercourse', i.e., an intergenerational goal of the world-historical development of humankind which is no less a critical standard for the success of communist society.

Modern social science knowledge has reduced its independence as a form of theoretical life to a rule of methodology founded upon the auspices of technical rationality. This results in a disenchanted objectivism or rationalization of the interest and values which guide technological domination as a form or 'conduct of life', to use Max Weber's phrase. However, Weber's formal rationality, so far from resting upon 'value-free' auspices, is in fact an historical constellation whose precondition is the separation of the orders of knowledge, work, and politics. In the period of the bourgeois ascendency, the value-free conception of rationality furnishes a critical concept of the development of human potential locked in the feudal world of 'traditional' values. Weber makes a fatality of technical rationality, thereby identifying its historical role with political domination as such,[16] whereas Marx's critique of class political economy showed the critical limits of economic rationality. Social science knowledge needs to be grounded in a limited but authentic reflexivity through which it recognizes its ties to individual values and community interests, notwithstanding its attempts to avoid bias and ideology.

Of course, Marx's notion of an essence of humanity (*Gattungswesen*) seems to continue the tradition of rationalist metaphysics rather than to deconstruct it and to contribute to scientific Marxism. But in fact the species-being of humanity is a thoroughly critical concept of a difference essential to a humanist socialism. It emphasizes that:

1 the human senses are historical;
2 human reason is practical;
3 human beings are thinking bodies inseparable from collective life;
4 human nature is the social product of an historically humanized nature;
5 the human development of human beings is the *telos* of socialist society and of socialist humanism;
6 since the history of humanity is a contingent achievement, its ratio of success depends upon a continuous struggle to deconstruct and resist all modes of discourse and praxis that separate humankind from the future of humankind;
7 discourse upon the human development of human beings (*Das Menschwerden des Menschen*) provides the practical norm of all social, economic, political, and communicative institutions.

The discourse of Marxist-humanism is predicated upon the suspension of every binarism that derives from the unquestioned separation (estrangement) of humanity and humane existence. It therefore rejects the dualist tradition of Western metaphysics through which humankind dispossesses itself of its proper essence in favour of every other sort of spiritual and worldly possession. But, as Marx observes, the new language of humanity is hard to understand by individuals who have yet to unlearn the grammar of possessive individualism and who cannot distinguish between *being* and *having* – whose god is still money and not humankind:

> The only intelligible language that we speak to one another consists in our objects in their relationship to one another. We would not understand a human speech and it would remain ineffective; on the one hand it would be seen and felt as an entreaty or a prayer and thus as a humiliation and therefore used with shame and a feeling of abasement, while on the other side it would be judged brazen and insane and as such rejected. Our mutual alienation from the human essence is so great that the direct language of this essence seems to us to be an affront to human dignity and in contrast the alienated language of the values of things seems to be the language that justifies a self-reliant and self-conscious human dignity.[17]

It still cannot be said that Marxism has learned to speak its own language. Indeed, nothing privileges it in this respect – certainly not its claims to make a science of human history. Every reading of history stands to be judged by history. This is not the conclusion of an historical determinism, as it might seem, but is rather a statement of the problematic of the philosophy of history. It calls for an account of the relation between knowledge and action in which we must avoid both the scientism and simplistic realism and the nihilism of subjective relativism, which equally destroy the hermeneutic of reason in history. Marxist rationalism is more than an epistemology because it is concerned with the human meaning of knowledge, and is therefore always critical with respect to the uses of science. At the same time Marxism does not reduce knowledge to a class practice because this would barbarize its humanist aims. We must avoid altogether the idea that history is governed either by scientific laws or by an occult logic that makes human events rational, whatever the appearances. But this means we need a proper conception of human knowledge and the historical space in which it unfolds. Hegel and Marx between them have taught us that the human spirit does not exist outside of history, any more than history itself can unfold except as the externalization (*Entäusserung*) of human subjectivity. Idealism and materialism are false alternatives. They fail to describe the constitution of historical space as a praxis determined by the affinity of choices (*Wahlverwandtschaft*) human beings make in their economic, political, and religious lives.

NOTES

1 *The New Science of Giambattista Vico* (1948) translated from the third edition by T. Goddard Bergin and M.H. Fisch, Ithaca: Cornell University Press, paras: 236–7. This reference also applies to subsequent appearances in this chapter.
2 Marx, K. (1971) *Early Texts*, trans. and ed. by D. McLellan, Oxford: Basil Blackwell, p. 169.
3 Marx, K. (1964) *The Economic and Philosophic Manuscripts of 1844*, trans. M. Milligan and ed. D.J. Struik, New York: International Publishers, p. 141. This reference also applies to subsequent appearances in this chapter.
4 Ibid., p. 162.
5 Hegel, G.W.F. (1910) *Phenomenology of Mind*, trans. J.B. Baillie, London: Allen and Unwin, p. 343. This reference also applies to subsequent appearances in this chapter.
6 Ibid., p. 343.
7 Ibid., p. 221.
8 Ibid., p. 234.

9   Ibid., p. 238.
10 Marx, K. *Early Texts*, p. 151.
11 Marx, K. (1964) *Pre-capitalist Economic Formations*, E. Hobsbawn, (ed.) London: Lawrence and Wishart, p. 84.
12 Marx, K. and Engels, F. (1976) 'The German Ideology', in *Collected Works*, London: Lawrence and Wishart, 5: 449. This reference also applies to subsequent appearances in this chapter.
13 O'Neill, J. (1982) 'Marxism and Mythology', pp. 43–58, in his *For Marx Against Althusser, And Other Essays*, Washington, DC: University Press of America.
14 Marx, K. and Engels, F. (1959) *Basic Writings on Politics and Philosophy*, L.S. Feuer (ed.) New York: Doubleday and Company, p. 247.
15 Ibid., p. 251.
16 Marcuse, H. (1968) 'Industrialization and Capitalism in Max Weber', in his *Negations: Essays on Cultural Theory*, Boston: Beacon Press.
17 Marx, K. *Early Texts*, p. 201.

Part II

The politics of mutual knowledge

Chapter 6

'Posting' modernity
Bell and Jameson on the social bond – with an allegory of the body politic

In contemporary cultural criticism, whether the figures are neo-conservative or neo-Marxist, it is generally agreed that our cultural malaise is at its height in postmodernism. But whereas Daniel Bell would argue that the collapse of the modern temper is to blame for the incivility of post-industrial society,[1] Fredric Jameson would consider late capitalism itself to be the source of the postmodern fragmentation of its cultural values.[2] However, despite this analytic difference and their opposing political values, Bell and Jameson are inclined to call for a renewal of religious symbolism to restore the social bond against postmodern values which undermine equally the conservative and Marxist traditions.[3] Postmodernism appears, therefore, to create a neo-modern opposition from both Left and Right. In turn it inspires a Durkheimian reflection on the sacred value of the social bond which is either backward looking, as in Bell's neo-conservatism, or else resolutely utopian, as in Benjamin, Bloch, Marcuse, and Jameson.

I think it is not unfair to Bell's argument to put it as follows: capitalism has successfully changed itself and the world without destroying itself through the class and ideological conflicts predicted by Marxists. Indeed, capitalism has successfully moved into a post-industrial phase in which its information sciences continuously revise its technological future, thereby solving the problem of crisis and again disappointing its Marxists critics. The post-industrial phase of the capitalist economy appears, however, to be threatened more by the contradictions which derive from its postmodern culture and policy than early capitalism was endangered by the cultural tensions of modernism. In short, late capitalism may prove unable to integrate its postmodern culture with its technological base. This is because the efficiency values of the latter are difficult to reconcile with a

culture of narcissism and a politics of egalitarianism. While Bell insists
that previous cultural critics were naïve in supposing that modern
society can collapse at any single point, his own articulation of the
triplex of economy, policy, and culture nevertheless envisages the
possibility of the post-industrial techno-culture being sapped by
postmodern hedonism and self-gratification. For, despite the contempt
which modernist artists expressed towards bourgeois scientism and
materialism, they nevertheless shared the same 'bounded' individualism exemplified in the Protestant ethic and its affinity for industrialism. That is to say, there existed a tension in modernism between
its religious and its secular values as well as between its attitudes
towards the self and towards society. But this tension has collapsed
in postmodernism and its lack threatens to bring down post-
industrialism. Bell, however, is quite unclear whether it is modernism
or the collapse of modernism (and thus postmodernism), which undermines late (post-industrial) capitalism. How do we choose between
the following observations?

> Today modernism is exhausted. There is no tension. The creative
> impulses have gone slack. It has become an empty vessel. The
> impulse to rebellion has become institutionalized by the 'culture
> mass' and its experimental forms have become the syntax and
> semiotics of advertising and *haute couture*. As a cultural style,
> it exists as radical chic, which allows the cultural mass the luxury
> of 'freer' lifestyles while holding comfortable jobs within an
> economic system that has itself been transformed in its
> motivations.[4]

Here, then, modernity is damned if it does and damned if it does
not underwrite capitalism. In the latter passage, however, we can
hear more clearly Bell's neo-conservative lament for the moral values
of a solidly bourgeois society in which the bond of religion is strong
and resilient enough to bear the creative tensions of bounded Protestantism and spirited capitalism. At bottom, Bell attributes the crisis
of capitalism to a crisis of religion, to a loss of ultimate meaning
which undercuts its civic will. By this he means that the obligations
of collective life are reduced to subjective rights, the will to endure
calamity is softened into the demand for instant gratification and
religion is replaced by the utopiates of progress, rationality, and
science:

The real problem of *modernity* is the problem of belief. To use an unfashionable term, it is a spiritual crisis, since the new anchorages have proved illusory and the old ones have become submerged. . . . The effort to find excitement and meaning in literature and art as a substitute for religion led to modernism as a cultural mode. Yet modernism is exhausted and the various kinds of postmodernism (in the psychedelic efforts to expand consciousness without boundaries) are simply the decomposition of the self in an effort to erase individual ego.[5]

Bell's conception of postmodernism seems to turn upon a rejection of everything in modernism except its puritanism as the matching ethic of bourgeois culture and mass industry. Everything else is thrown into a catch-all of hedonism, neurosis, and death which exceeds the bounds of 'traditional modernism' whose subversion, as he says, 'still ranged itself on the side of order and, implicitly, of a rationality of form, if not of content'. But, he continues, the vessels of art are smashed in postmodernism and religious restraint has vanished from the civil scene. Humankind itself disappears as a transcendental value. Worse still – for Bell is not worried so much by philosophical extravaganzas – postmodernism ushers in a crisis of middle-class values! Here bathos is the result of Bell's attempt to combine historical, philosophical, and sociological generalities to create a vision of cultural crisis which is universal and yet decidedly American.

What he gains in assigning a certain grandeur to the diagnosis of American problems, Bell loses when it comes to tackling them in any specific institutional setting. For example, he claims the road to post-industrialism involves three stages. In the first, we encounter a natural world; in the second, we deal with a fabricated world; whereas, in the third, our world is ourselves and our social interaction. Although one might have expected Bell to celebrate this last stage of sociability as a sociologist's (Simmel, Goffman) paradise, he finds instead that we have lost all sense of the social bond due to our progressive secularization:

The primordial elements that provide men with common identification and effective reciprocity – family, synagogue, church and community – have become attenuated, and people have lost the capacity to maintain sustained relations with each other in both time and place. To say, then, that 'God is dead' is, in effect, to say that the social bonds have snapped and that society is dead.[6]

Because he is at pains to avoid a Marxist (even a Critical Theory) analysis of the sources of 'instability' in the American social order, Bell is obliged to leave things at the level of a neo-conservative lament over contemporary neo-liberalism, hedonism, and postmodernism. Thus America's final crisis is blamed upon a moral crisis whose sources are found in any number of situations (ignorance, poverty, and now AIDS) which seek to exceed the social compact and the proper arbitration of public and private goods. Without naming the excesses of the corporate culture and its wilful barbarization of the masses, and by keeping silence with regard to the industrial military adventures that enraged American youth, Bell falls into dismissing the critical culture of the sixties in the same vein that Christopher Lasch trashes the culture of narcissism. Because they both suppress relevant distinctions regarding the systems of corporate power, whose production of the culture they despise determines its mass consumption, Bell and Lasch cannot avoid the voice of a genteel modernism lamenting its own lost contexts of value with the fall into postmodernism.

Overall, Bell is worried that the project of modernity will be overwhelmed by its own anti-nomianism. The latter may have served a positive good in its break with patriarchal and feudal authority, but without such authorities to kick against, anti-nomianism soon loses all sense of its own limitations and the result is that liberty turns to liberation against which we lack any overarching principle of legitimation. The death of God and now the death of humankind, rather than its expected resurrection, leaves society without value. This is the terrible price of the anti-bourgeois assault upon modernism. The curious thing, however, is that, despite Bell's vision of the erosion of authority, we have not seen any expansion of social revolutions other than in the name of the very bourgeois and Christian values discounted by postmodernism. The reason may be, as the Grand Inquisitor well knew, that the masses retain that coherence of meaning and value which Bell believes it is the task of his own exhausted élite to reimpose. Thus, whatever the changes in the institutions and rites of religion, its basic existential responses are perhaps less endangered because they are more necessary than ever.

Bell seriously underestimates the popular resistance (if not indifference) to the élite culture of unrestrained individualism, impulsive
art, and moral nihilism which he defines as modernity's gift to
postmodernism. Apart from remarking upon the resurgence of idolatry
in the Chinese and Soviet Party, he does not make enough of the
power of religious values to sustain resistance among intellectuals as
well as old women. Of course, one is not appealing to the current prevalence of cults and sects of one sort and another which flourish whilst
official religions appear to wane. Yet Bell is bold enough to forecast
the appearance of three new religions or types of religious practice:

1 **Moralizing religion:** Fundamentalist, evangelical, rooted in the
   'silent majority';
2 **Redemptive religion:** Retreating from (post) modernity, rooted
   in the intellectual and professional classes; and the growth of
   intellectual and professional classes; and the growth of 'mediating
   institutions' of care (family, church, neighbourhood, voluntary
   associations) opposed to the state;
3 **Mystical religion:** Anti-scientist, anti-self, past oriented, rooted
   in the eternal cycle of existential predicaments.[7]

If Bell's prediction were to be borne out, then we might hope for
(post) modernism to erase the 'beyond' of modernity, returning to
the limits which the great civilizations have imposed upon themselves.
To do so, however, (post) modernism would need to revive sacred
institutions while not sacrificing our commitment to cultural pluralism.
So far, no theorist has appeared with any positive vision of such a
society.

In the meantime, we may turn to Jameson's reflections on
postmodernism and his attempt to restore Marxism to what Bell would
call a redemptive religion since each of them is in fact aware of
his respective appeal to Walter Benjamin's insistence upon the
indestructibility of the aura of religion in human history. Ordinarily,
social scientists, and Marxists in particular, are not kind to messianism.
This has made the reception of Benjamin slower on this score than
the adoption of his studies of culture and society. In short, Benjamin's
analysis of commodity fetishism and his messianic response to modernism have been separated, either to be expropriated in the analysis
of postmodernism or else left to those whose sympathies lie with the
unhappy consciousness deprived of any hope of redemptive institutions. It is to Jameson's credit, therefore, that in a phrase reminis-
cent of Benjamin he entertains the possibility of a 'two-way street'

between religion and Marxism. And we shall look at this argument more closely in our conclusion. Meantime, as an unrepentant Marxist, Jameson draws some of the necessary distinctions we found lacking in Bell's account of the role of mass culture in late capitalism. Yet it can also be shown that, despite their opposing political values, Bell's neo-conservatism and Jameson's neo-Marxism derive equally from a Durkheimian lament upon the dissolution of the social bond. But whereas Bell's ancient liberalism separates him from the Marxist vision of community, Jameson can enthusiastically invoke this communal vision as the ultimate emancipatory drive in the political unconscious of our culture.

Postmodernism certainly reflects the sense of an ending. The question is – what has ended? Is it industrialism – in which case both capitalism and socialism are finished? Bell would probably take this view. Yet he can find nothing to celebrate in post-industrialism because in the end he remains a high priest of modernism. But then, Bell, Habermas, and Jameson, despite their differences, are all open to the taunts of Lyotard who finds everything to celebrate in the postmodern dissolution of right and left consensus.[8] For Habermas, too, is unwilling to abandon the modernist project to which Marxism is committed. With quite different values from those of Bell, Habermas has also set about the destruction of the French branch of postmodernism which currently infects North America and Western Europe. Between such figures, Jameson's position is a little difficult since certain aspects of postmodern cultural criticism continue to appeal to him inasmuch as it belongs to the received radicalism of literary studies, art, and architecture with which he identifies himself.[9] Overall, however, Jameson manages to extricate himself from the postmodern dissolution of grand narratives and to oppose it with an eloquent, even if surprisingly religious appeal on behalf of Marxism as the transcendental ground of all human culture and community.

It might well be argued that such sociologies as those of Bell's post-industrialism, Lasch's culture of narcissism, and Toffler's third wave are themselves prime examples of the postmodern exorcism of ideology and class struggle essential to the culture industry of late capitalism. Thus Jameson insists upon drawing a number of distinctions in order to avoid both cultural homogeneity and cultural heterogeneity as twin aspects of postmodern mass culture. He therefore argues that:

1 Cultural analysis always involves a buried or repressed theory of historical periodization;
2 Global and American, postmodern culture is the super-structural expression of American domination;
3 Under late capitalism aesthetic production has been integrated into commodity production;
4 Postmodernism cannot be treated as part of modernism without ignoring the shift from early to late capitalism and the latter's redefinition of the culture industry.

These distinctions enable Jameson, like Habermas, to argue that Marxism must survive as the neo-modernist opposition to late capitalism, absolutely opposed to its superficiality, its imaginary culture, and its total collapse of public and private history. Jameson and Habermas are therefore insistent that Marxist discourse cannot flirt with contemporary fragmentation and subjectlessness. Marxism is the transcendental story, a utopian gesture without which humanity is unthinkable.

However incapable it has become of shocking the bourgeoisie, postmodernism certainly seems to *épater les marxistes!* Consider how Jameson contrasts Andy Warhol's 'Diamond Dust Shoes' with Van Gogh's 'Peasant Shoes', or rather, Heidegger's reflections upon them.[10] Warhol's shoes are colourless and flat; they glitter like Hollywood stars, consumed by a light that bathes them in super-ficiality, denying them all interiority, making them appear crazy for want of any gesture that is rooted in a world beyond artifice. By con-trast, Heidegger claims that the peasant's shoes tell a story that involves ordinary people; they are continuous with institutions whose meaningful history is the broader framework in which they figure as human artefacts. According to Jameson, all this is lost in the world of video space-time, in the hyperspatiality of postmodern architecture, and in the self-consuming arts of postmodern literature and music.

Like Bell, Jameson refuses the postmodern celebration of the fragment, the paralogical and paratactical arts that dissolve the moder-nist narrative, dancing upon the grave of identity, rationality, and authority. Yet Jameson insists that postmodernism should not be considered solely as a phenomenon of style:

It [postmodernism] is also, at least in my use, a periodizing con-cept whose function is to correlate the emergence of new formal features in culture with the emergence of a new type of social life and a new economic order – what is euphemistically called modernization, post-industrial or consumer society, the society of the media or the spectacle, or multinational capitalism.[11]

Jameson's piling up of alternative epithets for the description of the socio-economic system leaves it unanalysed in favour of its exploration in terms of two cultural phenomena – pastiche and schizophrenia – to which we now turn. The fascination of these phenomena for postmodernist theorists is itself a sign of the inextricable sense and non-sense that characterizes the a-historical and an-ecological predicament of late capitalism. *Pastiche* involves the intertextuality, intermodishness of codes-without-context whose inappropriateness suggests they never had even a local value and hence always prefigured the contemporary value chaos. As I see it, such codes create the illusion that 'Bogart' experienced himself and his social institutions with the same affectation exhibited by today's *Rocky Horror Show* for kids without a society and for whom character cannot mean anything else than caricature. The illusion of recycled popular culture is that bourgeois capitalism never created the institutional settings in which 'Bogey' was taken by himself and others for real. This is appealing because in the bureaucratic contexts of late capitalism 'Bogey' could only be a pastiche/parody of lost subjectivity or individualism. Postmodern sophisticates would, of course, claim that 'Bogey' is all there was from the beginning, i.e., the essential myth of individualism. Hence all that remains is to democratize the myth – everyman his own 'Bogey', everywoman as 'Bacall'. All we can aspire to is auto-affection through style, fashion, fad, to the moment, the scene, regrouped on the collective level through nostalgia, and everyday life as an open museum, a junk store, a replay.

While drawing upon the evaluative connotations of *schizophrenia* as a diagnostic concept, Jameson nevertheless disavows any intention to engage in cultural psychoanalysis beyond the confines of the literary community. Thus schizophrenia, as Jameson takes it from Lacan, is a linguistic pathology, the inability – due to faulty oedipalization – to assign signifiers any temporal and spatial fixed points of identity and reference. Everything floats in an imploded present; action, project, and orientation collapse in the literal, nauseous, and real present in which teenagers are typically trapped. To keep them in this docile state is a task for our education system as a part of the larger system of mass culture to which it occasionally opposes itself, as I have argued earlier regarding the functions of the disciplinary society and its therapeutic apparatus. What Jameson (like Bell and Habermas, but from a different interpretation of the same materials) finds at work in pastiche and literary schizophrenia is the collapse of the oppositional culture of modernism so that these two cultural elements of postmodernism now feed the cultural style of late capitalist consumerism:

> I believe that the emergence of postmodernism is closely related to the emergence of this new moment of late, consumer or multinational capitalism. I believe also its formal features in many ways express the deeper logic of the particular social system.[12]

By foreshortening the production process to the management of consumerism, the more difficult analysis of the social relations of production, power, class, and racism is reduced to the operations of an imaginary logic of the political economy of signifiers, where everything floats on the surface of communication. Here Jameson's reliance upon Baudrillard's *For a Critique of the Political Economy of the Sign* commits him to the company of Daniel Bell in a lament over the flood of narcissistic consumerism deprived of the mirrors that reflected the old order identities of societies which subordinated exchange value to the higher symbolisms of gift, sacrifice, and community. Rather, postmodern consumers find themselves as mere switching points at video screens which miniaturize their lives in order to speed them up. The result is that their everyday lives are left devastated by the contrast between the archaic symbolic orders that consumers nevertheless inhabit and the imaginary flux in which they drift. Thus, inside those soft bodies which wander through our shopping malls and whose minds are operated upon from the outside world, desire is deprived of all intelligence:

> This is the time of miniaturization, telecommand and the microprocession of time, bodies, pleasures. There is no longer any ideal principle for these things at a higher level, on a human scale. What remains are only concentrated effects, miniaturized and immediately available. This change from human scale to a system of nuclear matrices is visible everywhere: this body, our body, often appears simply superfluous, basically useless in its extension, the multiplicity and complexity of its organs, its tissues and functions since today everything is concentrated in the brain

and in genetic codes; which alone sum up the operational definition of being.[13]

Here, then, we have a curious effect. How can analysts as varied as Bell, Jameson, Lasch, Baudrillard, and Habermas join common chorus against late capitalism when their politics vary so widely from Right to Left? The answer seems to be that as cultural critics of late capitalist consumerism they are all *neo-modernists*. In turn, Marx's own modernism may well be the guiding influence. The centrality of Marxism to the project of modernity, as argued for by Habermas and Jameson, can also be claimed on the consideration of Marx's writing, his imagery, style, and narrative conventions. Thus Berman has drawn attention to the modernist reading required in order to grasp Marx's polyvalent writings without reducing them either to narrow science or to mere mythology.[14]

What unites Bell and Jameson, despite the different nuances in their response to the culture of postmodernism, is the will to order. In Bell the order is backward-looking; in Jameson it is forward-looking. Both are in search of a new social bond and both believe that it cannot be discovered by severing our links with the past as the most mindless forms of postmodernism imagine. In this regard, even Lasch and Habermas share the same modernist sentiment, despite different ideas about its historical sources. Although orthodox Marxism and neo-conservatism are as opposed to postmodernism as they are to one another, with respect to the value of the past each is shot through with the contradictory impulses of modernism. Each may blame the self-consuming artefacts of postmodernism for their cultural malaise, but the fact is that it is industrialism which institutionalizes discontent and, so to speak, condemns us to modernity. Yet the neo-Marxists seem just as unwilling as the neo-conservatives to switch their gods. As Marcuse saw, both continue to cling to the old god Prometheus. Both fight to keep out the young gods Orpheus and Narcissus whose pre-modern and post-industrial figure still fails to seduce Habermas and Bell. This is so, even though the social forecast of post-industrialism calls for a more creative divinity:

In the light of the idea of non-repressive sublimation, Freud's definition of Eros as striving to 'form living substance into ever greater unities, so that life may be prolonged and brought to higher development' takes on added significance. The biological drive becomes a cultural drive. The pleasure principle reveals its own dialectic . . . the abolition of toil, the amelioration of the environment, the conquest of disease and decay, the creation of luxury. All these activities flow directly from the pleasure principle, and, at the same time, they constitute *work* which associates individuals to 'greater unities'; no longer confined within the mutilating dominion of the performance principle, they modify the impulse without deflecting it from its aim. There is sublimation and, consequently, culture; but this sublimation proceeds in a system of expanding and enduring libidinal relations, which are in themselves work relations.[15]

Given the neo-Marxist and neo-conservative refusal of the new god Eros, a void is created in which Jameson can work to refurbish the Marxist vision of a collective utopia. Thus he argues that the death of the subject, the end of humankind, the migration of reason into madness, the collapse of social and historical narratives into schizophrenic case histories, are only acceptable visions of postmodern critique if we work for a renewal of Marxist history and hermeneutics. Jameson, still apprenticed to Marcuse and Bloch, assumes the Promethean task of binding his own myth to the utopian future of industrialism. He thereby seeks to retain the historical identity of the original Promethean myth with its utopian science of action and community bound by hope and memory:

Now the origin of Utopian thinking becomes clear, for it is memory which serves as the fundamental mediator between the inside and outside, between the psychological and the poetical. . . . The primary energy of revolutionary activity, derives from this memory of prehistoric happiness which the individual can regain only through its externalization through its reestablishment for society as a whole. The loss or repression of the very sense of such concepts as freedom and desire takes, therefore, the form of a kind of amnesia . . . which the hermeneutic activity, the stimulation of memory as the negation of the here and now, as the projection of Utopia, has its function to dispel, restoring to us the original clarity and force of our own most vital drives and wishes.[16]

Whereas capitalism displaces is own myths with secular science, utopian Marxism keeps the bond between myth and science as a history-making institution. Utopianism, then, is not a romanticism or nostalgia that refuses to learn from history. Rather, what can be learned from history, which preserves rather than represses its own genealogy, is that romanticism and myth cannot be contained by secularism and that in the end they are to be joined to the sciences of action and collectivity that they prefigure:

> Thus, to insist upon this term of Breton which corresponds both to Freudian usage and to our own hermeneutic vocabulary . . . a genuine plot, a genuine narrative, is that which can stand as the very figure of Desire itself: and this not only because in the Freudian sense pure physiological desire is inaccessible as such to consciousness, but also because in the socio-economic context, genuine desire risks being dissolved and lost. . . . In that sense desire is the form taken by freedom in the new commercial environment.[17]

In short, Jameson argues that every genre of thought (myth, literature, science) has to be grasped as a psycho-historical master-narrative (the political unconscious) which when properly interpreted, is Marxism. Postmodernism cannot be a stage in this narrative because it abandons history as a human motive, i.e., as the motive to make ourselves human individually and collectively.

Whereas Bell and Lasch lament the dissolution of the social bond, Habermas and Jameson continue to affirm its ultimate historical, normative, and analytic primacy. Jameson's particular strength, it must be said, lies in his will to carry the burden of the dialectical switching between the secularization and the reenchantment of the life-world and its modern vocation while seeking to avoid Weberian pessimism as well as Nietzschean cynicism. He does so fully conscious that the age of religion has passed and that for this very reason we are tempted to produce an 'aestheticized' religion, an imaginary or hallucinated community, in an age that is neither religious nor social. How, then, can Marxism, exempt itself from such sentimentalism? Jameson's reply is that Marxism and religion can be embraced as elements of 'marital square' in which history and collectivity join individual and community action and understanding against inaction and ignorance that dispossess the community and exploits it in favour of its masters. Jameson's fundamental claim is that all forms of social consciousness – both of oppressor and of oppressed – are utopian, inasmuch as these groups are themselves figures for an unalienated collective life. Jameson is at pains to deny that such an affirmation merely represents a return to a Durkheimian symbolics of social solidarity, or to a neo-Marxist marriage of aesthetics and social hygiene. Marxism needs both a positive as well as a negative hermeneutics of social solidarity if it is not to degenerate into postmodern fragmentation, or into an absurd negativity that would separate forever its scientific utopianism from its primitive myth of communism:

> Only Marxism can give us an adequate account of the essential mystery of the cultural past, which, like Tiresias drinking the blood, is momentarily returned to life and warmth and allowed once more to speak, and to deliver its long forgotten message in surroundings utterly alien to it. This mystery can be re-enacted only if the human adventure is one; only thus – and not through . . . antiquarianism or the projections of the modernists – can we glimpse the vital claims upon us of such long-dead issues as the seasonal alternation of the economy of a primitive tribe, the passionate disputes about the nature of the Trinity . . . only if they are retold within the unity of a single great collective story . . . Marxism, the collective struggle to arrest a realm of Freedom from a realm of Necessity. . . . It is in detecting traces of the uninterrupted narrative, in restoring to the surface of the text the repressed and buried reality of this fundamental history, that the doctrine of a political unconscious finds its function and its necessity.[18]

Such passages are among the best in literary Marxism. Yet Jameson's claims are clearly exorbitant. They are so because he cannot identify any specific social forces to carry his utopianism – his proletariat is everywhere and nowhere – and so he throws the holy water of Marxist utopianism over any group, whether oppressor or oppressed, in so far as they are 'figures' of an ultimately classless society!

In effect, Jameson achieves a remarkable inversion of the position of both Althusser and Lyotard with respect to the allegorical cathexis of master narratives or ideologies. History, in the large sense, is taken by Jameson to move through four levels – from the collective to individual and from the individual to collective story, thereby refurbishing Marxism as the master narrative, albeit as the 'absent cause' or the political unconscious of our times. The shifts involved between the collective and biographical figures and between the individual and communal levels of the social are achieved through the ideological categories of class discourse in so far as its antagonistic figures are always framed in an ultimately utopian reversal that results in a transcendental community. The stages along the way, so to speak, require that nature never be outside the romance in which it can respond to our desire in figures of good and evil, of wildness and civilization through which we, in turn, educate our imagination, as Frye would say. Vico and Marx, as I have shown in the previous chapter, would have said something similar. That is, each would have insisted upon the positive continuity in the hermeneutics of the past and the present in recognition of the social debt which capitalism represses (as the basis of its unconscious) and which socialism recognizes as its humanist *point d'honneur*. From this standpoint, the Marxist critique of reification and fragmentation is not simply an exercise in dialectical epistemology. It represents an ethical rejection of every possessive appropriation of values and relationships which breaks off, interrupts, and represses the recognition of exchange, intergenerationality, and collective debt. It is from this point of view that we understand the affinity between capitalism and secularism. This unholy alliance is constituted precisely through its suppression of the sacred and its rituals for the redemption of humankind's debt to the creation. The shift from *gemeinschaft* to *gesellschaft* represents the reduction of social debt to the social contract as a device for the individual appropriation of the pre-contractual values of reciprocity and communal indebtedness.

It is time now to look a little closer at Jameson's attempt to open a 'two way street' between religion and Marxism. In turn this will oblige us to formulate an alternative allegory of the body politic in response to Jameson's efforts on these lines:

> I have throughout the present work implied what I have suggested explicitly elsewhere, that any comparison of Marxism with religion is a two-way street, in which the former is not necessarily discredited by its association with the latter. On the contrary, such a comparison may also function to rewrite certain religious concepts – most notably Christian historicism and the 'concept' of providence, but also the pretheological systems of primitive magic – as anticipatory foreshadowing of historical materialism within precapitalist social formations in which scientific thinking is unavailable as such.[19]

One might charitably interpret such passages as Jameson's effort to maintain solidarity with past societies and to recognize a certain indebtedness to them. But his benchmark of science in fact breaks the bond between them because it is still necessary for Jameson to consider Marxism a science, however riddled with hermeneutics and psychoanalysis. This is all the more curious since he is also engaged in the restoration of the sacred values which underwrite the Marxist text to make it central to humanity. By the same token, it should be noticed that Jameson treats only a very generalized concept of Christian history, abstracting from the rituals and communities in which Christian doctrine is practised – and the same can be said of his concept of Marxism and mass culture. In each case, Jameson holds to the utopian position that, however degraded these forms of human culture may be, they never quite erase the aspiration towards individual and collective transfiguration which constitute class consciousness:

> All class consciousness of whatever type is Utopian insofar as it expresses the unity of a collectivity; yet it must be added that this proposition is an *allegorical* one. The achieved collectivity or organic group of whatever kind – oppressors fully as much as oppressed – is Utopian not in itself, but only insofar as all such collectivities are themselves figures for the ultimate concrete life of an achieved Utopian or classless society.[20]

In this extraordinary embrace of class consciousness, Jameson appears to have exceeded even his own understanding of Durkheim's inscription of religious solidarity as the sub-text of all culture. His Utopianism demands an absolutely sublimated culture entirely free of any functionalist or ideological usage. Ultimately, this is achievable only on behalf of a totally collective subject who would entirely escape the arrows of the poststructuralist critique of subjective subjectivism. The only figure of such a collective subject that Jameson can produce at this point is the 'body of the despot' contributed by the Asiatic mode of production:

> In most of the *Asiatic* land forms, the *comprehensive unity* standing above all these little communities appears as the higher *proprietor* or as the *sole* proprietor. . . . Because the *unity* is the real proprietor and the real presupposition of communal property . . . the relation of the individual to the *natural* conditions of labor and of reproduction . . . appears mediated for him through a cession of the total unity – a unity realized in the form of the despot, the father of many communities – to the individual, through the mediation of the particular commune.[21]

Despite the potentially regressive features in this figuration of 'Orientalism', Jameson contents himself with noting the attendant controversy but does not consider whether any other figure of the symbolic enactment of social reciprocity might be drawn from elsewhere in our cultural heritage. Here I think we need to rethink the allegory of the body politic and to show how Jameson lets slip a figure that might well have served his purposes better than that of the despotic body.

The body politic certainly emerges from a long allegorical history of the desire for the representation of unity and difference in a just society. It contains both a myth and a metaphysic which has been appended to throughout the history of social and political conflict both for revolutionary and restorational purposes. It is a transgressive figure when opposed to caste interpretations of social division of labour, as well as a figure of difference and charismatic justice when opposed to the forces of rationalization and homogenization. It is above all, a figure operative on both levels of synchrony and diachrony, demanding reciprocity on the social level and intergenerational indebtedness on the level of history. Thus it may be said that the political community thinks itself as a community of difference and exchange, avoiding both any extreme naturalization of its difference and rejecting any hardened organic or totalitarian conception of its species existence. The body politic is not a purely natural figure because it already figurates the desire for political community whose infrastructures are already in place at the levels of work, family, and society. It is therefore an act of interpretative violence for any theorist to treat the body politic as anything less than a mode of collective knowledge. It is not a mode of unconscious or of natural desire. Yet it is a transgressive figure because of its power to integrate what has been separated and to differentiate what has been homogenized. The body politic is a civilizational concept, to use the language of Frye, and it functions on the highest level of allegory to transfigure society in terms of the human body itself, imaginatively conceived as the universe of human potentiality.

Here, however, Jameson loses nerve and objects that the figure of the body politic is reprivatized and can reflect only itself, losing its analogical power as a collective organism. But Marx never conceived of the natural body as the subject of history for the very reason that he considered nature part of human history: 'History is the true natural history of man.'[22] Thus the history of the human body belongs to a collective history in which the figures of the body politic and of the *sensus communis* sketch out strategies of community and difference in the articulation of social life, economy, and policy. Vico's two basic axioms provide an initial formulation of the hermeneutic principles of the allegory of the body politic:

1 Common sense is judgement without reflection, shared by an entire class, and entire people, and entire nation, or the entire human race.
2 Uniform ideas originating among entire peoples unknown to each other must have common ground in truth.[23]

Viewed in this fashion, the body politic requires that we construct scenarios for the mutual accountability of the communities of natural and social science within the larger democratic community of common-sense political and legal practice. The metaphor of body politics, in keeping with Vico's own views, would therefore replace the scientistic metaphor in the dominant imagery of the polity. In this way, we might restore the public functions of rhetoric in the rational advocacy of knowledge and values that address the three basic domains of the body politic, which we differentiate as follows:

		Levels	Institutions	Discourse
Body Politic	(i)	the bio-body	family	well-being
	(ii)	the productive body	work	expression
	(iii)	the libidinal body	personality	happiness

Figure 6.1 Body politic: body sites, body discourses

By differentiating these three levels of the body politic, we further separate ourselves from naturalistic accounts of the political legitimacy problem by introducing a logic of ethical development as the fundamental myth of political life. The three levels of family, economic, and personal life represent an historical-ethical development and also permit it to identify contradictions or constraints and regressions in the body politic. Thus, we can identify alienation as a complex phenomenon that affects not only the productive body but also the bio-body and libidinal body. Conversely, alienation is not solved merely by satisfying organic needs, nor by the smooth engineering of productive relations since these do not meet the demands of the libidinal body. By the same token, we cannot abstract the dreams of libidinal life from our commitments to familial and economic life. Thus a critical theory of the legitimacy problems of the body politic is simultaneously a constitutive theory of social development and of members' recognition of the places in their lives where this development is blocked and even deteriorating. Members' expression of their experience with the underlying logic of development that sustains political legitimacy will not be limited to official electoral conduct. It will include such subversive practices as strikes, family breakdown, crime, protest, lampoons, neighbourhood and street gatherings, music, song, poster, and wall art. A critical theory of political legitimacy does not discount the rationality of members' ordinary accounts of their political experience in terms of the vocabularies of family, work, and person. Moreover, it does not presume upon either the found rationality or irrationality of such accounts.

Each of the three levels of the body politic is represented in a characteristic institution which is in turn allocated its proper domain of discourse. Although the various institutional and discourse realms of the body politic are only analytically differentiated, they may be said to constitute an evolutionary process in which the congruency of the three discursive orders maximizes the commonwealth.[24] Every society needs to reproduce itself biologically and materially. These needs are articulated at the institutional levels of work and the family where discourse focuses upon the translation of notion of well-being, health, suffering estrangement, and self-expression. Here we cannot deal with the institutions that are generated at these two levels of the body politic. In the later evolutionary stages, the articulation of the libidinal body generates discourse demands that impinge differentially upon the institutions of family and work. To date, the institutionalization of these 'revolutionary' demands represents a challenge to all modes of scientistic, social, and political knowledge. Meantime, we can envisage an extension of Habermas' programme for the rational justification of the ideal speech community in terms of the specific discursive contexts of the tri-level body politic. It would be necessary to generate a topology of knowledge and evaluation claims with regard to the bio-body, the productive body, and the libidinal body at each appropriate institutional level, with further criteria for urgency, democratic force, and the like.

The libidinal body politic represents a level of desire that fulfils the order of personality in so far as it transcends the goods of family and economy. So long as humankind continue to be birthed and familied of one another, then the bodily, social, and libidinal orders of living will not be separable pursuits. By the same token, the body politic cannot be reduced to purely economistic satisfactions any more than to the dream of love's body. A distinctive feature of the metaphor of the body politic is that it allows us to stand away from the system, i.e., machine, cybernetic, and organization metaphors that reduce the problem of political legitimacy to sheerly cognitivist sciences. This shift in turn recovers the plain rationalities of everyday living, family survival, health, self-respect, love, and communion. Members are aware of the necessary interrelationships between their family, economic, and personal commitments. They judge the benefits of their labour in the productive sector of the body politic in terms of the returns to their familial and personal lives. They are willing to make trade-offs between the demands of family life and the ambitions of their personal and libidinal life. In short, members have a fairly complex understanding of their corporate life which is not reducible to the single pattern of utilitarian or decisionistic reasoning that governs calculations in the productive sector.

On the right and on the left, we are still waiting for history to deliver itself. Whether politics or religion will be the midwife remains undecided. After a bitter lesson, the sociologist puts his money on religion. Jameson meantime perseveres with the alchemy of a hermeneutics that will deliver history, politics, and religion. And so the stage of history takes another turn. The Ghost of Marx returns; there is much talk about talk in which Jameson is apparently more agile than Habermas who waits for a chance to articulate a final economy of truth, sincerity, and justice. Bell is silenced, but offstage the laughter of Lyotard still reaches us. Marcuse, Bloch – and perhaps ourselves – remain saddened.

NOTES

1 Bell, D. (1982) *The Cultural Contradictions of Capitalism*, New York: Basic Books; (1980) *The Winding Passage: Essays and Sociological Journeys*, Cambridge, MA: ABT Books.
2 Jameson, F. (1984) 'Postmodernism, or the Cultural Logic of Late Capitalism', *New Left Review* 146: 52–92.
3 Bell, D. 'The Return of the Sacred? The Argument on the Future of Religion', in *The Winding Passage*.
4 *The Cultural Contradictions of Capitalism*, p. 20.
5 Ibid., pp. 28–9. This reference also applies to the short quotation from Bell in the paragraph immediately after.
6 Ibid., p. 155.
7 *The Winding Passage*, pp. 334–5.
8 Lyotard, J.-F. (1984) *The Postmodern Condition: A Report on Knowledge*, trans. G. Bennington and B. Massumi, Minneapolis: The University of Minnesota Press.
9 Jameson, F. (1983) 'Pleasure: A Political Issue', in *Formations of*

Pleasure, edited by T. Bennet *et al*. London: Routledge and Kegan Paul, 'Architecture and the Critique of Ideology' (1985) in *Architecture Criticism Ideology*, J. Ockman (ed.), Princeton: Princeton Architectural Press.

10 'Postmodernism, or the Cultural Logic of Late Capitalism', pp. 58–62.

11 Jameson, F. (1983) 'Postmodernism and Consumer Society', in *The Anti-Aesthetic*, H. Foster (ed.), Port Townsend, WA: Bay Press, p. 113.

12 Ibid., p. 125.

13 Baudrillard, J. (1983) 'The Ecstasy of Communication', in *The Anti-Aesthetic*, p. 128.

14 Berman, M. (1982) *All That Is Solid Melts Into Air: The Experience of Modernity*, New York: Simon and Schuster.

15 Marcuse, H. (1962) *Eros and Civilization: A Philosophical Inquiry into Freud*, New York: Vintage Books, pp. 193–4.

16 Jameson, F. (1971) *Marxism and Form: Twentieth-Century Dialectical Theories of Literature*, Princeton: Princeton University Press, pp. 113–14.

17 Ibid., pp. 100–1.

18 Jameson, F. (1981) *The Political Unconscious: Narrative as a Socially Symbolic Act*, Ithaca: Cornell University Press, pp. 19–20.

19 Ibid., p. 285.

20 Ibid., p. 291.

21 Ibid., p. 295.

22 Marx, K. (1971) 'Economic and Philosophical Manuscripts', in *Karl Marx Early Texts*, trans. and ed. D. McLellan, Oxford: Basil Blackwell, p. 169.

23 *The New Science of Giambattista Vico* (1948) trans. T.G. Bergin and M.H. Fisch, Ithaca: Cornell University Press, pp. 142–4.

24 Habermas, J. (1979) 'What is Universal Pragmatics?' in his *Communication and the Evolution of Society*, trans. T. McCarthy, Boston: Beacon Press, pp. 1–68.

Chapter 7

On the regulative idea of a critical social science

Lyotard's brand of post-rationalism derives from a very reduced sense of Wittgenstein's concept of a language game as an injunction to 'just gaming'. In this way, he is able to scandalize Habermas's construction of an ideal speech community by apparently undermining its grounds in speech–act theory and separating it from its links to tradition and history – and thus from any metalanguage of universal reason and freedom. Lyotard's arguments in fact increase the terrorism they attribute to Habermas's bias to consensus because they neglect the double struggle to achieve ethical individuality and social reciprocity. To gain perspective with respect to this debate, I think it is valuable to look at Winch's development of the Wittgensteinian concept of language and its implications for social science hermeneutics, especially since these arguments are reasonably clear and can be given a *radical turn*, without embracing Lyotardian violence. Further features of the argument will be taken up in the following chapter where we consider Giddens's restrictions on common-sense social science and their limitation of civic democracy.

Some time ago Peter Winch rescued interpretative sociology from the clutches of scientism by arguing that its fundamental subject matter, as well as its method of investigation, need not wait upon the findings of empirical science.[1] This is because understanding is not a matter of looking for generalizations that can be applied to human action from the outside, as it were, in the same way that a physicist is free to apply the concept of gravity to the behaviour of falling objects. The concepts that explain human behaviour have rather an 'internal relation' to the conduct they account for and are essentially constitutive of the conduct that falls under them. But this means that, once sociologists see the mistake in their scientistic pursuits, they really have nothing to do since the task of clarifying the rules that are constitutive of human action is properly philosophical work:

> It is not a question of what empirical research may show to be the case, but of what philosophical analysis reveals about *what it makes sense to say.* I want to show that the notion of a human society involves a scheme of concepts which is logically incompatible with the kinds of explanation offered in the natural sciences.[2]

Winch, then, exacts rather a high price for his manumission of sociology hitherto enslaved by science. At the same time, he himself seems to realize that sociologists do not quit the field that easily. Much of Winch's argument can only be understood as providing precepts for a more responsible – and by no means subjectivist – conduct of interpretative sociology. Thus, in addition to the claim that to understand language and society is virtually the same thing, Winch argues that for this very reason the practice of sociology is subject to a 'double hermeneutic'.[3] In other words, sociology is doubly responsible both to the interpretative practices it encounters among its subjects of study, and to the standards of rational explanation that prevail in the community of sociologists:

> Reflective understanding must necessarily presuppose, if it is to count as genuine understanding at all, the participant's unreflective understanding. And this in itself makes it misleading to compare it with the natural scientist's understanding of his scientific data. Similarly, although the reflective student of society, or of a particular mode of life, may find it necessary to use concepts which are not taken from the forms of activity which he is investigating, but which are taken rather from the context of his own investigation, still these technical concepts of his will imply a previous understanding of those other concepts which belong to the activities under investigation.[4]

I believe that we can read Winch's appeal to what Schutz would call the *postulate of adequacy* as an attempt to ground interpretative sociology by making it responsible both to the requirements of professional practice and to the privilege of lay opinion in democratic societies. I also think that the the same can be argued for Schutz, and thereby some reply made to the criticisms that interpretative sociology is idealist and conservative in a way that blocks the development of *critical* social science.[5]

Several commentators argue that nothing can be raised from the ashes of Winch's argument since Gellner[6] last dealt with it. I should begin by showing why I still think there is something to build on. Gellner engages in a *reductio absurdum* of the argument that language and society are intrinsically tied realities. He finds in it nothing but a *collectivist anthropomorphism*[7] engaged in a regressive defence of the cherished illusion that the world cannot be meaningless:

> These thinkers are not concerned or able to demonstrate that the human world is a *moral* tale, with justice and truth vindicated and some noble purpose attained: but they are concerned to show that it is, at least, a *human* tale. They wish to defend *the anthropomorphic image of man* himself.[8]

In Gellner's view, Winch's argument on the social nature of language and the linguistic nature of society represents the latest form of the idealist separation of humankind and nature. It is intended to cut off our understanding of social behaviour from causal explanation of a naturalist kind. The implications of claiming that concepts are socially governed practices are best seen, according to Gellner, if we reverse the proposition: it can then be seen to amount to the claim that all social practices are meaningful. But that is clearly not so, given the manifest practices of deceit, interpersonal conflict and organized attempts to overthrow ruling but unjust social practices. While disclaiming this reversal of the sense of Winch's argument as nothing but an expository device – and one hardly intelligible at that! – everything in fact turns upon it for Gellner's own case:

> If 'meaning = use', then 'use = meaning'. Of course, no one acually formulated the first equation *as* a formal equation (which would give us the premise for the second, reverse other reading), and in any case, it is not very clear what the thing means when formulated in reverse order. Nothing in the present argument hinges on this: I use this merely as a kind of expository device, to bring out the underlying pattern of Winch's argument.[9]

Thus, by means of an entirely gratuitous imputation, Gellner is able to hang Winch for indifference to all the troublesome predicaments in the lives of persons and societies, pushing him into a sublime relativism. All this, because it is supposed to be implicit in Winch's view that forms of life cannot be criticized from an *external* (by which Gellner means a causal) point of view which would furnish a standard for judgements about what is real and rational and what is not.

Now, it may well be asked why a *critical* standpoint need be *external* to the reality it pronounces upon. There seems to be a surreptitious reliance upon the notion of the natural scientist's external standpoint *vis-à-vis* nature (a somewhat old-fashioned view, in view of more recent social studies of science).[10] Moreover, what does it mean to say the scientist is unbiased towards nature, as though this were in any way like the lack of moral bias? The whole point is that nature's indifference to scientific formulation puts moral questions out of court. But the social world is not similarly indifferent to social science formulations of it since its members have an ethical as well as cognitive investment in their own versions of their world. This does not mean, however, that there are no socially instituted practices of criticism and evaluation internal to social institutions. Indeed, so far from being *external* to its institutions, criticism is deeply institutionalized in Western society.[11] Such criticism is not restricted to social science analysis, nor to Popperian critical rationality. It pervades our ethical, religious, legal and political institutions. It may be that within these institutions we *dramatize* right and wrong, good and evil, left and right, conservative and radical as though we had some radically external viewpoint upon ourselves. Among such practices are Gellner's own rhetorical arts. But a society that changes its religious, political and economic institutions over time does not do so because it is always looking outside of itself toward some external standard of reality. A society changes in view of its own grammar of change and improvement:

> To be emphasized are not the actual members of any 'stock' of descriptions; but the *grammar* which they express. It is through this that we understand their structure and sense, their mutual relations, and the sense of new ways of talking and acting that may be introduced. These new ways of talking and acting may very well at the same time involve modifications in the grammar, but we can only speak thus if the new grammar is (to its users) intelligibly related to the old.[12]

A society changes by redeploying its own moral and material resources. How this happens is formulated by its historians and social scientists who may well find certain institutional arrangements more fundamental than others in the narrative they recount. But it is far from obvious that human history is the study of a reality behind the affairs people take themselves to be engaged in, albeit without complete control. Historical study is rather like Max Weber's study of the relationship between capitalist economic behaviour and certain Protestant beliefs. Thus, as Louch points out in a grudging defence of Winch, Weber's study is misconceived as a project of discovering statistical relations between capitalism and Protestantism, and yet it is not simply an exercise in a priori conceptual analysis.[13] Weber to the contrary, his own explanatory practice was neither statistical nor empathetic *verstehen*. It was *reasoned inquiry* into the moral consequences of holding certain religious beliefs, like the doctrine of predestination and the calling, which could then be used to justify the cycle of saving and investment in profit-making industries. So conceived, history and sociology are *ethical* studies. They seek to show the logical relations – Weber spoke of affinities (*Wahlverwandschaften*) – between important practices in a society that are explained by showing how certain principles at work in it could justify the particular practice that comes under study:

> If this is the way the historian and sociologist go about their business, their explanations do not require further evidence in the way that an account of physical movement is acceptable only if it extends to or embraces further cases. The way in which the background relates to the actions within which they are performed is not causal or statistical. Nor does it have the kind of opacity which requires the invention of theoretical 'models' to render the relation between them intelligible. *The explanation is instead moral; i.e., it presents features of the background as justifying or providing grounds for the action.*[14]

In respect of Winch's claim that inasmuch as sociological understanding involves conceptual analysis it is more like philosophy than empirical science, Louch makes the following observations.[15] Winch's argument is strongest where sociological understanding involves *ad hoc* reference to settled institutions, conventions, rules and habits. But it does not tell us how the sociologist or anthropologist goes about acquiring knowledge of institutions and practices that are removed from everyone's knowledge and not clearly formulated even among members whose lives and occupations may be patterned by them. Moreover, institutions and conventions, while superficially the same, change over time and from society to society. Winch's method of conceptual analysis does not help with empirical studies of historical and comparative variations in conventions. Indeed, it seems as though in stressing the contextual features of explanation and understanding, Winch has lent to Wittgenstein's insistence upon their function an a prioristic rather than strictly empirical injunction to look and see how they work in practice. Weber could not presume upon capitalist institutions for the background sense of Calvin's *Institutes* and Franklin's autobiography. The issue is how well it can be argued that these texts exhibit ways of ethical reasoning that might be used to justify or legitimate a mode of practical reasoning about the primacy of profit in economic affairs. The cogency of Weber's argument is not rendered by trying, as he himself did in his methodological writings, to cast it in the form of a causal/probabilistic design. Nevertheless, it was necessary for Weber to do a great deal of historical research into the nature of markets, money, rent and property in order to grasp the nature of the institutional developments in the rise of capitalism. This enabled him to discern the points at which capitalism both required and fostered certain ethical justifications that later on it could do without. Thus Weber was well aware that profit-making was an activity engaged in throughout the ancient and medieval world. What he set himself to explain was how profit-making came to be justified on ethical grounds. The comparative perspective, once narrowed in terms of specific Protestant doctrines like those of predestination and the calling, allowed him to identify a non-sacramental redemptive activity – saving-and-investing – which eased Protestant anxiety at the same time that it oiled the wheels of capitalist industry. We see, then, that Weber's argument had to meet certain restraints furnished by the materials of inquiry and that the plausibility of his famous theorem on the Protestant ethic and the spirit of capitalism lies very much with its very own economy of argument.

We might say, then, that a society is a set of internal moral relations, never wholly coherent, yet such that any direction of change it assumes cannot impinge upon it from wholly external sources. Thus, while there was a huge shift from feudalism to industrial capitalism, that was morally offensive to many, it was a shift mediated by changes in the religious consciousness of Western Christianity. The specific nuances of this development are available to us only through historical and sociological study. Gellner, however, reifies social change into a conflict between guardians and martyrs, in which the guardians fight hopelessly and blindly against wave after wave of deviants without whom the European tradition is unthinkable. Winch, then, is on the side of the Pope and the Inquisition. Gellner stands, if not with the angels, at least with the prophets and martyrs. They come from two different camps. But *there is nothing to explain their encounter* unless we withdraw Gellner's assumption that different societies, or stages of the same society, can be isolated by some comparative standpoint entirely external to them. But the sources of social change are found *within* societies. In other words, the critical practices of any society are not external to it, except for the romantic and alienated postures of its artists and scientists. This becomes all the more obvious once Gellner himself moves in on Winch for the kill. Then we find that what condemns Winch is that it is he who, after all, seems to have challenged the evident external standard of the *cognitive inequality of cultures* – a challenge that Gellner views only as an affectation of the study, having nothing to do with real life:

> The philosophical significance of the scientific industrial 'form of life', whose rapid global diffusion is the main event of our time, is that for all practical purposes it does provide us with a solution of the problem of relativism – though a highly unsymmetrical one. (It is for this reason that no symmetrical solution can be entertained.) The cognitive and technical superiority of one form of life is so manifest, and so loaded with implications for the satisfaction of human wants and needs – and, for better or worse, for power – that it simply cannot be questioned.[16]

Winch, if we believe Gellner, is blind to reality and fails to comprehend the real working methods whereby social scientists lead men out of the closed society.[17] There is no word in Gellner about how it is that in fact so many critical theorists have turned to the Wittgensteinian analysis of language as an institution which might furnish a more radical grasp of the problems of power and repression in modern society.[18] In doing so, they have all treated Winch with more care than Gellner. And it is this aspect that we must try to understand. For I think there is a critical basis to Winch's view of the relation between language and society which can be developed to answer such critics as Gellner, whether or not in a version that Winch would necessarily adopt. Even the latter reservation might be withdrawn once we have elaborated Winch's position in terms of some Schutzian arguments.

From the very start, sociologists have wondered whether they had a method of their own. In their worst moments, they are inclined to wonder even whether they have a distinctive subject matter. The wolves at the door assure them that they do not have any worries not taken care of by history or economics. These cries make sociologists more nervous and even more determined to find their own way. But the severest temptations come from those who,

like Peter Winch, help sociology to fight off the wolves of science
by showing that human conduct cannot be represented in any other
language (physicalistic, sociological or whatever) than persons
ordinarily use to convey the sense and purpose of their activities.
The price of such defence is that sociology is subsumed by philosophy,
once we see that the analysis of linguistic meaning is a philosophical
and not a scientific undertaking. At first sight, Winch comes as an
ally since he liberates philosophy from its self-imposed task as a
scientific underlabourer, clearing the way to knowledge by stripp-
ing language of its idols, and reducing it to patterns of efficient
communication, free of the knots of ordinary language. But this is
a conception of philosophy that depends upon a false view of the
relation between language and the world. It may well be that there
is a contingent relation between the language of science (it is really
a notation system) and the processes of nature. At least, it is quite
possible to imagine nature outside of scientific representations, though
perhaps not apart from religious, magical and poetic conventions.
Scientists themselves are fond of speaking of the power of science
to refer to its findings as in some sense independent of their expression.[19] They have spoken this way, however, not because it represents their actual practice but because it defends their interests against
religion and the arts which they sometimes consider sheer word play.
Inasmuch as the social sciences have been concerned to fight for
ideological autonomy, they too have tried to reduce the language of
the social sciences to a notational system for the definition and
explanation of social processes that are conceived as an extra-linguistic
material of investigation. Now that sociologists begin to weary of
scientism, Winch is there to explain to them that they need to recover
the autonomy of language and with it the competence of social actors.
Once they see that there really are no scientific windmills to tilt at,
they can sit at home with the good sense of philosophy's Sancho
Pancho.

   Winch's story has been told often enough. It amounts to this: what
we call 'the world' has no existence for us apart from the language
that provides the conceptual machinery whereby we articulate the
world, its objects, persons, interests, values and evils. Indeed, as
Schutz argues, we actually deal with several 'worlds'. This is evident,
once we stop to think of the worlds of our friends, relatives and
children; the world of the sick and dying; the world of fashion; the
worlds of the particular sciences, physics, biology, economy,
literature; the worlds of religion, magic, alchemy and so on.[20]

We know that we cannot gain access to these worlds without acquiring their language, just as a child senses he or she will never grow up unless they learn to talk like those around them. Of course, we still persist in talking about 'the world' and 'language', as though we all spoke a common language with reference to a single external reality. In practice, however, we know that the world is 'my word' and its extent limited by my command of language. We don't know what we can't talk about, although we may talk about things we don't understand very well, whether from reading newspapers, going to lectures, watching television and travelling abroad. We inhabit small worlds on the basis of a fine command of language that is nevertheless far below the requirements of scientific and literary discourse. No one agonizes about this in the ordinary course of affairs, although we may well admire and encourage anyone concerned to increase their knowledge and command of the language of particular sciences:

> Remember that the language-game of everyday life underlies the various language games of science. And while each concrete scientific discipline and each sub-speciality has its own grammar, there is some overlap among these extraordinary (technical) languages and also an overlap with the language-game of everyday life.[21]

This is not to say that we are not sometimes limited in our enterprises because we lack the requisite conceptual discriminations. On such occasions, we may stand in need of science. Or there may be other occasions where we sense we are in trouble because the expressions we make use of go contrary to our intentions, or exceed the limits of our language. This is frequently the case between children and their parents. The child's question, 'If God made everything, who made God?' will usually produce a parental grunt, eked out with a grudging recognition of the logical fervour of children. But it is hardly likely to result in linguistic therapy to reduce the child's illegitimate totality claims. This is work for philosophers and is perhaps satisfying to them alone.

What is not the case is that our use of 'ordinary' language in the conduct of our affairs which obliges us to be intelligible to others and responsible towards them for our actions – in other words, to risk the negative sanctions of being found incomprehensible or irresponsible – is totally inadequate for these very purposes. On the contrary, ordinary language is designed for nothing else and is therefore not to be regarded as a weak form of scientific language.

The latter may well be suited to the pursuit of specific cognitive interests, but is not adequate to the articulation of our everyday affairs:

> When I talk about language (words, sentences, etc.) I must speak the language of everyday. Is this language somehow too coarse and material for what we want to say? *Then how is another one to be constructed*? – And how strange that we should be able to say anything at all with the one we have![22]

As Schutz observed, the questions that are real and important in everyday life do not require any philosophical or scientific address.[23] They are given to us as the framework of the linguistic community in which we grow up. They are not issues that, as it were, lie behind language. Rather, they arise only for persons who are *sociolinguistically competent*. Such persons seek to convince others of their participation in communal tasks as a moral accomplishment that confirms their own identity while simultaneously affirming the collective way of things. In short, there are no private ethics, any more than there are private languages. This does not mean, however, that a community may not differentiate public and private spheres, as well as articulate a language of rights and obligations respective to each domain. What it does mean, despite Rousseau, is that no one has a language of the heart that is prior to the social contract. On the contrary, as Durkheim saw better than Rousseau, we need a complex division of social labour in order to create a society with the moral density that permits the quest for personality and authenticity for some, if not for everyone.

Winch builds upon Wittgenstein's notion of rules that claim that language is a constitutively social achievement and not the work of private persons. It is necessary to be very clear about what this involves. It means that we never deal with human conduct as though it were something with an inside all of its own that has to be deciphered in any way that an ingenious social scientist can devise in order to bring it to a public level of understanding. An action, an emotion, an idea, a promise, or an insult counts as nothing unless it has a social setting of which the agent is cognizant and towards which he or she is oriented, as though towards a rule of expression. This does not mean that an action or emotion may not be misunderstood. Indeed, it is only in terms of the notion of a rule that it makes sense to speak of a misunderstanding, or a misfiring; but that is not the same thing as an act whose idiosyncrasy condemns it to meaninglessness:

Imagine someone using a line as a rule in the following way: he holds a pair of compasses, and carries one of its points along the line that is the 'rule', while the other one draws the line that follows the rule. And while he moves along the ruling line he alters the opening of the compasses, apparently with great precision, looking at the rule the whole time as if it determined what he did. And watching him we see no kind of regularity in this opening and shutting of the compasses. We cannot learn his way of following the line from it. Here perhaps one really would say: 'The original seems to *intimate* to him which way he is to go. But it is not a rule'.[24]

What Wittgenstein or Winch might have added, is that anyone who was found to be playing with the notion of the rule in this way would risk his or her claim to moral seriousness. If not discovered after all to be joking, and then willing to concede the discovery, he or she might then face charges of stupidity and thereby enter the party of moral degradation which is the price of toying with collective representations. We see, then, that the idea of human behaviour standing in need of sociological clarification because it is otherwise inherently confused at the base level is just a myth of social science and its search for a dumb material of representation. In the social world conduct that fails to be inherently meaningful, even if misguided or awkward in some fashion, falls outside the pale of society. But this is ignored by social agents to their cost. It may sound banal to recall the story of the boy who cried 'wolf' too often. It is hardly so to children or to members of minority groups whose experience of language convinces them of its sanctioned use. It could only be overlooked by someone bewitched by the scientific use of language in which such identity concerns are supposedly absent.

Wittgenstein's conception of language consists in the discovery of the irreducibility of the connection between language and society. Language is a social institution and it is the accomplishment of individuals oriented *ethically* as well as cognitively to its rules of usage. It is part of this position that society does not wait upon the discoveries of science for its intelligibility. The *constitutively spoken nature* of social life means that its massive and ordinary *intelligibility* consists of the very same practices which comprise its members' *sociolinguistic competence*. This saves sociology from scientism. For Winch, however, it justifies the dismissal of sociology altogether in favour of the philosophy of ordinary language as the proper instrument of social intelligence. Here, then, we have a potential double bind which I think Schutz can resolve for us. On the one hand, it is necessary to defend the autonomy of lay social theorizing *vis-à-vis* the pretensions of scientistic sociology. The latter requires that its 'materials' be free of any prior interpretation other than the formulation provided by sociological concepts. In this struggle critical sociology is happy to make alliance with the ordinary language philosophy of action, especially in its Wittgensteinian emphasis upon the social contexture of language. However, once it appears, to Giddens for example, that critical sociology thereby risks an 'idealist' alliance with the self-sufficiency of lay versions of society and personality, the professional power of sociological language *vis-à-vis* ordinary language will be invoked:

> Winch does not wish to argue that the sociological observer, in his attempts at explaining social conduct, must confine his vocabulary to that used by lay actors themselves. But apart from a number of passing comments, no indication is given of the relationship which exists between lay and technical concepts, nor, indeed, is it very clear why the latter should be called for at all.[25]

Winch takes it that the most general task of sociology is to examine the very notion of a 'form of life', i.e., the definite modes of meaningful action that prevails under specific forms of human association. However, rather than develop this line in accordance with a formal sociology such as that of Simmel or Goffman,[26] Winch chooses to rest upon Wittgenstein's formulation: 'what has to be accepted, the given, is – so one could say – forms of life'.[27] He uses this formulation in order to make the claim that the heart of sociology is philosophical business and that it is entirely misplaced elsewhere. Of course, it is necessary for Winch to show that Wittgenstein's analysis of language can be extended to treat other forms of social interaction. So he chooses to deal with Max Weber's conception of specifically human action defined in terms of conduct to which an agent assigns a subjective sense that in the light of the agent's circumstances appears as the 'reason' for the agent's behaviour. One is sometimes mistaken about one's reasons for acting, both in the sense that what one takes to be the outcome of one's action, say, bringing about industrial peace by voting for the Labour Party, and that one's motives for voting Labour, which may be less than purposive in the first sense, perhaps express merely sentimental ties to one's father's values. But such cases, in the first instance, only make sense provided that there are occasions when an agent's actions *do* have the sense the agent gives to them, and, in the second case, where it is possible for an agent to understand what it means for an observer to say that the agent voted from habit, sentimental ties, or even unconscious aggression towards the agent's father:

> If you are led by psychoanalysis to say that really you thought so and so or that really your motive was so and so, this is not a matter of discovery, but of persuasion. In a different way you could have been persuaded of something different. Of course, if psycho-analysis cures your stammer, it cures it, and that is an achievement. One thinks of certain results of psycho-analysis as a discovery Freud made, as apart from something persuaded to you by a psycho-analyst, and I wish to say this is not the case.[28]

An action may be counted meaningful in a technical language other than that of the agent, provided the agent can understand the observer's use of such concepts. Thus, it is not possible to understand the therapeutic goals of psychoanalysis unless the patient is accorded the ability to understand the concepts of Freudian analysis, although the patient would never use them in first-order expressions of motive. It is this requirement of social science explanation that lacks any counterpart in natural science. Schutz speaks of this principle as the *postulate of adequacy*, and makes it a requirement of the proper conduct of interpretative sociology:

> Each term in a scientific model of human action must be constructed in such a way that a human act performed within the life-world by an individual actor in the way indicated by the typical construct would be understandable for the actor himself as well as for his fellow-men in terms of commonsense interpretation of everyday life. Compliance with this postulate warrants the consistency of the constructs of the social scientist with the constructs of common-sense experience of the social reality.[29]

This, of course, is a postulate that the protagonists of scientistic sociology would be unwilling to observe. They would see in it nothing but a hindrance to the formation of scientific theories which cannot possibly be tied to commonsense in this way. They might well be confirmed in this belief, in view of Winch's use of the postulate of adequacy to deny to sociology any other status than a philosophical enterprise. Indeed, I am arguing that Winch, by overlooking his relation to Schutz, misses the fully critical implication of his own arguments.

Consider once again Winch's voting example. Suppose we say an agent voted Labour as an act of unconscious aggression towards the agent's father. Is such aggression a reason or a motive for acting in this way? Winch would say it is not a reason in the sense of a *cause* for action inferred by the agent from what the agent knows about the relations between voting, the agent's father's expectations and the like.[30] He says that it might well be a motive, however, in the sense that to vote contrary to the father's expectations was something the agent wanted without either knowing exactly why or being able to give any justificatory reasons. Winch believes that when we find an action condemnable we are more likely to look for its motives than its justifying reasons. In the present example, it would be odd for the agent to justify disappointing voting behaviour as the result of 'unconscious' aggression – though one can imagine the agent seeing anger at the father as something making sense of many seemingly odd acts committed previously, but without any such confrontation as in the voting case. Now Winch wants to say that an action done from condemnable motives, while not being reasonable in the sense of justifiable, may none the less be *intelligible* in terms of modes of behaviour familiar in our society. Thus, in view of the way fathers can abuse the authority given to them, and in so far as their children are often lacking in resources for self-expression and are tempted to blame this upon their niggardly fathers, a child might well vote Labour in the hope of threatening the father with some redistribution of power between them. Anyone living under such institutions would find this intelligible. In my view, they might even find it *reasonable* in the sense of justifiable because they believe that paternalism is intolerable and should be removed. It then depends upon which side of the convention one stands as to how one characterizes the agent's aggression. Given the *status quo*, it is a condemnable 'motive' which will be regarded as irrational, if not unconscious, by those in authority. In this context, the submissive agent will be encouraged to speak of his own motives as 'unconscious'. However, once there is a general challenge to paternal authority, it becomes liberating to recognize the sources of one's anger, and therapeutic to vent it upon an appropriate figure rather than to be consumed by it. In short, *there are changeable ratios in the grammar of reason, motive and cause which depend upon the degree of reflexivity in individuals and the openness of their institutions to such critical appraisals*. In the voting example, because of the interpretation of everyday language by at least vulgar Freudian concepts, most

people would find it intelligible to connect political behaviour with
the oedipal relations between father and child, for example, at least
in so far as questions of general resources are concerned, whether
or not they would consider access to mother to be the cause of causes.
Where serious differences over the logic of political institutions or
the property system might occur, there would be in differential evalua-
tions regarding strategies of reform. Given that family life and the
property system are intimately related, what is the best way to achieve
an analytical understanding of these relationships, and what, in
practice, is the best place to attempt changes?

We should set aside this rather overburdened case for now. Suffice
it to say, that the critical discussion suggested by it becomes wholly
fictitious unless we devise discursive scenarios for an exchange
between the relevant parties to the case, where each is considered
competent to address his own motives, and reasons, and each is aware
of the interplay between individual and institutional resources,
including the problem of asymmetry, oppression and unequal power.
In short, it would be necessary to pursue the discussion in the
framework of what Habermas has called an *ideal speech situation*.[31]
Only in that way can we grasp the dialogic preconditions of critical
reflexivity either as therapy or as institutional reform.

This is not the direction taken by Winch. He is concerned to limit
the scientistic ambitions of sociology but not, on balance, to discourage
the possibility of a critical interpretative sociology. Towards this end,
Winch makes a double appeal to the *postulate of adequacy*, though
he does not use this expression or in any way connect his argument
with Schutz's formulation. Winch nevertheless imposes the adequacy
rule upon the social scientist in relation both to the community of
study and his relations to his own professional community: 'So to
understand the activities of an individual investigator we must take
account of two sets of relations: first, his relation to the phenomena
which he investigates; second, his relation to his fellow scientists'.[32]
The regularities that a social scientist claims to find in the world can
only be understood relative to given institutional contexts that provide
the framework within which human beings act in such a way that
it is in turn possible for the social scientist to speak at all plausibly
of investigating the regularities of human behaviour.[33] The social
scientist, however, misinterprets these regularities as naturalistic
events when in fact they are nothing but the sedimentations of the
reasoned conduct of persons in society. But more. The social scientist's
own conduct in making judgements about the sense and uniformity

of human conduct is itself subject to similar interpretative rules. The scientific behaviour of the sociologists can only be understood relative to the maxims of scientific procedure that prevail their own professional community. Indeed, it is the consensus prevailing in the community of scientists that enables the investigator to engage meaningfully in the work of first-order observation. However, we cannot speak without a regress when referring to the scientist's grasp of his own community's procedures for sense-making as itself based upon observation:

> The phenomena being investigated present themselves to the scientist as an *object* of study; he observes them and notices certain facts about them. But to say of a man that he does this presupposes that he already has a mode of communication in the use of which rules are already being observed. For to notice something is to identify relevant characteristics, which means that the notices must have some *concept* of such characteristics; this is possible only if he is able to use some symbol according to a rule which makes it refer to those characteristics. So we come back to his relation to his fellow scientists, in which context alone he can be spoken of as following such a rule.[34]

What follows from this, although it is Schutz rather than Winch who saw it, is that the *rationalist assumption* applied by sociologists to bring order into their observation of human nature ought to be regarded as *a rule of procedure for the production of knowledge satisfying the standards prevailing for the production of the sociological corpus*.[35] Rationality is therefore not a uniquely first-order construct of human behaviour which the sociologist simply abstracts from their observations of persons in society. But Winch, unlike Schutz and Garfinkel, turns away from the study of the social sciences regarded as courses of practical reason.[36] This is because Winch believes that the double requirement of sociological explanation, namely, that, in addition to being referred back to sense-making procedures in the scientific community, it must also be referred back to the rules of sense-making in the community which is his field of study – and to which there is no self-interpreting counterpart in the objects of natural science investigation – puts an end to sociology. It certainly places a particular *hermeneutic obligation* upon sociology and, to the degree that it is honoured, it makes it impossible to proceed with a scientistic version of sociology. At the same time, Winch anticipates that this obligation will in fact be shrugged off by social scientists, if the price of its observance is to reduce their practice to the kind of unreflective understanding that characterizes lay persons caught up in custom and in ultimate ignorance of the social forces shaping their lives. Winch must then rescue his own philosophical expropriation of social phenomena from the charge that it merely endorses common-sense address of persons and society and abjures anything like the reflexive task of the social sciences. So he insists that all he is saying is that, while the social sciences must use technical concepts not to be found in lay language (and here he seems to concede the continued existence of the social sciences), the use of these concepts, unlike those of the natural sciences, implies a previous understanding of the lay concepts that are constitutive of the phenomena of social investigation. Thus, while businessmen do not use such a technical concept as 'liquidity preference', it only has explanatory value because it is logically tied to the notions businessmen do make use of in the conduct of their affairs. Winch is not, incidentally, claiming that the economist's use of technical concepts presupposes anything like an empathic understanding of business affairs. What he means to say, I think, is that there is nothing in principle that prevents the businessman giving a first-order account of his operations intelligible to the economists who, in turn, ought in principle to be able to communicate the sense of such concepts as liquidity preference to their business clientele. Indeed, such translations[37] go on all the time in consultancy, journalism and conferences. I think we can best understand the sense of Winch's relativism, which has so exercised his rationalist critics, if we take it as part of his recognition of the ethics of social science investigation made necessary by its expanding practice that shows no signs of abating due to philosophical exorcism of any kind.

Winch is opposed to the ironies of the social sciences – their so-called estrangement-effect. Their practice is to ignore the competing ways of life in human society and to subject their different standards of self-interpretation to the overriding social science assumption of *utilitarian rationality*. Winch discusses the rationality assumption in connection with Pareto's distinction between logical and non-logical action:

> A logical action then is one that fulfills the following conditions:
> (a) it is thought of by the agent as having a result and is performed by him for the purpose of achieving that result; (b) it actually does tend to have the result which the agent envisages; (c) the agent

has (what Pareto would regard as) good (i.e., 'logico-experimental') grounds for his belief; (d) the end sought must be one that is empirically identifiable.[38]

The presumption of scientific explanation – its imperialistic rationalism – requires that magic be treated as poor science or that martyrs be considerd hedonists in the next life if not this one. Indeed, everyone can furnish his or her own pet example of the kind of irony today's public is supposed to swallow, setting aside its own good sense in favour of the accounts of crime, perversion and idleness favoured by social scientists as keepers of the standards of social rationality.

Winch objects to the social scientist's practice of *decontextualizing* lay reasoning in order to make human behaviour nothing but a sequence of strange uninterpreted events whose sense is then re-attributed to them in so far as they approximate the rationality model of action favoured by the social scientist. Thus we might experiment – as comedians do – with an account of men running after a piece of pigskin filled with air, risking great injury to themselves in order to produce alternations of joy and misery in a crowd of bystanders who are otherwise engaged in eating and drinking to cool themselves in summer or warm themselves in winter. Such accounts by systematically exploiting the removal of the rules of the game that give these events the sense of a game of football may be useful as an exercise in comparative sociology, as well as in the practice of comedians or dramatists. Indeed, such *incongruity procedures* are a powerful instrument for displaying the massive trust that persons have in the unchallenged course of their lives. Precisely because of our ordinarily unthematic grasp of social practices, there is a considerable danger in the use of such dramaturgical concepts as that of 'role' when employed by sociologists to suggest that social realities require of us none of the sincerity we ordinarily invest in them.[39] In this respect, Winch's position represents a strong moral defence of the *prima facie* reasonableness of everyday practices: 'The only legitimate use of such a *Verfremdungseffekt* is to draw attention to the familiar and obvious, not to show that it is *dispensable* from our understanding'.[40]

Winch perhaps goes too far in separating understanding and causal explanation. In practice, the two may be seen to be *complementary* aspects of human knowledge – excluding but presupposing one another.[41] We might think of the process of the quasi-objectification of behaviour through the use of statistical data, psychoanalytic and sociological concepts as a methodological device – a temporary estrangement of interpretative meaning – which is then reintegrated with the subject's understanding once the social scientist provides his or her final analysis. This is clearer in the practice of psychoanalysis than in sociology where so much investigation is never reported back to those affected by the studies. All the same, what the sociologist neglects to do in this direction, he or she is obliged to do on behalf of those who commission their studies. Here we have a political asymmetry and Schutz's postulate of adequacy, or Apel's complementarity thesis serves to point this out. By the same token, we allow for the expansion of common-sense understanding through the accumulation of objectified scientific data, avoiding the false impression that interpretative understanding is always self-sufficient. Winch overstresses the internal relation between language and experience in order to defend lay understanding from external scientific explanation. In practice, common-sense understanding is capable of critical comparison, reflection upon facts and removal of obvious contradictions. And the scientific community is not worlds ahead of it in this regard. Winch's objection to the exploitation of the *Verfremdungseffekt* is not simply an endorsement of unenlightened common-sense. It is not a question of praising common sense rather than science. It is instead the insistence that *common-sense knowledge of persons and society is a structure of ethical competence* that could not conceivably be replaced by social science programmes.[42] Winch defends this position, as I understand him, in his *doctrine of the internality of social relations*, although he risks giving it an idealist formulation, upon which Gellner seized: 'If social relations between men exist only in and through their ideas, then, since the relations between ideas are internal relations, social relations must be a species of internal relations too'.[43] We cannot separate language and social relations. For example, the difficulty we sense in answering today whether we are 'real' citizens arises because we sense that modern political relations are governed by instrumental considerations, subject to welfare repairs, that hardly meet the criteria for the old notion of citizenship. The term survives but we sense its hollowness, without being able to abandon the values it connotes. It is not that we think that our fellow men and women are only 'pretending' to be citizens. We are expressing a common plight: those who wish to be citizens in modern society have particular trouble to realize the depths of that experience. The concept of citizenship, then, both generates and is generated by the particular conduct it describes/prescribes. Those who understand themselves to be citizens will in a variety of circumstances expect of one another certain acts that in turn are taken as evidence and confirmation of their citizenship. Thus it is possible to look at the particulars of behaviour as descriptive evidence for the relations between citizens and to appeal to the concept of citizenship to accept or reject actions proffered as instances of it. This is not to deny that there is no behaviour independent of the concept. It is rather to say that what behaviour *counts* as citizenship rests upon the criteria of what is appropriate to citizens in a given society. What looks like an instance of war may simply be a skirmish, a patrol error, a reprisal, depending upon how governments choose to find things. Thus, in practice we observe complex arguments, exchange of missions, cease-fires, peace talks, all involved in finding whether or not countries are at war. Anyone who remembers his or her youth will remember similarly complex negotiations over whether so-and-so was really his or her friend and, of course, even greater discriminations to decide whether he or she was in love.

No one would think of calling in a social scientist – or a philosopher – to decide the issue of war or love. And this, as Winch would say, is because to make these discoveries is not like discovering that the law of gravity obtains with respect to the fall of objects within the earth's sphere. Furthermore, these examples may serve to show just how false it is to underestimate the complexity and reflexiveness that enter into lay reasoning. There may in fact be a desirable reversal of the status of common-sense and scientific reasoning. In a democracy, we take it that such decisions as whether to go to war may be reached with technical advice duly weighed, but not decisive. There seems to be little reason why this should not be the same for social scientists when advising governments. Indeed, it is essential to the preservation of parliamentary democracy. Likewise, in our personal lives we would regard it as pathetic to find a man or a woman consulting a psychoanalyst in order to come to the decision to fall in love, or to have children and raise a family. This does not mean to say that family psychologists may not have advice to offer on the problems of marital and parental relations. It is rather that we only resort to this advice when our own competence falters and that we should only contract to the therapeutic relation with the intent to restore our ordinary competence in everyday living. If social scientists have advice to offer us, it is because the social sciences are themselves practices that are part of the very culture they seek to analyse. It is this relationship which makes it practical and sensible for members to make use of them. Not some other grammar of society.[44]

There is after all no intrinsic hostility between common sense and scientific knowledge once we understand these to be historical acquisitions, always relative to one another. Unfortunately, social phenomenologists have emphasized the static, if not conservative aspects of what Schutz called 'the stock of knowledge'.[45] But Schutz himself has warned against this static bias:

> A word of caution seems to be needed here. The concept of finite provinces of meaning – world of art, of science, of work, of everyday life – does not involve any static connotation as though we had to select one of these provinces as our home to live in, to start from or to return to. That is by no means the case. Within a single day, even within a single hour our consciousness may run through most different tensions and adopt most different attentional attitudes to life. There is, furthermore, the problem of 'enclaves', that is, of regions belonging to one province of meaning enclosed by another. ... To give an example of this disregarded group of problems: any projecting within the world of working is itself ... a phantasying, and involves in addition a kind of theoretical contemplation, although not necessarily that of the scientific attitude.[46]

Inasmuch as science and common sense build upon one another, common sense can only be ignorant in its mockery of scientific failure, just as science would be blind to ignore common sense as an essential resource in its own working practices. There are, of course, social scientists who do not share any of these worries. They presume upon the subject/object model of investigation in which other subjects, persons like themselves, are reduced to objects of study, interview and tabulation. Furthermore, the palpable sense of lay persons' activities in their own minds is made to appear strange, confused and in essential need of reformulation according to scientific standards of adequate sense and rational efficiency. That social scientists are partner to these very standards of common-sense rationality and procedure which they judge to be nothing but poor science, is either overlooked or else recognized in the *role-split* between the scientist's own civic and professional attitudes. This split is often referred to as the *value neutrality* of the scientist. It represents his or her commitment to lines of scientific argument regardless of where they led them and their fellow citizens whose moral beliefs, families, pace of work, urban environment and the like are subjected to the privileged pronouncements and interventions of the social

sciences. Today it is clear that citizens, consumers, workers and
students, as well as ethnic minority groups and the women's movement, do not easily accept the implicit silence imposed upon them
by those who claim to have the blueprint for their lives. Those who
are the guardians of the official institutions that have been subject
to citizens' questions, demonstrations and civil disobedience are likely
to see in these events evidence only of the need for securing order
through even more rational social planning and legislation. But what
is really at stake in these political confrontations is the breakdown
of the privileged say-so of the applied social sciences, whose
dependence upon the physical science paradigm prevents them from
making any accommodation to the lively, self-interpreting, presence
of persons whose moral competence with their own affairs is injured
by the passivity required of them by social science intervention. It
is to such a critical common sense and its appropriate subordination
of the practice of the social sciences within democratic institutions
that we think Winch's idea of a social science makes a defensible
contribution. But we need to expand upon it in terms of Schutz's
postulate of adequacy as rule for delimiting the privilege of social
science discourse. We may then reformulate Winch and Schutz in
terms of the following regulative principles for the production of a
democratic knowledge-society:

1 recognize the moral/rational competence of individuals;
2 recognize that institutions are not on an entirely different rational/
   moral level from individuals;
3 find a language of translation between institutional discourse and
   individual discourse;
4 find a language of translation between scientific discourse and
   common-sense discourse;
5 treat the institutionalization of the two languages of translation (3
   and 4) as fundamental to the practice of democratic institution;
6 treat the rule of translation as a cross-cultural imperative in order
   to minimize the cultural imperialism of Western institutions and
   scientific discourse.

What Schutz's postulate of adequacy emphasizes is the fiction-
ality of scientific reasoning and its ultimate dependence upon the
common-sense communicative competence of the community of
scientists in general and the larger lay society in which they live and
work. Although Schutz's phenomenological descriptions may suggest
a static division between scientific and common-sense knowledge,

he in fact insisted upon the need to create mediating institutions between them. For each is 'impossible' without the other. That is to say, in Western industrial democracies we are bound – in terms of our own 'form of life' – to cross-fertilize common sense and science in every domain of experience. In this our science and our morality are inseparable. Yet we know that we increasingly suffer from the subordination of common sense and morals to expert knowledge and scientific neutrality. We do so at great peril to democratic institutions. It is precisely at this juncture that it is valuable to link Winch and Schutz to arrive at a set of regulative principles and practices which would confirm our will to democracy which is currently the weak link in liberal and socialist societies. It needs to be recalled that Schutz saw each of us as simultaneously (i) the man or woman on the street; (ii) the expert; (iii) the well-informed citizen.[47] Thus each of us possess a good deal of knowledge that is a collective legacy and not particularly the result of any inquiry of our own. We owe such knowledge to our family, school, community, newspapers, radio, television, books and theatre, as well as the life's smaller conversations and experiences. Yet each of us possesses some specifically occupational or scientific knowledge in virtue of which we claim competences and rights on our own behalf, while making similar concessions with respect to other's claims to expertise. At this level, we separate ourselves from common-sense street knowledge in order to amplify the total knowledge of society through specialization. Then, again, as well-informed citizens we seek to re-embody in ourselves the best knowledge we can acquire in the general conduct of our affairs. But if this is to happen we need mediating institutions like public education, honest journalism and parliamentary democracy through which we may join in a common civic effort to enhance our humanity.

NOTES

1 Winch, P. (1958) *The Idea of a Social Science, and its Relation to Philosophy*, London: Routledge and Kegan Paul. A convenient collection of papers around Winch's argument and a bibliography is available in *Understanding and Social Inquiry* (1977) F.R. Dallmayr and T.H. McCarthy (eds) Notre Dame: University of Notre Dame Press, Part Three, 'The Wittgensteinian Reformulation'. See also, A. MacIntyre (1978) 'The idea of a social science', pp. 211–29 in his *Against the Self-Images of the Age: Essays on Ideology and Philosophy*, Notre Dame: University of Notre Dame Press.

2 Ibid., p. 72.
3 Giddens, A. (1976) *New Rules of Sociological Method*, London: Hutchinson University Library, p. 79. See also J. O'Neill (1983) 'Mutual Knowledge', pp. 53–70 in *Changing Social Science: Critical Theory and Other Critical Perspectives*, D.R. Sabia and G. Wallulis (eds) Albany: State University of New York Press.
4 Winch (1958) Op. cit., p. 89.
5 See the following chapter on mutual knowledge in this book.
6 Gellner, E. (1974) 'The New Idealism – Cause and Meaning in the Social Sciences', in *Positivism and Sociology*, A. Giddens (ed.) London: Heinemann, pp. 129–56. For a defence of radical anthropomorphism as a necessary communicative practice, see J. O'Neill (1985) *Five Bodies: The Human Shape of Modern Society*, Ithaca: Cornell University Press.
7 Despite his appeal to physical and medical models, Freud seems also to have believed that psychoanalytic understanding depends upon the agent's linguistic competence. He put it as follows: 'Our understanding reaches as far as our anthropomorphism', *Minutes of the Vienna Psychoanalytic Society, Vol. 1, 1906–1908*, H. Nunberg and E. Federn (eds) (1962) New York: International Universities Press, p. 136.
8 Gellner (1974) Op. cit., p. 131.
9 Ibid., pp. 133–4.
10 O'Neill, J. (1981) 'Marxism and the Two Sciences', *Philosophy of the Social Sciences*, Vol. 11(3) Autumn, pp. 1–30.
11 For an account of how moral change arises within social systems, see, P.F. Strawson (1974) 'Social Morality and Individual Ideal', pp. 26–44 in his *Freedom and Resentment, and other essays*, London: Methuen and Co. Ltd.
12 Winch, P. (1977) 'Understanding a Primitive Society', in Dallmayr and McCarthy, Op. cit., p. 174.
13 Louch, A.R. (1963) 'The Very Idea of a Social Science', *Inquiry*, 6, pp. 273–85.
14 Ibid., p. 276. My emphasis. Louch then says that the relationship between moral facts while being *logical*, and thus seeming to support Winch, is nevertheless only discoverable *empirically*, or else history and sociology fudge their obligation to provide descriptions and comparisons which provide intelligible grounds for explaining conduct by appeal to conventions or justifying practices prevailing in a given society.
15 Louch, A.R. (1966) *Explanation and Human Action*, Berkeley and Los Angeles: University of California Press, pp. 164–5; also 'The Very Idea of a Social Science' (1963) *Inquiry*, 6, pp. 273–86.
16 Gellner, Op. cit., p. 155.
17 I have expressed my position on the question of the comparative inequality of cognitive cultures in my introductory essay, 'Scientism, Historicism and the Problem of Rationality', in *Modes of Individualism and Collectivism* (1973), J. O'Neill (ed.) London: Heinemann.
18 See A. Wellmer (1976) 'Communication and Emancipation: Reflections on the Linguistic Turn in Critical Theory', in *On Critical Theory*,

J. O'Neill (ed.) New York: The Seabury Press, pp. 231–63; J. O'Neill (1986) 'Decolonization and the Ideal Speech Community: Some issues in the theory and practice of communicative competence', pp. 57–76 in *Critical Theory and Public Life*, J. Forester (ed.) Boston: MIT Press.

19 O'Neill, J. (1983) 'Some issues in the realist use of science', pp. 64–70 in *Realizing Social Science Knowledge*, B. Holzner, K. Knorr, and H. Strasser (eds) Vienna: Physica-Verlag.

20 O'Neill, J. (1985) *Five Bodies: The Human Shape of Modern Society*, Ithaca: Cornell University Press.

21 Phillips, D.L. (1977) *Wittgenstein and Scientific Knowledge, A Sociological Perspective*, Totawa, N.J.: Rowman and Littlefield, p. 109.

22 Wittgenstein, *Philosophical Investigations* (1953) Oxford: Basil Blackwell Publishers, 1: 120.

23 Schutz, A. (1964) 'The Problem of Rationality in the Social World', pp. 64–90 in his *Collected Papers II: Studies in Social Theory*, The Hague: Martinus Nijhoff.

24 Wittgenstein (1953) *Philosophical Investigations*, I, p. 237.

25 Giddens (1976) Op. cit., p. 49.

26 O'Neill, J. (1973) 'On Simmel's Sociological Apriorities', pp. 91–106 in *Phenomenological Sociology, Issues and Applications*, G. Psathas (ed.) New York: John Wiley and Sons.

27 *Philosophical Investigations*, II, XI, p. 226e.

28 Wittgenstein, L. (1972) *Lectures and Conversations*, Berkeley and Los Angeles: University of California Press, p. 27.

29 Schutz, A. (1962) 'Common-sense and scientific interpretation of human action', *Collected Papers*, The Hague: Martinus Nijhoff, 1: 44.

30 The analysis of the relation between reason, cause and motive is not settled and I do not pretend to contribute to it. However, I do not think that the ordinary sense of reason and cause need to be separated. See, D. Davidson (7 November 1963) 'Actions, Reasons and Causes', *The Journal of Philosophy*, LX(23) pp. 685–700. I also think that the self-interpretative or teleological nature of ordinary discourse makes it unnecessary to separate desire, sensation and intention. See, C. Taylor (1970) 'Explaining Action', *Inquiry*, 13, pp. 54–89.

31 Habermas, J. (1970) 'Toward a Theory of Communicative Competence', pp. 115–48 in *Recent Sociology*, 2, 'Patterns of Communicative Behavior', H.P. Dreitzel (ed.) New York: The Macmillan Company. See also, J. O'Neill (1985) 'Decolonization and the Ideal Speech Community: Some issues in the theory and practice of communicative competence', in *Critical Theory and Public Life*, J. Forester (ed.) Cambridge: MIT Press.

32 *The Idea of a Social Science*, p. 84; see also note 4.

33 See, H.T. Wilson (1984) *Tradition and Innovation: The idea of civilization as culture and its significance*, London: Routledge and Kegan Paul, for a remarkable reading of Wittgenstein and Weber on our form of life and its conception of scientific rationality and technical progress.

34 *The Idea of a Social Science*, p. 85.

35 Garfinkel, H. (1967) *Studies in Ethnomethodology*, New Jersey: Prentice-Hall; A. Cicourel (1964) *Method and Measurement in Sociology*, New York: Free Press.
36 O'Neill, J. (1980) 'From Phenomenology to Ethnomethodology: Some Radical "Misreadings"', pp.7–20 in *Current Perspectives in Sociological Theory*, 1, S.G. McNall and G.N. Howe (eds) Boston: JAI Press, Inc.
37 Turner, S.P. (1980) *Sociological Explanation as Translation*, London: Cambridge University Press, nicely defends Winch to a considerable degree along these lines.
38 *The Idea of a Social Science*, pp. 97–8.
39 For an appraisal of the emancipatory and destructive options in the dramaturgical approach to persons and society, see J. O'Neill (1972) 'Self Prescription and Social Machiavellianism', pp. 11–19 in his *Sociology as a Skin Trade, Essays Towards a Reflexive Sociology*, New York: Harper & Row. This essay treats the works of Erving Goffman and Peter Berger.
40 *The Idea of a Social Science*, p. 119.
41 Apel, K.-O. (1967) *Analytic Philosophy of Language and the Geisteswissenschaften*, Dordrecht: D. Reidel Publishing Company, p. 23.
42 This is argued at length in J. O'Neill (1974) *Making Sense Together, An Introduction to Wild Sociology*, New York: Harper & Row. See also, A.W. Gouldner (1975) 'Sociology and the Everyday Life', in *The Idea of Social Structure, Papers in Honor of Robert K. Merton*, L.A. Coser (ed.) New York: Harcourt Brace Jovanovich, pp. 417–32.
43 *The Idea of a Social Science*, p. 123.
44 O'Neill, J. (1986) 'Sociological Nemesis: Parsons and Foucault on the Therapeutic Disciplines', pp. 21–35 in *Sociological Theory in Transition*, M.L. Wardell and S.P. Turner (eds) Boston: Allyn & Unwin.
45 Berger, P.L. and Luckmann, T. (1967) *The Social Construction of Reality, A Treatise in the Sociology of Knowledge*, New York: Doubleday and Company, Ch. II, 'Sedimentation and Tradition'.
46 Schutz (1962) 'On Multiple Realities', *Collected Papers I*, p. 253.
47 Schutz, A. (1964) 'The Well-Informed Citizen: An Essay on the Social Distribution of Knowledge', pp. 120–34 in his *Collected Papers, II*.

Chapter 8

Mutual knowledge

THE LINGUISTIC TURN IN THE SOCIAL SCIENCES

Human societies are self-interpreting institutions. Historically, this hermeneutical work has fallen to priests, philosophers, and artists who were gradually usurped by scientists, lawyers, economists, and sociologists. This, of course, is not an undisputed shift, although we generally accommodate to it by allowing scientists their say-so with respect to nature, while clinging to our own right to an opinion on religion, politics, business, and the arts. In these areas, too, there are advocates for the dominance of scientific discourse, who seek to persuade us that laymen can at best chatter upon the nature of society. Those who favour the analogy between nature and society as the dumb material of science are therefore inconvenienced by the seemingly inextricable relation between ordinary language and social reality. Indeed, they are likely to consider those who stress the constitutively spoken nature of human society to be idealists, romantically tied to convention and conservatism. In practice, the scientistic ambitions of sociology are well entrenched in Western societies, politicians having persuaded laymen and themselves that the complexities of modern living can only be settled through a trustful delegation of analysis and initiative to the technical sciences. But today there is a civic tendency to question the bureaucratic processing of everyday life. To keep pace, professional voices have risen to question the scientistic model of constructivist sociology as an expropriation of an ordinary civic competence with the sensible conduct of human affairs. To keep on top of these developments, even self-styled critical sociologists find themselves having to straddle the double claims of scientific and common-sense accounts of social life. In this way, they hope to preserve professional face by chastising their colleagues while also instructing them in new methods of holding on to what they may have lost forever.

Something like this provides the background to Anthony Giddens' persistent, if not repetitive, attempts to refurbish the grounds of the mutuality of common sense and sociological knowledge, or what he calls the 'double hermeneutic' of the social sciences.[1] It is necessary to examine Giddens' argument, because it betrays a fundamental ambivalence towards common-sense knowledge even where he, as a sociologist, has tried to bring about a *rapprochement* between the moral claims of lay and expert knowledge. Giddens thereby misses a serious communicative issue in the power relations of political democracies. Since he draws heavily upon what we may call *the linguistic turn in the social sciences*, we should recall the basic propositions on which Giddens constructs his argument:

1 (a) Social science must treat action as rationalized conduct ordered reflexively by human agents;
   (b) It must grasp the significance of language for the practical accomplishment of rational and reflexive action.
2 (a) The recognition of the linguistic accomplishment of the reflexivity of human conduct ought also to be introduced into the conduct of sociological research and method;
   (b) Social science theories are not simply neutral 'meaning frames' but moral interventions in the life of the society they propose to clarify.[2]

In themselves these prescriptions are hardly news and, in fact, are recognized in the daily practice of sociological research that is quite ignorant of the tradition of European social theory – or at best happy to leave it on the mantelpiece, along with the bric-à-brac of early science. Nothing, then, is to be gained from elaborating upon these mnemonic devices as they stand.

It is therefore in another way that we must be concerned with the *constitutively spoken (sprachlich) subject matter of sociology*. The purely methodological issue is that the social sciences, while aspiring to the practice of the natural sciences in their operations of definition and generalization, lack an analogously dumb material of reference. That is to say, while the natural sciences benefit from the indifference of natural and physical processes to scientific formulation, the social sciences are not similarly privileged in their encounters with persons and institutions. This is not simply the complaint, revelled in by British critics of the jargon of the social sciences, that the latter have yet to reach that stage of scientific maturity where their language cannot be found to be a thin disguise for common-sense expressions. While this is often the case, and might be taken to defend us against the pretensions of the social sciences, it is not an argument we wish to use. Our purpose is not to enter a plea for the preservation of sociology but to confront the *political ambivalence in its critical practice*, let alone in its scientific versions. As I understand it, the seriousness of the political issues to which we are led by the communicative reflexivity of common-sense knowledge of social structure derives from the concern it holds for the public in Western democracies. Here it is the voice of the social science experts and technicians in the service of the Party, whether right or left, which threatens to erode civic competence and political responsibility.

COMMON-SENSE SOCIABILITY AS COMMUNICATIVE COMPETENCE

What has evolved from the phenomenological and neo-Wittgensteinian critique of positivism is a shift from compliance theories of knowledge and social reality to a competence model of the pretheoretical and sentimental foundations of everyday social life.[3] To the extent that this existential or phenomenological shift in the validation of common-sense structures of knowledge and values that turn upon native linguistic competences represents a 'radical' break with scientistic sociology, Giddens needs to endorse it. But because he suspects Idealism in the linguistic turn, he introduces some further propositions for a constructivist critical sociology whose central concepts of structure, power, and change might render common-sense knowledge more rational.

We need first to set out what is attractive in the sociology of everyday life, and then we shall see how Giddens manages his ambivalence with regard to *the critical problem of the radical relativization of scientific and everyday accounts of persons and society*. Although Schutz himself seems not to have had any political ambitions for interpretative sociology, I believe that it is not difficult to provide one for the *critical turn in phenomenological sociology*.[4] Here I am at odds with Giddens. I shall argue that common-sense knowledge and values do not depend upon scientific reconstruction for the exercise of critical reflection. It is a prejudice of science and philosophy to think of common sense as a poor version of reason. On the contrary, the practice of science is enriched and would be quite impossible without its ties to the practices of common-sense reasoning. Moreover, the strict subordination of common-sense knowledge to the social sciences would constitute a political practice so far envisaged only in philosophical and science-fiction utopias. Indeed, it is a mark of the latter that they abjure common sense. The essential distinction between the natural and social sciences, which makes the standard of rationality fostered by the social sciences intrinsically a problem of the *politics of knowledge*, is that human relationships, customs, and institutions are not merely 'orders' produced by scientific reconstruction. The human order is initially a *pretheoretical institution*, resting on the unarticulated 'common-sense' knowledge of others as 'kindred' with whom we experience dependable needs and wants, expressed in the 'relevances' of time, place, and the human body. The nature of this order cannot be settled through a dogmatic rationalism that subordinates common-sense knowledge of individual and social life to the standards of realism and objectivism. The latter are maxims of scientific conduct but not obviously normative for all social praxis. Indeed, a fundamental task of the sociology of knowledge must be its reflexive concern with the grounds of *communication* between everyday common-sense reason and scientific rationality. Such a concern would contribute to the possibility of a democratic society in the modern world by defending the fundamental grounds of social life as the *inalienable competence of individuals* exhibited in their everyday lives together.

It is quite unthinkable that society could ever be a construct of sociological reasoning alone.[5] In Marxist terms and, I believe, Schutzian (implicit in his preference for such metaphors as 'the stock of knowledge'), common-sense knowledge of social structure supplies an enormous *surplus value of meaning and value* without which analytic social reasoning would itself be entirely unworkable. Thus the primacy of the everyday world as a self-interpreted structure of practical knowledge and values is fundamental to the investigative procedures of interpretative sociology. It is the foundation of the universality of experience that eludes both a transcendental ego, and the covenants of an empirical ego locked in the pursuit of self-interest.

Schutz, Simmel, and George Herbert Mead all agree that the social world is the product of an essentially human capacity for adopting the attitude of the *generalized other* towards oneself (Mead), and thereby building up a structure of *typifications* and *relevances* (Schutz) whereby we are able to interact without solipsistic anxieties as to the ordinary and dependable course of our interaction with our fellows:

In abstract thought the individual takes the attitude of the generalized other toward himself, without reference to its expression in any particular other individuals; and in concrete thought he takes that attitude insofar as it is expressed in the attitudes towards his behaviour of those other individuals with whom he is involved in the given social situation or act. But only by taking the attitude of the generalized other toward himself, in one or other of these ways, can he think at all; for only thus can thinking – or the internalized conversation of gestures which constitutes thinking – occur. And only through the taking by individuals of the attitude or attitudes of the generalized other toward themselves is the existence of a universe of discourse, as that system of common or social meanings which thinking presupposes as its context, rendered possible.[6]

Like Mead, Simmel rejects any notion of the construction of a common social world as the product of scientific abstraction and synthesis: the unity of society needs no observer. It is directly realized by its own elements because these elements are themselves conscious and synthesizing units. Nor does Simmel see the synthesis of social life as the direct focus of individual action, but as the by-product of innumerable specific relations governed by 'the feeling and knowledge of determining others and being determined by them'. This is not to say that the sociologist for his own specific purposes may not elaborate an 'additional' synthesis. But the problem here is that the synthesis of external observation which takes as its paradigm the observation of nature is not analogous to human unity, which is grounded in understanding, love, or common work. The social synthesis is the work of individuals for whom others have the same reality as themselves and are not reducible simply to the contents of individual consciousness, but function to orient language, thought, and conduct toward the social world. We *think* the other but at the same time we are so *affected* by them that sociation is better regarded as a 'knowing' than a 'cognizing', says Simmel. But neither is sociation simply an emphatic projection of psychological similarities:

We see the other not simply as an individual but as a colleague or comrade or fellow party member – in short, as a cohabitant of the same specific world. And this inevitable, quite automatic assumption is one of the means by which one's personality and reality assume, in the imagination of the other, the quality and form required by sociability.[7]

Schutz has examined in detail the range of typifications, from face-to-face to increasingly anonymous situations, removed in time as well as space, that provide the framework of the ordinary person's social repertoire of relevances, interests, and values. These he can pursue in common with others, without any radical break in what can be taken as matter of course and what needs particular reflection because of contradictions, deceits, and puzzles. In short, the social world is not, as constructivist analysts wish to make out, an intrinsic puzzle that requires scientific mediation and reconstruction in order to make rational sense.

As we have seen Peter Winch argue, it is only permissible for social scientists to make culture strange in order to reveal the massive trust and unchallenged sense that members invest in it.[8] And indeed the deep sense of the *incongruity procedures* of Goffman and Garfinkel is to show that the sense of social possibility, and its techniques of face and impression management, is false to the unarticulated structure of our *everyday trust and social competence* with one another.[9] In contrast with manipulative and expert knowledge, our mundane experience of the self and its social situation is given to us through the same set of typifications and motives that are the convenience of anyone. It is only by some incongruity of experience, some outrage or manipulation, that I discover that my self is not synonymous with selves in general, or that what I take to be the perceivedly normal and typical features of my situation are not in fact shared by or available to anyone like me. Thus it is the starting assumption of every social relationship that each of us knows with whom he is interacting. This involves the typification of each partner's actions, motives, and situation. What is required is that each person be able to observe the rules of *self-respect* and *considerateness* that sustain the ritual of social interaction:

A person's performance of face-work, extended by his tacit agreement to help others perform theirs, represents his willingness to abide by the ground rules of social interaction. Here is the hallmark of his socialization as an interactant. If he and the others were not socialized in this way, interaction in most societies and most situations would be a much more hazardous thing for feelings and faces. The person would find it impractical to be oriented to symbolically conveyed appraisals of social worth, or to be possessed of feelings – that is, it would be impractical for him to be a ritually delicate object.[10]

It is not necessary that the typifications of respect and consideration be accessible in a perfectly *reciprocal* way in order to sustain
social interaction. Person and action typifications are *corrigible*
through experience and interaction. But what is not true, is that we
withhold our trust in others until we have *absolutely* certain grounds
for it. Socially speaking, seduction precedes both deduction and
induction as the basis of our experience with others. Thus, in the
ordinary course of life we take others at face value, and expect to
be sustained in the face that we ourselves project. In these exchanges,
the primary focus of social interaction is the expressive communication between self and other. We must then regard language, gesture,
task, motive, and situation as primary resources for social bonding,
and as the *precontractual basis* for all other covenants, even those
in which we deceive one another.

Interpretative sociology, therefore, treats the natural attitude of
daily life as *generative maxims of conduct* whereby social agents derive
their ordinary sense of competence from the practices of their
surrounding institutions as a claim to moral membership in those
institutions. In other words, the way social agents have of deciding
the sensible status of their own actions or of events in their lives is
to refer to the particulars of these events as the *occasioned evidence*
of their grasp of the institutions of language, work, family, or school.
In turn, these institutions furnish the *indexical grounds* of their actions
and talk, whose sense therefore is never *wholly* at stake in members'
questions, answers, descriptions, and the like. The maxims of
common-sense social interaction and communication permit ordinary
persons to locate themselves and others in meaningful schemes of
action. Their sense is generalized due to a common ability to locate
the *occasional*[11] or *indexical*[12] properties of talk and behaviour as
an essentially unthematic accomplishment:

> In exactly the way that persons are members to organized affairs,
> they are engaged in serious and practical work of detecting, demon-
> strating, persuading through displays in the ordinary occasions of
> their interactions the appearances of consistent, coherent, clear,
> chosen, planful arrangements. In exactly the ways in which a setting
> is organized, it consists of methods whereby its members are pro-
> vided with accounts of the setting as countable, storyable, proverbial,
> comparable, picturable, representable – i.e., *accountable events*.[13]

These basic ethical features of common-sense social and communicative competence are precisely the grounds presupposed

by Habermas's ideal speech community.[14] The critical task of this community would be seriously limited if it could not depend upon the vital competences of the everyday life-world:

> Such communication must therefore necessarily be rooted in social interests and in the value-orientations of a given social life-world. In both directions the feedback-monitored communication process is grounded in what Dewey called 'value beliefs'. That is, it is based on a *historically determined preunderstanding*, governed by social norms, of what is practically necessary in a concrete situation. This preunderstanding is a consciousness that can only be *enlightened hermeneutically*, through articulation in the discourse of citizens in the community.[15]

THE MUTUALITY OF COMMON SENSE AND SCIENTIFIC RATIONALITY

The common-sense attitude of everyday life is not just a given. It is something that is evinced in social conduct as part of an agent's grasp of how things are, as his or her ability to handle their social surroundings, relevant others, and their own 'face'. The attitude of everyday life is thus not simply a cognitive attitude, but also an expressive or *ethical competence*, which Garfinkel refers to under the concept of *trust*, that is, 'a person's compliance with the expectations of the attitude of *daily life as a morality*'.[16] Given that everyday action reveals an intrinsically ethical competence, we cannot submit it to the ironies of scientific reconstruction without altering the moral universe that is the field of social investigation. Thus it is necessary to come to understand the social scientist's conduct as itself a *form of life*,[17] governed by its own maxims for the conduct of rational inquiry. We cannot impose these standards upon lay members, as though the latter were otherwise incapable of meaningful action. Schutz formulates the structures of scientific interest and relevance as dependent upon maxims of conduct that require a radical break with the everyday life-world. The scientist suspends the spatiotemporal relevances motivated by his or her own presence in the world. They adopt a timeless and objective stance, in which space-time coordinates function solely to state the conditions for repeating an experiment. Because the scientist has no 'here' within the world, and is immune to the reciprocity of viewpoint, with its horizons of intimacy and generality, he or she is obliged to construct a *model actor*, to whom they impute a *rational consciousness* interacting with others destined similarly to act like any rational person:

> The homunculus is invested with a system of relevances originating in the scientific problem of his constructor and not in the particular biographically determined situation of an actor within the world. It is the scientist who defines what is to his puppet a Here and a There, what is within his reach, what is to him a We and a You or a They. The scientist determines the stock of knowledge his model has supposedly at hand. This stock of knowledge is not socially derived and, unless especially designed to be so, without reference to a social approval. The relevance system pertinent to the scientific problem under scrutiny alone determines its intrinsic structure, namely, the elements 'about' which the homunculus is supposed to have knowledge, those of which he has a mere knowledge of acquaintance, and those others he just takes for granted. With this is determined what is supposed to be familiar and what anonymous to him and on what level the typification of the experiences of the world imputed to him takes place.[18]

Schutz, however, is not content simply to cordon off lay practices of social theorizing from interference by the practice of scientific sociology. Rather, he insists that inasmuch as social scientists have no other subject matter than the self-interpreting practices of lay social interaction, they are obliged in their own accounts of social behaviour to meet the requirement of *the postulate of adequacy*:

> Each term used in a scientific system referring to human action must be so constructed that a human act performed within the life-world by an individual actor in the way indicated by the typical construction would be reasonable and understandable for the actor himself, as well as for his fellow-men. This postulate is of extreme importance for the methodology of social science. What makes it possible for a social science to refer at all to events in the life-world is the fact that the interpretation of any human act by the social scientist might be the same as that by the actor or by his partner.[19]

Giddens finds it difficult to accept the Schutzian postulate of adequacy. Taken along with the generally static conception of the stock of knowledge – although this is unfair to Schutz, as we shall see – the postulate of adequacy seems to limit sociology to the representation of received knowledge, which hardly seems useful to its critical purpose.[20] Because it focuses attention upon action as meaning rather than action as praxis, i.e., the practical realization of interests, it fails to give sufficient attention to *the problem of power* in social life. Moreover, these two issues are interrelated, inasmuch as the operation of power and the conflicts that arise over it are issues of differential interpretation of the 'same' idea system. Since the postulate of adequacy restricts the formation of technical concepts to the level of lay comprehension, it would hinder the development of a critical social science as the necessary instrument of social and political change. Giddens therefore seeks to reformulate the adequacy postulate in a more progressive version:

> The conceptual schemes of the social sciences therefore express a *double hermeneutic*, relating both to entering and grasping the frames of meaning involved in the production of social life by lay actors, and reconstructing these within new frames of meaning involved in technical conceptual schemes.[21]

The double hermeneutic of the social sciences may be given a progressive rather than conservative turn, Giddens argues, provided we take the actor's first order meanings to rest upon a shared symbolic framework which provides for the *communicative intent* of his actions to be given a conventional sense. Human interaction is successfully coordinated because all subjective meaning is logically and socio-logically dependent upon a shared but inarticulable background of *mutual knowledge*. How this differs so far from Schutz's or even Winch's position is hard to see, even supposing we accept the insistence upon the passivity of common-sense knowledge. It is with two further claims that Giddens believes his position to be quite distinct: 'The production of interaction has three fundamental elements: its constitution as 'meaningful'; its constitution as a moral order; and its constitution as the operation of relations of power'.[22]

In speaking of the *moral order of interaction*, Giddens argues that it is necessary to distinguish the *enabling* and the *constraining* features of norms and not to emphasize one aspect at the expense of the other. Interaction as a moral order involves a system of rights and duties which can be negotiated by actors, since its enforcement is dependent upon sanctions that do not fall upon them in the same way that the sun destroyed the wings of Daedalus. Thus it is clear that anyone breaking the law enters into a complex series of negotiations whereby the nature of the sanctions to be applied is determined with respect to the rights of both the plaintiff and the defendant. Furthermore, it is mistaken to assume that actors internalize the moral order without reservations. Social norms may be observed cynically, they may be exploited, subverted, or reformed. Indeed, as I have shown elsewhere,[23] we may expect these responses. Because the reflexive elaboration of the normative system of values, knowledge, science, law, and art is tied to the institutions of power, authority may be challenged by anyone decoding the official definition of reality, order, meaning, and value. Despite Giddens, an important element in the radical protest of the sixties, at least, was furnished by the subversive practices of interpretative sociology.

But rather than forget these efforts, we must face part of their lesson in what we may call *the paradox of social reform*. It is that we need to lean upon institutions in order to change them. Therefore, to some extent they must always be open to change, even when we find fault with them. What this means, as the New Left discovered, is that we cannot gain a leverage upon institutions by standing entirely outside of them. It is necessary, therefore, to avoid the absolute antithesis of good and evil attributed respectively to the conservative and radical positions, since this only forces a confrontation which narrows the available space for negotiation.[24] Worst of all, as in acts of terrorism, it may weaken the very fabric of society. In other words, then, even when we differ, we are obliged not to destroy the fundamental background assumptions of our society. Admittedly, this may involve moving to very general principles of agreement, but it may be preferable to the violence of civil war and terrorism.

The paradox of social reform, then, involves the avoidance of a reified version of social institutions which cuts off their members from morally intelligent dialogue about the values, directions, and capacities of these same institutions. The political arts involved here may be compared to the art whereby as speakers we turn language, which as an institution always precedes us, into a personal articulation of meaning and expression through which we realize ourselves. Although he protests against the analogy, Giddens has no better way than to appeal to the relation between language and speech in order to correct what he perceives as the failure of interpretative sociology to take account of the influence of large institutions of society. This is because he, too, needs some way to express a non-reified approach to the relations between structures and agency whereby he can account for the coexistence of order and change:

Interaction is constituted by and in the conduct of subjects; *structuration*, as the reproduction of practices, refers abstractly to the dynamic process whereby structures come into being. By the *duality of structure* I mean that social structures are both constituted *by* human agency, and yet at the same time are the very *medium* of this constitution. In sorting out the threads of how this happens we can again profit initially by considering the case of language. Language exists as a 'structure', syntactical and semantic, only insofar as there are some traceable consistencies in what people say, in the speech acts which they perform. From this aspect, to refer to rules and syntax, for example, is to refer to the reproduction of 'like elements'; on the other hand, such rules also *generate* the totality of speech acts which is the spoken language. It is this dual aspect of structure, as both inferred from observations of human doings, and yet also operating as a medium whereby those doings are made possible, that has to be grasped through the notions of structuration and reproduction.[25]

It is therefore curious that Giddens should want to locate the reification of institutions solely in the life-world of lay actors. His critique of interpretative sociology as an idealist hindrance to critical social analysis seems to rest upon nothing else than this scientist prejudice towards common-sense language. He believes that lay language alone refers to social institutions in a reified mode. It therefore fails to distinguish institutions as necessary *objectifications* of social interaction with their untoward consequences as *estranged, thing-like* obstacles to human purposes.[26] Yet he also notices that common sense is not impervious to expert knowledge and, thus, in his own words:

> This therefore raises the crucial questions: *In what sense are the 'stocks of knowledge'*, which actors employ to constitute or to make happen that very society which is the object of analysis, *corrigible in the light of sociological research and theory?*[27]

With this question Giddens turns full circle to reconsider the implications of the postulate of adequacy and the double hermeneutic of the social sciences. He rests his case on the claim that every competent social actor is him or herself a social theorist engaged in the ordinary course of their affairs in rational and instrumental appraisals of their actions. This is normal practice in Western societies, which are also characterized by the practice of social science: hence the two, after all, do have a certain affinity.

THE RADICALIZATION OF THE POSTULATE OF ADEQUACY

Giddens worries that Schutz's postulate of adequacy may lead sociology into the backwoods. Admittedly, Schutz's clarification of the postulate is minimal. But it surely is not intended to unstick sociology or economics, for which Schutz had an obvious admiration. What he had in mind is that all human sciences are just that – human achievements that in the most radical sense can never be totally alienated from ordinary human intelligibility and competence. Now, Schutz knew that none of us participates equally in the production and consumption of human knowledge, goods, and services. Indeed, in this regard he laid the foundations for a fundamental sociology of the social distribution of knowledge which would be the missing link in externalist, Marxist approaches to this problem.[28] Giddens is concerned with only one small linkage in this chain, whereas Schutz's canvas is very broad. For our purposes, it will be enough to draw upon his remarks upon the epistemological status of the well-informed citizen.[29] What Schutz has in mind is not just an attitude or a social type but a dimension of knowledge that in any individual may coexist with several others, which he differentiates as follows:

1 *the expert*: The expert's knowledge is restricted to a limited field, but therein it is clear and distinct. Expert opinions are based upon warranted assertions; judgements are not mere guesswork or loose suppositions;

2 *the man on the street*: The man or woman on the street has a working knowledge of many fields which are not necessarily coherent with one another. . . . This knowledge in all its vagueness is still *sufficiently* precise for the practical purpose at hand;

3 *the well-informed citizen:* On the one hand, the citizen neither is, nor aims at being, possessed of expert knowledge; on the other, the citizen does not acquiesce in the fundamental vagueness of a mere recipe knowledge or in the irrationality of unclarified passions and sentiments. To be well informed means to arrive at *reasonably founded* opinions in fields which are at least mediately of concern to the citizen.

Each of us may be a composite of these attitudes. In a complex society, depending upon achieved levels of education and access to publications and media, it is more likely that even the expert will be relatively ignorant of others' expertise. Hence we have the option of living with the imposition of others' knowledge that each of us accepts as a common citizen, or else we must strive to achieve some sort of educated understanding of matters outside our strict competence because of their general bearing upon our community. As I understand Schutz, he considered the attitude of the well-informed citizen to involve a special duty, if the political life of modern democracies is not to be handed over to technical experts. The duties of the well-informed citizen are:

1 to consider oneself perfectly qualified to decide who is a competent expert, and
2 to make up one's mind after having listened to opposing expert opinions.

Giddens never considers that the professionalization of the social sciences in the service of the administrative state maximizes the bureaucratic ethos and undermines the civic competence that Schutz and many others consider vital to democratic life. Incidentally, Schutz sharply distinguished the debased politics of public opinion from a democracy built upon the well-informed citizen. The latter is not just a romantic or populist construct of interpretative sociology. To become well-informed required that the citizen recognize his or her own laziness and prejudices. The same is true of the expert whose professionalized expertise renders him or her just as vulnerable as the man on the street with respect to specialities outside his own. Schutz states:

> A certain tendency to misinterpret democracy as a political institution in which the opinion of the uninformed man on the street must predominate increases the danger. It is the duty and the privilege, therefore, of the well-informed citizen in a democratic society to make his private opinion prevail over the public opinion of the man on the street.[30]

What the postulate of adequacy may be seen to require is *the institutionalization of the translatability and thereby accountability of expert knowledge* in order to raise the level of the well-informed citizen. Several institutions are potentially relevant: the schools and universities, the press, radio and television, trade unions, and political parties. In short, the postulate of adequacy implies the need to create a pedagogy that will subordinate expert knowledge to the needs of political democracy. Habermas has described the basic issues here,[31] although Giddens' account ignores this concern of critical theory;

and O'Neill has described the complementary colonial context of such a pedagogy, emphasizing that the issue of *relative illiteracy* can be generalized to urban, industrial problems.[32]

What the postulate of adequacy reminds us of is that what 'we' sociologists call society is in fact a plurality of worlds, each with its own lively structures of practical reasoning and belief. Thus, as everyone knows, we do not easily move from one little world to another in anything but a superficial way, as much dependent upon the tolerance of our hosts as on the superiority we attribute to ourselves as visitors and observers. This is true not only of travel, but *vis-à-vis* any trade, craft, or profession whose practices are not known to us firsthand. Inasmuch as social scientists are professionally devoted to crossing such frontiers, they need to remember that in broadening their minds they may well know less about everything. In fact, if we compare the practices of so-called comparative sociology with those that obtain in classical studies, very few sociologists have anything like the skills required to master local histories, languages, philosophies, art, and literature that are the basis of the monumental studies in these fields. Part of the professional sociological uneasiness with ethnomethodological studies, in my own opinion, derives from their commitment to the study of the orderliness of absolutely local phenomena, that is to say, with the fine arts whereby institutions come to have for their members a here-and-now objectivity that is for them 'the world'. This humbles sociological ambition. Moreover, I think, it challenges the deepest prejudice of all constructivist sociology, whether critical, Marxist, or whatever.

What Schutz, Garfinkel, and Marx all rejected is the prejudice that the everyway world is meaningless unless categorized by the social scientist. What underlies this prejudice is the expropriation of the Kantian discovery that nature is a subjective construction. Positively, the Kantian discovery *vis-à-vis* society, which is a *moral phenomenon* and not a natural phenomenon, is that the social world is an inter-subjective construction, a kingdom of ends that each wishes for all. It is curious that sociologists should indulge in ironies upon the poverty of common-sense knowledge and values when their own practices are unthinkable without such a background. In short, then, *we need to relativize science and common sense*, to allow for the positivity of common sense and to avoid the negativity of science in relation to it, thereby checking the pretension of science to absolute knowledge. Science waits no more than common sense upon logic for the construction of what is to be known in a manner external to the multiplicity of pratices whereby we come to treat things as real, unreal, true, false, efficient, consistent, and the like. Sociologists are quite mistaken in imagining that natural scientists apply to their own practices of discovery standards of rationality that are wholly external to the standard of *normal practice* prevailing in the community of science.[33] Moreover, as Schutz shows, we can account for how persons accommodate or deviate from the standards of their community of belief and action through the use of the notion of normal practice as a *regulatory concept* that is implicit in the very claim to membership in any epistemic community.[34] The postulate of adequacy reminds the sociologist that it is abortive to seek a standard of rationality that is external either to the community of belief and action under study, or to his or her own practices as a member of a scientific community.

Indeed, there is a considerable irony in the sociologist's self-exemption from the standards of common-sense knowledge and action, when, in fact, their own marginality may render them the least able to understand them, let alone see through them. Moreover, only a moment's reflection is required to recall the variety of opinion and belief within the sociological community as to the worth of its own enterprise. It cannot be sufficiently stressed that *the common-sense world is not a reified and unreflexive praxis*. It is full of art and humour, it is explored in literature, art, song, film, and comic strips. Common-sense knowledge is far from being a poor version of science. It is self-critical and, above all, capable of dealing with the contradictions and paradoxes of social life that otherwise drive sociologists off into utopias, anachronisms, and nostalgias that make ordinary people suspicious of the intellectual's grasp of reality. We ought to reject the social science stereotype of the rigidity of custom, habit, and instinct in human affairs. It involves a false contrast between traditional and modern societies, as well as an arrogant moral posture. As Michael Oakeshott has very well observed:

> Custom is always adaptable and susceptible to the *nuance* of the situation. This may appear a paradoxical assertion; custom, we have been taught, is blind. It is, however, an insidious piece of misobservation; custom is not blind; it is only 'blind as a bat'. And anyone who has studied a tradition of customary behaviour (or a tradition of any other sort) knows that both rigidity and instability are foreign to its character. And secondly, this form of the moral life is capable of change as well as of local variation.

Indeed, no traditional way of behaviour, no traditional skill, ever remains fixed; its history is one of continuous change.[35]

The liveliness and self-organizing nature of practical reason with respect to the contexts and local relevances of everyday life, is the fundamental ground of all sociological reflection and the touchstone of its praxis. This is not a rule of blind conservatism. It is rather a *conservationist argument*, one essential to the defence of the rationalities of everyday living against the inroads of scientistic sociology and its expert interventions that so often presume upon their privileged sense of the orders of living. The postulate of adequacy is therefore a basic proposition in what I have called *wild sociology*,[36] which ought to be understood as a great insistence upon *the kinship between sociology and common sense*.

Common-sense knowledge has been the butt of philosophy and science from the very beginning. It is only when philosophy and science reach the absurd heights of rationalism, scholasticism, and crippling asceticism that the voice of common-sense everyday knowledge gets a hearing. Then we look around for the suppressed resources of that other side of our moral tradition that has always been at grips with the dominance of scientism in philosophy, art, literature, and politics. In this tradition, as Gouldner suggests, the concept of everyday life has been an instrument as well as itself an object of struggle.[37] Throughout the ages, everyday life has been the source of resistance to the extraordinary, the mystifying, and the destructive heroism of the élites of religion, war, and commerce. The virtues of the everyday life are anti-heroic, unseen, and enduring. Gouldner likens everyday life to the kind of life Western societies have imposed upon women, and I have compared it to the family of man. In either case, everyday life does not simply lead us away from politics, as Giddens and others fear.

Rather, then, everyday life points up the nature of the realm of politics and history as a realm of crisis, of constant departures from ordinary life which is at the same time leaned upon for these very departures, sending its sons to war and its food to the towns, and suffering destruction or neglect in return. The sociologist who neglects the claims of everyday life promotes the realm of crisis. Forgetful of one's own attachment to everyday life, he or she then speaks of 'discovering' social reality. This way of talking, however, merely overlooks the massive fact of the *already known* everyday world. In viewing the very same considerations as those summarized in the postulate of adequacy, Gouldner joins his earlier conception of the reflexive sociologist to the task of defending everyday life from the critical neglect of the commonplace by social scientists.

The alternative to this attention to the commonplace is to treat people as things, which is to ally sociology with the forces that already seek to dominate them or to bring about their compliant subjugation. Much of the 'scientificity' of the study of humans is already in the paid service of this project of political control. Moreover, it is this ambition to subjugate people that makes it necessary for scientistic sociology to express so much concern with the construction of external accounting systems for discovering patterns or order and deviance in its subject populations. This is, admittedly, the hard work of normal sociology. It is, however, not welcome to the people. For as Gouldner argues, at best the findings of such sociology will seem 'obvious' or 'ordinary' to them. In this, however, they reject not only the narcissism of the sociologist but also his or her pretended omnipotence, their claim to have reached the bottom of lives and institutions from the outside and without the pains of ordinary existence. Is there any other way? This question will always divide sociologists, for it lies at the heart of the Western embrace of domination and its increasingly ambivalent response to its own success. In the meantime, the defence of everyday life, of common-sense knowledge and values constitutes the radical task of interpretative sociology. It requires that sociologists be prepared to set aside their narcissism in order to work as the underlabourers in the world of everyday life with which in all other respects they retain kinship.

NOTES

1 Giddens, A. (1976) *New Rules of Sociological Method*, London: Hutchinson University Library. This project is dependent upon his previous volume, *Capitalism and Modern Social Theory* (1971) Cambridge: Cambridge University Press, and his *Studies in Social and Political Theory* (1977) London: Hutchinson.

2 Giddens (1976) *New Rules of Sociological Method*, Op. cit., p. 8. These propositions are set down as the 'new' rules of sociological method in Giddens' concluding chapter. What is worse, his bald formulation of these propositions is unlikely to please even those within the field of interpretative sociology who take these propositions as something more than shibboleths and are by now involved with much more intricate issues of methodological procedure in their daily work as sociologists. For these practitioners, Giddens' critical comments merely summarize the normal

troubles of sociological work that cannot be escaped even in the resolutely quantitative practice of sociology.

3   O'Neill, J. (1980) 'From Phenomenology to Ethnomethodology: Some Radical "Misreadings"', in *Current Perspectives in Social Theory*, I, S.G. McNall and G. Howe (eds) Greenwich, Conn.: JAI Press, pp. 7–20.
4   O'Neill, J. (March 1972) 'Can Phenomenology Be Critical?' *Philosophy of the Social Sciences*, 2: 1–13; reprinted in *Phenomenology and Sociology: Selected Readings* (1978) T. Luckmann, (ed.) New York: Penguin, pp. 200–16.
5   Berger, P.L. and Luckmann, T. (1967) *The Social Construction of Reality*, New York: Doubleday, p. 15.
6   Mead, G.H. (1967) *Mind, Self, and Society*, ed. and Introduction C.W. Morris, Chicago: University of Chicago Press, pp. 155–6.
7   Simmel, G. 'How Is Society Possible?', in *Essays on Sociology, Philosophy and Aesthetics*, trans. and ed. K.H. Wolff, New York: Harper and Row, p. 344.
8   For an excellent discussion of Winch, see S.P. Turner (1980) *Sociological Explanation as Translation*, Cambridge: Cambridge University Press.
9   O'Neill, J. (1972) 'Self-Prescription and Social Machiavellianism', in his *Sociology as a Skin Trade*, New York: Harper and Row, pp. 11–19.
10 Goffman, E. (1967) *Interaction Ritual: Essays on Face-to-Face Behavior*, New York: Doubleday Anchor, p. 31.
11 Husserl, E. (1970) *The Crisis of European Sciences and Transcendental Phenomenology: An Introduction to Phenomenological Philosophy*, trans. D. Carr, Evanston, Ill.: Northwestern University Press, p. 122.
12 Bar-Hillel, Y. (1970) 'Indexical Expressions', in his *Aspects of Language*, Jerusalem: The Magnes Press, pp. 69–88.
13 Garfinkel, H. (1967) *Studies in Ethnomethodology*, Englewood Cliffs, NJ: Prentice-Hall, p. 34.
14 Habermas, J. (1979) 'What Is Universal Pragmatics?', in his *Communication and the Evolution of Society*, trans. T.A. McCarthy, Boston: Beacon Press, pp. 1–68.
15 Habermas, J. (1970) 'The Scientization of Politics and Public Opinion', in his *Toward a Rational Society*, trans. J.J. Shapiro, Boston: Beacon Press, pp. 68–9.
16 Garfinkel, H. (1963) 'A Concept of, and Experiment with, "Trust" as a Condition of Stable Concerted Action', in *Motivation and Social Interaction*, J.O. Harvey (ed.) New York: Ronald Press, pp. 187–238.
17 Weber, M. (1958) 'Science as a Vocation', in *From Max Weber: Essays in Sociology*, trans. and ed. H.H. Gerth and C. Wright Mills, New York: Oxford University Press, pp. 129–56. Cf. H. Martins (1972) 'The Kuhnian "Revolution" and Its Implications for Sociology', in *Imagination and Precision in the Social Sciences*, T.J. Nossiter, A.H. Hanson, and S. Rokkan (eds) London: Faber and Faber, pp. 13–58.
18 Schutz, A. (1964) 'Concept and Theory Formation in the Social Sciences', *Collected Papers*, I, Natanson, M. (ed.) The Hague: Martinus Nijhoff, pp. 41–2.

19 Schutz, A. (1964) 'The Problem of Rationality in the Social World', *Collected Papers*, II, ed. and intro. A. Brodersen, The Hague: Mouton, pp. 85–6.
20 See Giddens' remarks on the problem of adequacy in his *New Rules*, Op. cit., pp. 148–54, and in his *Central Problems in Social Theory* (1979) London: Macmillan, pp. 245–53.
21 Giddens, *New Rules*, p. 79.
22 Ibid., p. 104.
23 See J. O'Neill (1972) 'Part II: On Language and the Body Politic', in his *Sociology as a Skin Trade*, Op. cit.
24 The problem of the nature of violence in liberal society and the criteria for the use of violence in a socialist revolution is treated at length, from a phenomenological perspective, in J. O'Neill, 2: 'Merleau-Ponty's Critique of Marxist Scientism', *Canadian Journal of Social and Political Theory* (Winter 1977–8), 33–62.
25 Giddens, *New Rules*, pp. 121–2.
26 For an analysis of the notions of objectification, reification, and estrangement, see J. O'Neill (1972) 'The Concept of Estrangement in the Early and Later Writings of Karl Marx', in his *Sociology as a Skin Trade*, pp. 113–36.
27 Giddens (1974) *New Rules*, p. 115; my emphasis.
28 Schutz, A. and Luckmann, T. *The Structures of the Life World*, trans. R.M. Zaner and H.T. Engelhardt, Jr., London: Heinemann.
29 Schutz, A. (April 1979) 'The Well-Informed Citizen: An Essay on the Social Distribution of Knowledge', *Collected Papers*, II, pp. 120–34. Cf. Roger Jehensen, 'The Social Distribution of Knowledge in Formal Organizations: A Critical Theoretical Perspective', *Human Studies*, 2: 111–29.
30 Schutz, 'The Well-Informed Citizen', p. 134.
31 Habermas, 'The Scientization of Politics and Public Opinion', pp. 62–80.
32 O'Neill, J. (1974) 'Le langage et la décolonisation: Fanon et Freire', *Sociologie et Sociétés*, VI, pp. 53–65.
33 O'Neill, J. (1981) 'The Literary Production of Natural and Social Science Inquiry', *The Canadian Journal of Sociology*, 6, Spring, pp. 105–20.
34 Barnes, S.B. (1972) 'Sociological Explanation and Natural Science: A Kuhnian Reappraisal', *Archives Européennes de Sociologie*, XIII: 373–91.
35 Oakeshott, M. (1948) 'The Tower of Babel', *Cambridge Journal*, 2, as quoted in Winch, *The Idea of a Social Science*, pp. 62–3.
36 O'Neill, J. (1974) *Making Sense Together*, New York: Harper and Row.
37 Gouldner, A.W. (1976) 'Sociology and the Everyday Life', in *The Uses of Controversy in Sociology*, L.A. Coser and O.N. Larsen (eds) New York: Macmillan, pp. 417–33.

Chapter 9

The mutuality of science and common sense
An essay on political trust

Here I want to return to the question of the constitutive grounds of society and the life-worlds of knowledge and trust. I do so because there is a considerable danger that the post-rationalist critique of the metaphysics of presence (Derrida) and consensus (Lyotard) will convey the impression that human institutions can be contracted in mistrust and intractable minoritarianism – a view that Giddens courts as a consequence of (post) modernity. The latter view might represent a viable strategy on the level of secondary, bureaucratic institutions, but it cannot be generalized to the level of primary institutions and life-world relationships. I think it necessary, as I have said earlier, for us to present our own analysis of the grounds of sociability rather than to trade upon the social and political fall-out from post-rationalist theory. This exercise will also prepare the ground for our arguments regarding the mutuality of knowledge, common sense and science and for our views on the basic communicative ethics of civil institutions and our social debt to past and future generations.

Before any consideration of the question 'How is Society Possible?' we should note that this is not merely a problem sociologists raise when haunted by the ghosts of philosophy. Thus those who dismiss the question as 'philosophical', because of its kinship with Kant's speculations on the a priori constitution of nature, might be reminded that the same question concerned both the practical Hobbes and Machiavelli. These two for all their tough-mindedness, answered the question in terms of a theory of human nature which still left the preconditions of order, or the inter-subjective bases of recognition and virtue, undetermined by the protocols of violence and divine fiat on which they rested the social order.

The problem of order is, of course, as much a question about the subjective nature of social reality or its meaningfulness and value as an inquiry into the nature of the moral and political order. These questions in turn involve us in a conception of knowledge and rationality that implicitly determines the theory of conduct and congruent social order, as we have seen in Chapter 4. Thus the question of the possibility of society poses simultaneously a problem in the sociology of knowledge. It raises questions concerning the ultimate legitimacy of the formal and substantive modes of rationality as well as questions concerning the institutionalization of the sentimental bases of rationality, contract, and order, examined in Chapters 2 and 3.

It is no longer obvious how we should relate the moral claim of everyday conceptions of identity and order to the sociological reconstruction of these phenomena determined by the standards of scientific rationality and its own organizational claims. The problem here is not simply that the paradigm of natural science observation and theory construction does not answer to the interference problem produced by the interaction between the social scientist and the object of study, for similar effects can be found in experimental science. The essential distinction between the natural and social sciences which makes the standard of rationality fostered by the social sciences intrinsically a problem of the sociology, if not the politics, of knowledge is that human relationships, customs, and institutions are not merely 'orders' produced by scientific reconstruction. The human order is initially a pretheoretical conduct resting on the unarticulated 'common-sense' knowledge of others as 'kindred' when they experience dependable needs and wants expressed in the 'relevances' of the human body, time, and place. The nature of this order cannot be settled through a dogmatic rationalism which subordinates common-sense knowledge of individual and social life to the standards of realism and objectivism which are maxims of scientific conduct but not obviously normative for all social praxes. Indeed, a fundamental task of the sociology of knowledge must be its reflexive concern with the grounds of *communication* between everyday common-sense reason and scientific rationality. Such a concern would answer to the needs of a democratic society. By the same token, this civic concern cannot be ruled by antagonism and minoritarianism.

I will relate ever so briefly the desirable relationship between scientific knowledge and common-sense knowledge. At the same time, I want to raise the larger question of political trust invested in the social sciences by democratic societies. In order to bring these issues into focus, I shall raise a question which I refer to as the problem of the mutuality of accounts. I raise this question because I think it requires us to see the everyday practices of common-sense knowledge and the rational procedures of scientific method as interdependent practices. I want to argue that it is false to separate social rationality into rigid categories of common-sense and scientific knowledge, but most important, I believe that we cannot rely upon the presumption of an unexamined subordination of common-sense knowledge to scientific knowledge. Today, we must recognize that knowledge, whether in the hands of party bureaucrats or professional experts, is a political trust that must be made accountable, legally and morally speaking, to popular understanding. The issue of what information we should act on is not decidable on the grounds that the procedures of science are superior to those of common sense and lay practice, merely because the latter do not meet the same standards of rational or methodic accountability. I shall deal first with the purely methodological issue before turning to the problem of the ways in which institutions shape scientific knowledge and public opinion.

COMMON SENSE AND SCIENTIFIC ACCOUNTS

I propose now to contrast 'accountable' common sense, or the natural attitude of daily life, and the 'accountable' rational procedures of the scientific attitude.

We owe to Schutz a basic attempt to restore the rationality of everyday life and to show how it could never be replaced by the paradigm of scientific rationality. His argument should not be interpreted as an espousal of irrationalism or as anti-science; it simply advocates a responsible tension in the life of reason that is shared by all, without being peculiar to the calling of science. Schutz points out that in order to interpret human action, to evaluate its empirical adequacy, its delusions and errors, sociologists, of whom Weber and Parsons are the outstanding examples, have conceived of action in terms of the paradigm of instrumentally rational activity, i.e., conduct that for any external observer is directed to the 'best' adaptation of given resources to given ends. Before we dismiss people's ordinary, but largely unexamined and untaught, competences as inferior reasoning, we need, Schutz argues, to distinguish between various elements of common-sense rationality.[1] We can then see whether they are reducible – or whether they even need to be reduced to the pattern of scientific rationality. We may distinguish the following cases:

1 Where 'rational' is synonymous with reasonable, the common-sense use of cookbook knowledge is certainly rational.
2 Rational action may be equated with deliberate action. There are, however, general senses of the notion of deliberation:
   (a) Common-sense action is deliberate in so far as it invokes the considerations upon which its practices were originally based.
   (b) Common-sense action is deliberate where it sees the applicability of past knowledge to a present situation.
   (c) Common-sense action is deliberate in the same sense as is any action that is motivated by some anticipated end.
   (d) Common-sense action, by its very nature, is not deliberate in the sense of engaging in an elaborate rehearsal of competing lines of action.

In stricter terms scientifically rational action may be understood as:

1 Planned action.
2 Predictable action.
3 Logical action.
4 Decision-ruled action.

The last four items are quite problematic in themselves. We can hardly doubt that everyday life involves planning and predicting. The trouble is that people are committed to schemes and projects that involve long spans of time and encompass roundabout means to their ends. At any time we cannot, as a scientific observer hopes, easily carve out the 'unit-acts', i.e., the simple means–end scheme that would account for everyday conduct. By the same token everyday life cannot rely upon the ideals of conceptual clarity and the distinctions espoused by logicians, since people advance ideas and employ talk only within the limits of their own situations. Finally, the concept of action based upon rational choice is applicable to everyday life in that it refers to choices best directed to serve an actor's purposes, provided the actor has given knowledge. But if this means choice guided by the rationality of the knowledge on which the very choice is based, then this is not a practice of everyday life, nor can it provide a methodological principle for the interpretation of everyday conduct. This is because the postulate of rational action presupposes that the observer:

1 Has knowledge of the place of the actor's end in terms of his or her overall plans, which must also be known to the actor.

2 Knows the relationship of the actor's end with his or her other ends and its compatibility or incompatibility.
3 Has knowledge of the describable and indescribable consequences that might arise for the actor in achieving this end.
4 Has knowledge independent of the actor of all the technically possible means of achieving this end, as well as of all their mutual interferences.
5 Has knowledge of all the means of accomplishing this end that are actually within the actor's reach.
6 Has knowledge, in view of the social nature of action, of the interpretations and misunderstandings of the actor's conduct by his or her peers.
7 Has knowledge of the ends of the reactions of these peers to the actor.
8 Has knowledge of all the elements (1–5) that the actor attributes to others.
9 Has knowledge of the overall structure of the levels of intimacy and anonymity within which the actor pursues his or her ends among his or her peers.

Schutz concludes that the notion of rational action is so idealized that it is not to be found anywhere in the world, and so it cannot be used either to fault everyday standards of practical reasoning or to provide a model for their interpretation. Where, then, do we find use for the notion of the rational actor? Schutz answers that the model of the rational actor is to be regarded as a theoretical construct through which sociologists seek to give to their own knowledge and interest in the analysis of social order the status of scientifically rational knowledge. In other words the postulate of rational action is a maxim of sociological analysis. It requires that the steps to the solution of a sociological problem be constructed in such a way that:

1 They remain in full compatibility with the rules that define scientifically correct decisions of grammar and procedure.
2 All the elements be conceived in full clearness and distinctness.
3 The clarification of the body of knowledge, as well as the rules of investigative and interpretative procedure, be treated as a first-priority project.
4 The projected steps contain only scientifically verifiable assumptions that have to be in full compatibility with the whole of scientific knowledge.

The premise that instrumentally rational action is the dominant sociological frame of reference is thoroughly dependent upon the institutions of exchange, economy, and legal-rational bureaucracy that are the setting of modern society. Furthermore, scientific conduct is, in fact, ruled only by the norms of empirically adequate reasoning. This claim is hotly disputed, however, particularly when we conceive the broad process of scientific imagination and discovery and look closely at the processes of argument and proof in the community of scientists.[2] Thus, we cannot hastily accept the idea that scientific rationality and everyday reasoning are the same. Moreover, since sociology has as its subject matter the everyday self-interpreted conduct of humankind, and not an external nature that is indifferent to scientific formulations of it, we may find that we have to treat sociological reasoning as yet another practice of rationality. If we are not aware of these differences, we simply conspire with the most general process of rationalization in our lives, namely, that increasing organization and predictability, which Weber himself regarded as the 'disenchantment of the world', and the iron cage of bureaucracy. We succumb to the institutions which take the magic out of living, depriving life of its charm and excitement as well as of its ordinary but manageable muddles.

THE POLITICS OF RATIONAL ACCOUNTS

To this point we have examined the presumptions of rationality in the theories and methods through which sociologists seek to produce scientific knowledge of persons and society. We have tried to show the principal differences between modes of rationality that constitute everyday, common-sense knowledge and sociological knowledge of social action. An educated person must learn to bring together the claims of these two rationalities, so that they do not ignore common sense in favour of science, or indulge a blind faith in the authority of science, ignoring its working difficulties. The issue here, then, is that of the political accountability to which experts must be held, and to which they should be open in order to preserve a democratic community. In complex societies there is a great need for specialized knowledge; usually this can only be acquired by full-time social scientists. Inevitably, professional scientists want to formulate and apply their knowledge to problems of urban development, race, or family disorders, but in a democracy we are committed to the belief that judgement of human conduct is best regarded as a common affair, as in trial by jury. We surrender to experts and élites only at great risk to the republic.

We can perhaps now bring together our earlier discussion of common-sense knowledge and values to show how they bear upon the politics of defining the situation, the goals and means, in which lay populations come to deal with professional social scientists and social planners. A proper respect for the lay community's sense of reasonableness and responsibility would lead to the following observations:

1 The sociologist must in the first instance study lay versions of social problems and remedies.
2 Lay versions of social problems will be found to be highly problematic.
3 The problematic nature of social problems means that basic conflicts will exist between sociological and lay definitions of social problems.
4 In view of these conflicts inherent in lay definitions of social problems and remedies, the sociologist cannot treat his or her own objective formulation of problems and remedies as completely free of continued discussion and dispute.

The problematic nature of social problems and their remedies is inherent in common-sense sociability. Thus, we tend to locate troubles and remedies as matters of individual responsibility, although we also hold to the view that sociability itself implicates us in chains of events for which we may be held responsible only in a general way. In America this is especially the case, since American freedoms and civil rights were originally built upon the responsibilities of private ownership and decentralized forms of government. As business and government move into centralized and large-scale corporate organizations, America faces the dual problems of the erosion of lay opinion and common-sense morality while struggling to develop responsible central government and corporate business practice. It is, therefore, presumptuous of social scientists to imagine that they can inhabit the middle ground, and from there, hold the nation together. Yet, there is a serious sense in which this is precisely the challenge of the social sciences, provided it can be taken up with humility and consideration for the differences in communities and persons that still exist despite the massive centralizing forces within modern society.

SCIENCE AND PUBLIC KNOWLEDGE

We are faced with the enormous task of finding communicative institutions that can mediate the authority of science and technology. These institutions must be geared to the essentially administrative tasks of the state, as well as the ideals of civic understanding and the consensus that motivates democratic societies. This problem is stated in the sharpest terms by Jürgen Habermas:

> But if technology proceeds from science, and I mean the technique of influencing human behavior no less than that of dominating nature, then the assimilation of this technology into the practical life-world, bringing the technical control of particular areas within the reaches of the communication of acting men, really requires scientific reflection. The pre-scientific horizon of experience becomes infantile when it naively incorporates contact with the products of the most intensive rationality.[3]

It should be clear, then, that the preceding argument has not distinguished the methodological standing of common sense and scientific reasoning simply to indulge the 'infantile disorder' of left-wing phenomenology. The argument is also intended to contribute radically to the place of common-sense communicative competence in the political processes of modern democracy. This is, however, too large a matter to settle, and for the moment what we wish to show are the general outlines of the problem, which we think underlies a shift in perspective that may be addressed as the linguistic turn in the social sciences. This shift represents the combined effect of ordinary language philosophy, particularly after Wittgenstein, phenomenology, hermeneutics, and critical theory, especially Habermas's theory of communicative competence. Leaving aside the intricacies of these developments, what they permit us to do is to formulate the communicative relation between social science and democracy as the proper background for the specific role of sociology's particular ambivalence with regard to the relative claims of scientific and common-sense accounts of persons and society. Within the limits of the present inquiry, we cannot do more than indicate the general features of the communicative approach to political resources and locate the problem of fostering mediating institutions of public discussion called for by the relativization of common sense and scientific knowledge of social structure and social change:

Such communication must therefore necessarily be rooted in social interests and in the value-orientations of a given social life-world. In both directions the feedback-monitored communication process is grounded in what Dewey called 'value beliefs'. That is, it is based on a *historically determined preunderstanding*, governed by social norms, of what is practically necessary in a concrete situation. This preunderstanding is a consciousness that can only be *enlightened hermeneutically*, through articulation in the discourse of citizens in a community....

Weber's thesis of the neutrality of the sciences with regard to preexisting practical valuations can be convincingly employed against illusionary rationalizations of political problems, against *short-circuiting* the connection between technical expertise and a public that can be influenced by manipulation, and against the distorted response which scientific information meets with in a deformed public realm.[4]

THE COMMUNICATIVE MODEL OF DEMOCRACY

Without underestimating the complexity of social and political decision making – any more than it should be pessimistically overestimated – we may formulate the problem of the relationship between science and democracy as a communicative task addressed to the mobilization of members' commitment to the goals and institutionalized allocations of scientific and technical resources employed to translate social goals into daily conveniences, rewards, and deterrents. Thus, the legitimacy of a democratic political system consists of the processes that lead to the achievement of the following descriptive states:

1 Its members have access to the information channels whereby social goals are articulated.
2 In varying degrees, its members are aware of and feel entitled to exercise their rights in the translation of subjective needs into specific and local allocations of resources.
3 Its members' troubles with the determinate processes of resource allocation establish prima-facie claims for reforms at level 2 or change of social goals at level 1.

The interrelationship, or loop effect, between these three processes represents the democratic legitimation process as the constitution of a communicative community, in which the channels between scientists and politicians are opened to responses and reformulations directed through the channels of public opinion.

The validity of a democratic political system rests in the reference of its goals and resource allocations to parliamentary and electoral ratification, which brings political decisions within the social contract. Characteristically, the processes of political legitimation in capitalistic society involve public debate, public information, news media, journalism, and the institutions of public education. These institutions are conceived mostly to reinforce the belief that political life can be exemplary of rational and just conduct, at the same time that the polity accommodates the sheer necessities and incommodities of economic and social life.

The processes of legitimation and delegitimation, however, assume particular features in the present context of state-administered capitalism. In this situation the legitimation process becomes an intrinsic function of political economy and not an epiphenomenal exercise, as Marxists might argue. A large part of the present capitalist economy consists in the activity of state enterprises that do not merely complement or correct the private-market system but which largely determine the parameters of economic activity. Therefore, an essential task of the legitimation process is to secure allegiance to the new schedule of public and private production. A second major feature of this process is the political socialization of large numbers of persons who enjoy goods and services without direct employment in either sector of the economy. In short, employment in the public sector and consumption of health, education, and welfare from that sector without corresponding inputs defines a large population whose loyalty to the political system cannot be identified in terms of previous class and motivational attitudes.

Under these conditions the legitimation problem in which the social sciences are involved acquires the following distinct features:

1 The market system can no longer be legitimated in terms of its power to mobilize the bourgeois ideology of private exchange.
2 The central administrative role of the state in the economy must be legitimated.
3 The administrative role of the state must be maintained independently of the mechanisms of formal participation in democratic politics.
4 The legitimation process requires the mobilization of diffuse mass loyalty without direct participation.
5 The depoliticization of the public realm requires (a) civic privatism, i.e., the pursuit of consumption, leisure, and careers in exchange

for political abstinence; (b) the ideological justification of public depoliticization by means of élitist theories of the democratic process or by technocratic and professionalized accounting practices that rationalize administrative power.

The social sciences are engaged at all levels in the administration of the large institutions of industrial democracies. Numerous commentators have drawn attention to the consequent problems of trust and accountability involved in the practice of sociology. Sociologists, like everyone else, have a self-image: they are themselves as inheritors of the Enlightenment legacy of liberal rationalism; they challenge the authority of high places, and the ignorance of the lowly, in order to bring us all into the republic of knowledge and freedom. Sociologists like to think of themselves as a free-floating, intellectual élite, working on behalf of a demystified society in which human energies are committed to reaching their fullest potential. Sociologists claim to challenge the system, to question authority and convention. They are the friends of the poor, the exploited, and of all who suffer social injustice. Yet sociologists, for the most part, live middle-class lives and are dependent upon establishment institutions for their employment and also for the huge sums of money required to conduct their research. These requirements, in fact, penetrate to the very core of the ways in which sociologists *do* sociology. The administrative demands, then, of the social sciences impose the following conditions upon the formulation of sociological knowledge:

1 The rationalization of the administered society requires that scientific discourse be problem-specific and subject to decision making.
2 The very nature of the language and reportage of the social sciences contributes to the administrative effort to manage behaviour and institutions according to maximum efficiency standards.
3 The ability of the administered society to command allegiance in exchange for goods and services reduces political participation to the demand for information and to the residual right to withdraw loyalty in elections.
4 The combined effects of these processes (1–3) on the communicative competence of citizens is that discourse about the ideal values of political, economic, and social life is seen as irrelevant to the management of modern states.

To many critics the jargon of the social sciences is a laughable matter. To others, who also recognize it as the pretension of an immature science, there is the more sober conviction that as the social sciences achieve political recognition, their rhetoric will grow more modest:

> The maturity of a science may be measured not only by its power, but by its discrimination in knowing the limits of its power. And if this is so, the layman does not need to worry lest the social sciences, as they become more scientific, will be more likely to usurp political authority. On the contrary, they will stop short of trying to solve completely our major political problems not because they are unlike the natural sciences, but to the extent that they are like them. And the more they get to be like them, the more they will be of a specific service to the policy maker, and the less they will pretend that their methods can measure all relevant aspects of any concrete problem and supply its final answer.[5]

THE LIMITS OF SOCIOLOGICAL KNOWLEDGE

We cannot be sure, however, that the limits of science will be remembered by sociologists as they get closer to the centres of political power. It is likely, too, that politicians will find the rhetoric of a pseudoscientific sociology more congenial than the rigorous language of science. It is, therefore, incumbent upon sociologists to monitor their own rhetoric, to keep what is properly sociological in their speech along with the broader understandings and values of the democratic society to which they owe their existence. Sociologists must strive to increase human understanding and self-control, not for the purpose of making a small part of the earth or one class of persons more precious than others, but in order to mine the inexhaustible resources of humanity. In this task sociology must try to build up sure knowledge that is free from prejudice and jargon. Still, it cannot blindly pursue science's dominion over nature. Sociology has no external referent; it is only another way of addressing people, who do not wait on science, still less on sociology, for their living. Nor are they likely to set aside everything they have found valuable in the plain course of living in favour of a partial speech and minor knowledge. To remember this subjects sociology to a pedagogical rule of limit and dialogue. Sociology should not aspire to domination, or technical control over humans, because the human collectivity is properly motivated only through a consensus of unarticulated affinities and shared deliberations. Such a collectivity does not destructively deny its past ways, nor is it blind to the present, but it does distrust manipulation and is wary of those without local allegiances or any limits.

People are more likely to welcome sociology if it avoids criticizing others as a means of placing itself above others. And perhaps because sociology lacks the élitist tradition of humanist culture and the power and authority of the physical sciences, it may well prove to have an average self-consciousness that resists splitting humans into either scientists or laymen. Ideally, sociology should be a popular science. It may be subverted by its own professional concerns, but this makes sociology no worse than any of the sciences that claim to serve humans. The roots of sociology's problem lie in political economy. We cannot extrapolate the benefits of science, industry, and education from the system of political economy, class, and international stratification in which they are embedded. It is quite easy to devise scientific utopias that are unrelated to the harsh world of political economy. Occasionally, sociology has appeared capable of providing a neutral administrative science of human organization that could cut across these problems, but sociology has had to learn that it cannot work upon society's problems without being part of society – and that this involves the risk of being absorbed into the goods and evils of the very society it seeks to remedy.

It may be said that I have set sociology against its subjects without addressing how its subjects are to be set against sociology – as would suit current perceptions of the irremediably ideological nature of all sciences. But I do not believe in the current version of the difference between the sciences and the life-world. This is because I believe that the forgetfulness of science may be corrected by common-sense memory and tradition which remain the necessary carriers of the arts and sciences. However, nothing corrects the forgetfulness of our contemporary ideologies that rewrite history, gender, and race. Our current minoritarian moralities expropriate the suffering and hopes of humankind. The sorrow of humankind exceeds all disadvantage and disability and lays upon us an historical debt that cannot be repaid through contemporary declarations of intolerance whose indifference to the dark corners of the world is deepened by the light which minor morality plays now attract to themselves.

NOTES

1   Schutz, A. (1964) 'The problem of rationality in the social world', in his *Collected papers, II, Studies in Social Theory*, ed. and introduced by

A. Brodersen, The Hague: Martinus Nijhoff.
2 Phillips, D.L. (1972) *Wittgenstein and Scientific Method: A Sociological Perspective*, Totowa, NJ: Rowman and Littlefield.
3 Habermas, J. (1970) *Toward a Rational Society: Student Protest, Science and Politics*, trans. J.J. Shapiro, Boston: Beacon Press, p. 56.
4 Habermas, J. (1976) *Legitimation Crisis*, trans. T. McCarthy, Boston: Beacon Press, pp. 69–70.
5 Price, D.K. (1965) 'The established dissenters', in *Science and Culture: A Study of Cohesive and Disjunctive Forces*, G. Holton (ed.) Boston: Houghton Mifflin, p. 133.

Conclusion
The common-sense case against post-rationalism

In the last decade, we have witnessed a considerable celebration of
the collapse of Western metaphysics. Philosophers and literary
theorists have persuaded social and political thinkers that they have
been working with contaminated concepts, discourses and texts that
are rotten with false binarisms, outworn subject and object representations and, worst of all, full with a phallic-physics whose power
is now spent. The collapse of Western metaphysics should bring down
with it, of course, both capitalism and communism. Thus postmodern
celebrants can congratulate themselves upon a doubled criticism which
appears to have had an historical effect beyond anything dreamed
of by the *ancien régime* of critical thought and enlightened reason.
Anyone who remains doubtful about whether binarism and phallicism
are the pillars of the Western tradition without which it will collapse
as soon as their rotten core is exposed shows that they have been
asleep during the most excited period of critical thought. Once awake,
however, common-sense sceptics will have to dance the dance of difference, breakdown and discontinuity with nothing to hold on to –
no tradition, no text, no subject and no story to remember. Their
eyes will have to adjust to the bright lights of postmodernism with
its sparkling signifiers flashing out momentary values against a great
black sky of nonsense.

I have tried to make the counter argument to post-rationalism from
the twin standpoints of *common-sense values* and *embodied rationalism*
that I have drawn from the cross-fertilization of phenomenology and
Marxism. I believe that the perspective of phenomenological Marxism,
which I have developed in the preceding chapter devoted to the theme
of mutual knowledge, cannot be so readily disposed of as we might
believe were only the siren voices of Derrida, Foucault and Lyotard
to prevail.[1] Since I have paid considerable attention elsewhere[2] to

these writers, I should say that on this occasion I have been concerned with them only in the same rough and ready way that oppositional figures deserve. In short, I am 'just gaming' with them as do Lyotard or Derrida with the tradition to which they are opposed.[3] I have not taken them on with anything like the effort made by Habermas[4] in his twelve lectures designed to sink French poststructuralism in the bog of German Romanticism and its gaseous byproducts of nihilism and fascism. Like his opponents, Habermas is a strong 'misreader' and I have commented upon his work in other contexts.[5] Here I have tried to show how we might retain Habermas's critical programme with the help of the phenomenological emphasis upon radical structures of common-sense knowledge and values and at the same time point to the search for community and history against the postmodern abandonment of the great history of knowledge and freedom.

Edward Said claims to have discerned within the general weakening of the will to 'filiation' that characterizes modernism – and hence the fall into postmodernism – a reverse movement towards what he calls 'affiliation'. The latter movement seeks to rethink human relationships and to remove them from the exclusionary model of the colonial canon of what constitutes humanism:

> Thus if a filial relationship was held together by natural bonds and natural forms of authority – involving obedience, fear, love, respect, and instinctual conflict – the new affiliative relationship changes these bonds into what seems to be trans-personal forms – such as guild consciousness, consensus, collegiality, professional respect, class and the hegemony of a dominant culture. The filiative scheme belongs to the realms of nature and of 'life', whereas affiliation belongs exclusively to culture and society.[6]

Although Said's concept of affiliation is a step in the right direction, it is weakened through what it loses by its abstraction from the sociological events upon which it draws. We therefore cannot expect to be enriched by re-importing this notion rather than replacing it with our own sociological account. Despite his considerable flirtation with postmodernism, Jameson has the merit of drawing more deeply upon the sociological tradition in a surprising blend of Durkheim and Marx which we have examined because of its bold invocation of the *sacred* as the unsurpassable figure of human community:

> Durkheim's view of religion (which we have expanded to include cultural activity generally) as a symbolic affirmation of human relationships, along with Heidegger's conception of the work of art as a symbolic enactment of the relationship of human beings to the nonhuman, to Nature and to Being, are in this society false and ideological; but they will know their truth and come into their own at the end of what Marx calls prehistory. At that moment, then, the problem of the opposition of the ideological to the Utopian, or the functional-instrumental to the collective, will have become a false one.[7]

Whatever sympathy we may have for the attempts by Said and Jameson to pull back from the postmodern surge, we cannot borrow from them what they have picked from sociology. We must therefore address postmodernism, post-rationalism and post-Marxism on our own ground. At stake in the current wave of post-rationalism, as I see it, are the following issues:

1 Can there be a radical historical narrative?
2 Is there a radical agent – the artist-hero, the proletariat, humanity – of the humanization of man/woman-kind?
3 Has Marxism lost all credibility as the hermeneutical science inscribed within the emancipatory history of humanity?

Cutting across these questions is the failed history of Communism and perhaps of Christianity, although there is a vast difference of scale involved – which has obliged the Left to elaborate an auto-critique on the following issues:

4 Marxist scientism.
5 Communicative ethics.
6 The colonization, or reduction of the life-worlds of the city, family, gender, nature and 'other' worlds to their vicarious versions replayed in a mass culture generated by multinational corporate capitalism which systematically forecloses the double question of stratification and colonialism internal and external to nation states.

It would be foolish for anyone to attempt to present all of these issues in a single synthesis. Each of us works with as much or as little of the synthesis of knowledge that our competence permits, so long as we do not ignore the synthesis as a regulative principle of knowledge. In my opinion, Lyotard's views of the postmodern condition are outrageous because they glibly violate the regulative principle of socio-historical synthesis in a Pacman, video-game distortion of Wittgenstein's deference to the limits of the life-world as the limit of sceptical violation. Lyotard plays Lilliputian games on the Habermasian corpus as though Habermas were a Gulliver incapable of feeling any part of his body because of his Hegelian gigantomania. Lyotard's phraseology whips around the regulative ideal of the speech community as though the latter were a communist jukebox with only one record to play. The fault of totalitarianism or 'exclusionism' is thrown at every vision of community in the strangest of all claims, namely, that it is foolish, on the one hand, to believe that capitalism can ever exhaust heterogeneity, and criminal, on the other hand, to embrace socialism because it necessarily excludes heterogeneity. Capitalist economics are presumably easier on the libido than communist economics. Similarly, Lyotard recommends abandoning the grand Enlightenment story of emancipatory knowledge because this no longer frames the strategic inquiries of the information sciences in late capitalism.[8] Lyotard's Marxism and Freudianism are thus doubly positivist. This, as I see it, is the brunt of *'Lyo-retardism'* and of what must be resisted in his brand of post-rationalism.

Deconstructionism and poststructuralism have advanced postmodernism by benefiting from the embarrassment of representationism. Having discovered the fictional element in realism, postmodernists challenge anyone to cling to objects, meanings or even to themselves – as though such demands upon sense and intelligibility represented nothing but an anaclitic disorder or an ability to enter the game of Fort/Da! Lyotard taunts us with the search for 'signs' – nothing more – that our humanity furnishes its own norm. Any desire to prove this, or to ground it outside the practice of writing, would domesticate the postmodern sublime and offend its aesthetics of a warring justice that never builds a home or a polis where, like love, justice might once again be blind. The suspension of a common sense and of public discourse fractions human speech into aggressive 'mini-logues' that, in my view, distract us from the corporate monologue which is, in fact, well served by the postmodern babel of tongues. This latest form of the *trahison des clercs*[9] is, of course, eminently suited to their proliferation by means of thread-pulling from the text(ure) of tradition treated as though it were nothing but a mental blanket. The slide from Kant to cant to can't, polished by Lyotard, turns politics into a playground rather than returning us to 'paganism'. This is because Lyotard's paganism no longer has any institutional authority outside of a weakened secularism.

Lyotard's debile imperative, 'Be Just!', lacks any interpretative rules.[10] It is a commandment that will only sound out to those bewitched by a praxis without either a subject or a community that might offer any model of being true, or free, or just. Having stripped the life-world of any dimensions of value, Lyotard then reassigns it the 'pagan' values of impropriety and contrariety. But this represents a parody of what is always idiomatic in the life-worlds of the family, or of gender, or of knowledge and freedom, where properties are commonly assignable and foolishness, cruelty and deceit readily recognizable. Having suppressed all general interests, Lyotard can only recollect them as style – as Chanel No. 5 – the 'linking' (*enchainement*) of things that the French do so well, like finding '*le mot juste*'. In this Lyotard is fun but not serious, while Habermas remains serious but not fun. Yet too much else is occluded between these options.

Life-worlds cannot be subject to remorseless parody or to an unremitting gaze of alienation without this impulse turning against itself and poisoning its original desire to show how things and relations between people might have been. The desire to be reconciled through such original or post-revolutionary fantasies is part of humankind's legacy that is figured in Marx's notion of our 'species-being' (*Gesamtwesen*). But there are other figures on this ground that critique cannot undermine without offering humankind stones in place of bread. The 'piety' of Lyotardism consists in allowing oneself to be slapped on one cheek by fictionalism and on the other cheek by fractionalism, thereby losing all sense of the great tradition that bore us and of the hope for a freedom that will deliver us. Lyotard loses the radicalization of history that is distilled into the Ten Commandments, and of their overriding injunction that we love one another, precisely because he works from their Kantian abstraction which as such is no better than Bentham's universal utilitarianism. Such abstractions have already cut their ties with the life-worlds within which they had acquired some parochial sense. But ethical maxims without rituals are no better – and probably worse – than rituals without ethics. Moreover, the places of our worship cannot be limited to the memorials of the holocaust since the grave of anyone is neither more holy nor less holy than the grave of any other of us. Lyotard dances over the long history of the holiness of anyone's death that is the beginning of those grand narratives he considers extinct.

Post-rationalism represents another turning point in the impoverishment of reason by an intelligent despair that undermines itself by the very gesture of pointing to reason's exaggeration. But what has been claimed by a few on behalf of reason has still to be enjoyed by the many on whose behalf reason's declaration was first pronounced. The latter are not well served by the announcements of reason's death, or of the impossibility of truth and justice except as the prevalence of a temporary aesthetic. Too much of the world still starves, dies young and is wasted by systematic greed and evil for anyone to write the obituaries of philosophy, ideology and humanism. Rather, our task must be to keep alive our common-sense ability to discern truth and falsity, freedom and slavery, justice and injustice and to hold these distinctions on behalf of anyone, anywhere, defended and preserved in any future legacy of humankind. It is the will to preserve such charitable translation of the ideals of philosophy, religion and morals that is the mark of phenomenology in the tradition of later Husserl, Merleau-Ponty and Schutz. It is into this tradition that I have woven a thread from Vico to Marx into my own embroidery of their concepts of embodied mind and a civil history that together constitute the great legacy of humanism. I belive that in this tradition the voca- tion of reason is honoured as a responsible enterprise that cannot be overwhelmed by its weakness for the very reason that irrationalism can only be identified within reason's own history. At the same time, I have tried to give a more common-sense and civic interpretation to this ideal in the light of work by Schutz and Winch. In this vein, I have also given Marx's concept of alienation what I have called an Orphic rather than a Promethean interpretation, insisting thereby on the civilization of the senses that is integral to reason's history. It will be obvious that I give quite a different sense to the linguistic turn in the social sciences than it has taken in literary criticism. Thus I have insisted upon the constitutive ground of trust in society and its discourses and in turn I have defended common-sense sociability as a primary mode of communicative competence which must be honoured by a practice of translation between scientific and common- sense accounts of our institutions which I may repeat as follows:

1 recognize the moral/rational competence of individuals;
2 recognize that institutions are not on an entirely different rational/moral level from individuals;
3 find a language of translation between institutional discourse and individual discourse;
4 find a language of translation between scientific discourse and common-sense discourse;

5 treat the institutionalization of the two languages of translation (3
   and 4) as fundamental to the practice of democratic institutions;
6 treat the rule of translation as a cross-cultural imperative in order
   to minimize the cultural imperialism of Western institutions and
   scientific discourse.

In this way, I have reformulated the regulative principles of Habermas's ideal speech community into a set of decolonizing practices
that elsewhere I have related to the contexts of class and imperial
violence where the task is to devise brave pedagogies to nurture the
culture of communicative competence as the seed of local democracy.
This is not to hide from the world of bureaucratic discourse, on the
one hand, nor from brute violence, on the other. It is rather to
strengthen reason by giving it a limit in the recognition of the parochial
intelligence and good sense of local institutions which are the enduring places of human history.

It is a conceit of postmodernists that they are charged with survival
on behalf of a humanity whose gods they alone have declared dead.
What is extraordinary in this is that it breaks faith not simply with
modernism but with the whole of humankind which has always defended itself through its institution of religious rites, marking the triangle
of birth, marriage and death as the frame of all civilized life. It is
only with respect to this intergenerational structure of life and death
that anyone 'comes after' or 'before'. But, of course, this is not even
a possible perception unless we project upon all previous culture our
own exhausted lineages. The irony here is that postmodernism jet-
tisons sacrificial cultures with its own abandonment of indebtedness.
What is degenerate about much postmodern celebration is that it lacks
any religious sense of space and time. Contemporary design is to
be rejected because it constructs monuments to itself without place
or time. Contemporary design is surrendered to processing signs outside of any embodied or parochial usage of signs. To reduce the
ennervation involved in such sign-processing, postmodernism makes
reference to itself as a new village, or a polis but seen from a sky-
light. In practice, the footings of postmodernism are sunk in fast food,
information desks, rattling waterfalls, lifeless plants and indifferent
elevators that marry time and money to the second.

The postmodern celebrants of the irreal, of the screen and its
simulacra ought to be understood as religious maniacs, or as
iconoclasts breaking the gods, and not at all as sophisticates of modern
science and art. The reason why this is so is that there never was

a time when the arts and sciences were not aware of their fictional status. Even when they settled into a comfortable realism, there always arose a philosopher, an artist or a scientist to smash the icons and to renew the fictions. In short, what is to be remembered is not that our signs are empty shadows but that we must never lose our imaginative capacity for bringing light out of darkness and for renaming things in accordance with our own genesis.

Postmodernism addresses us with a series of one-line observations – always borrowed or recycled – to which are attached pictures that claim to re-present nothing but re-production. In addressing us – men or women – these one-liners repeat the ideological voice of the system they cannot describe or analyse. Otherwise Marx might have bought a camera. The monotony of postmodernist aesthetics is bearable only in the circles of radical chic. Lacking patronage, these groups massage the market with its own products seen from a different angle in the same museums and galleries seen from the same angle of radical chic. In all this, nothing is learned except the conscription of the cave which disciplines us through the eye's ignorance. Capitalist rhetoric cannot be imploded by the rhetoric of capitalism in which the techniques of critical analysis are themselves hostage to the debasement of vision without knowledge. The claim that there are no longer any grand stories capable of under-writing common sense – and that the situation is even worse in the arts and sciences – gives comfort only to those who lack community at any level of society other than intellectual fashion.

The new illiterati who espouse the postmodern condition are, of course, extraordinarily agile in the composition of the age of decomposition. They consume an extraordinary literary diet in the production of illiteracy or the cerebral celebration of the audio-visual masses. The paradox here is grounded in their own socio-economic dilemma. As members of a class whose literacy privileges them even more in the stage of late capitalism than it did in the modernist period, they are obliged to catch up with an intensification of sensationalism that has exceeded anything Baudelaire or Benjamin might have imagined. Just as rock musicians drown language in the auto-copulatory gestures performed before bodies without carnal knowledge, so postmodern theorists destroy knowledge by separating language in gestures that play out sensations without context or sense.

Postmodernism cannot genuinely embrace difference because it is split both from its future and its past without thereby intensifying its present. In all previous generations – indeed, this is constitutive of the very notion of generation, which is not a sexual but a cultural concept – life was sacred because it enjoyed ritual recognition of its wholeness through the displacement of suffering, gifts and death upon a sacrificial victim. This has no counterpart in the horror of war, urban crime or terrorism because the randomization of these events by definition breaks the civilized frame of life exchanged against the death of previous generations among whom we shall be remembered. What every generation owes to each other is that no one ever dies once because our death is marked and remembered in narratives that are never lost to the human family. This is another way of recollecting how the life-world gives meaning and value to its members in contrast with the horror of excommunication. By contrast, postmodernists utterly deceive themselves with the posture of victimage as a personal ideology that could be borne without the rituals of a sacred community. This is the zero-point of post-culturism.

My own observations draw continuously upon a distinction between language and vision, between élites and masses. In this respect, they appear to lag behind the postmodernist transgression of such differences. To this I reply that where everything is equal nothing is equal. Moreover, the postmodernist celebration of difference is disingenuous since its own aspirations soon exhaust themselves in the tribalism of cliché. Hence the anxiety experienced by postmodernists conscious of their temporal prefix – they fear that they have set themselves up for supersession. Having mocked tradition and intergenerationality, postmodernists can only fear their own posterity – why should they be remembered? Indeed, why should anyone dismiss an already dead moment of the mind – except to reaffirm the life of the mind?

NOTES

1 Carrol, D. (1987) *Paraesthetics: Foucault, Lyotard, Derrida*, New York: Methuen; *Diacritics*, 14(3) (Fall 1984), A Special Issue on the Work of Jean-François Lyotard.
2 O'Neill, J. (1992) *Critical Conventions: Interpretation in the Literary Arts and Sciences*, Norman: University of Oklahoma Press.
3 Lyotard, J.-F. and Thébaud, J.-L. (1985) *Just Gaming*, trans. W. Godzich, Minneapolis: University of Minnesota Press.
4 Rachman, J. (1988) 'Habermas's Complaint', *New German Critique*, 45, Fall, pp. 163–91.
5 O'Neill, J. (ed.) (1982) *On Critical Theory*, Washington, DC: University Press of America.

6 Said, E. (1983) *The World, the Text, and the Critic*, Cambridge: Harvard University Press, p. 20.
7 Jameson, F. (1981) *The Political Unconscious: Narrative as a Socially Symbolic Act*, Ithaca: Cornell University Press, p. 293.
8 Benhabib, S. (1984) 'Epistemologies of Postmodernism: A Rejoinder to Jean-François Lyotard', *New German Critique*, 33, Fall, pp. 103–26.
9 Bauman, Z. (1987) *Legislators and Interpreters: On modernity, postmodernity and intellectuals*, Ithaca: Cornell University Press.
10 Altièri, C. (1989) 'Judgment and Justice Under Postmodern Conditions; or, How Lyotard Helps Us Read Rawls as a Postmodern Thinker', pp. 61–91 in *Redrawing the Lines: Analytic Philosophy, Deconstruction, and Literary Theory*, Reed Way Dasenbrock (ed.) Minneapolis: University of Minnesota Press.

Index